The Kentucky Derby

The Kentucky Derby

How the Run for the Roses Became America's Premier Sporting Event

James C. Nicholson

Foreword by Chris McCarron

UNIVERSITY PRESS OF KENTUCKY

Copyright © 2012 by The University Press of Kentucky

Scholarly publisher for the Commonwealth,
serving Bellarmine University, Berea College, Centre
College of Kentucky, Eastern Kentucky University,
The Filson Historical Society, Georgetown College,
Kentucky Historical Society, Kentucky State University,
Morehead State University, Murray State University,
Northern Kentucky University, Transylvania University,
University of Kentucky, University of Louisville,
and Western Kentucky University.
All rights reserved.

Editorial and Sales Offices: The University Press of Kentucky
663 South Limestone Street, Lexington, Kentucky 40508-4008
www.kentuckypress.com

16 15 14 13 12   5 4 3 2 1

Cataloging-in-Publication data is available from the Library of Congress.

ISBN 978-0-8131-3576-2 (hardcover : alk. paper)
ISBN 978-0-8131-3577-9 (ebook)

This book is printed on acid-free paper meeting
the requirements of the American National Standard
for Permanence in Paper for Printed Library Materials.

∞

Manufactured in the United States of America.

 Member of the Association of
American University Presses

To the memory of my grandfather, Shultz,
who brought me to the racetrack

Contents

Illustrations

Illustrations

Foreword

The sport of horse racing has provided me with the opportunity to journey all around the world. During my travels as a professional jockey in a career that lasted nearly four decades, I was often conspicuous because of my size, my build, and the riding crop that stuck out of the "tack" bag that I carried onto airplanes. Upon learning that I rode Thoroughbreds for a living, people I met would invariably ask me if I had ever ridden in the Kentucky Derby. Their next question would be, "Have you ever won it?"

The Kentucky Derby is, without question, the most sought-after prize in this magnificent sport, which originated over four hundred years ago. When I was growing up in Dorchester, Massachusetts, my parents and grandparents always watched the Derby on television. I first became interested in the Derby at the age of fourteen in 1969, the year Majestic Prince won. The big chestnut colt was trained by Johnny Longden, a former jockey who retired with the most wins in the history of American racing (and the only man to win the Run for the Roses as both a jockey and a trainer). Majestic Prince was ridden by Bill Hartack, whose fifth win that day tied Eddie Arcaro's record for most career Derby wins for a jockey. I have watched every running of the Derby since that first Saturday in May—except when I was participating in it as a rider myself.

My first opportunity to ride in the Derby came in 1976. The thrill I felt at my first Derby start in the 102nd Run for the Roses was only enhanced by the fact that I would be competing against my older brother Gregg, who was also a jockey and who had introduced me to the sport of horse racing only a few years earlier. Our dad was in attendance, and words cannot describe the look on his face when Gregg and I walked past him on the way to the track. There was never a prouder father. My mount, Cojak, had a moderate chance to win, but we finished sixth, just behind my brother. When I returned to the unsaddling area, I dismounted by leaping into the air as I shouted, "I just rode in the greatest race in the world!" Despite our somewhat disappointing finish, I was almost as excited as if we had actually won the race. Riding in my first Kentucky Derby was an experience I would never forget.

In 1983, I got a little closer to smelling those famous roses, finishing second on Desert Wine. Three years later I again finished second, this time behind one of the best race riders in the history of the sport, Bill Shoemaker, who was then fifty-six. In October of that year, I suffered a fractured left femur in a racing accident, which sidelined me until early April 1987.

As I was preparing to return to racing, Hall of Fame trainer Jack Van Berg asked me if I thought I would be fit enough to go a mile and a quarter on the first Saturday in May. I answered, "Of course I will." But in the back of my mind I was not really sure. However, I knew he was thinking of letting me ride Derby contender Alysheba, so I stepped up my exercise regimen to make sure I would be ready. Hall of Fame jockey Pat Day had been riding Alysheba but had committed to ride the eventual favorite Demos Begone instead. What a stroke of luck for me.

I was well enough to ride Alysheba in his final Derby prep, the Blue Grass Stakes, which in those days was contested only nine days before the Run for the Roses. We crossed the wire in first place but were disqualified and placed third by the stewards, who felt that we had interfered with another horse in the homestretch. Although I was disappointed in the decision, I still liked our chances in the Derby.

Alysheba again found trouble in the homestretch on the first Saturday in May, but this time he took the worst of it—clipping heels, stumbling, and almost falling. However, he was such a gifted athlete that he regained his balance and his footing in time to charge by Bet Twice en route to victory. When we reached the winner's circle the crowd went nuts. I felt like a rock star as security guards and police officers escorted me up to the press box for the postrace comments. Fans were grabbing, screaming, and asking for (or more like demanding) autographs. Chris McCarron was finally on the map!

Although it is a prize universally coveted by those involved in Thoroughbred racing, the Derby has eluded some of the finest horsemen, the wealthiest people, and the most hard-working individuals in the racing and breeding industries, both here in the United States and abroad. When Alysheba got me to the finish line in front of sixteen other colts in the 113th running of this historic fixture, I couldn't believe it had actually happened to me. I could finally answer, "Yes!" when fellow airline travelers asked if I had ever won the Run for the Roses. Most of the time, the ensuing conversation would last until we reached our destination, and I never got tired of speaking about the experience.

Two weeks before the 1994 Derby, I received a phone call in the jockeys' room at Santa Anita Park. It was Hall of Fame trainer Nick Zito. Nick needed a rider for Go for Gin. Hall of Fame jockey Jerry Bailey had been riding Go for Gin that whole spring but opted to ride another horse in the Derby. Nick had me fly to Louisville a week before the race to exercise the colt at Churchill Downs. The workout the colt put in gave me goose bumps. He worked incredibly well and provided me with a tremendous feeling of confidence. As soon as I dismounted, I phoned my wife and told her to buy a ticket for a flight to Louisville.

Go for Gin validated my confidence by winning in virtual wire-to-wire fashion on a sloppy track before 120,000 screaming fans who were drenched by the day-long storms. I never felt a drop of rain. After my victory on Go for Gin, when anyone asked if I had ever won the Derby, I would stick out my chest, raise my head, and say with great pride, "Yup, twice."

But just as there is no better feeling in racing than winning the Kentucky Derby, losses in America's greatest race are the toughest to swallow. In the 1996 running my mount was a fine California-bred gelding named Cavonnier. When we reached the final sixteenth of a mile, I could smell those roses yet again, as we were a length in front. Then Grindstone came flying down the middle of the track and nailed us right at the wire. I was devastated! I think it took me a year to psychologically recover from that defeat. I rode in four more Derbies but never again made it to that coveted winner's circle in the shadows of the famous twin spires.

I retired from riding in 2002 but I have attended every Derby since. I especially enjoy bringing friends and family into the stable area and leading them from barn to barn to introduce them to the Derby trainers, owners, and jockeys before the big race. I have been told countless times that the Kentucky Derby is the most exciting sporting event they've ever attended. When the paddock judge announces, "Riders up" and the horses head out to the track and "My Old Kentucky Home" is sung, it takes my breath away. Every time I hear that legendary song, my eyes well up with tears. Every time.

I have always been fascinated by the history of Thoroughbred racing, and I love to read about how horse racing became a popular sport in the United States. More specifically, the Kentucky Derby unfailingly interests and inspires me. This book provides more insight into the Derby than any other I have read.

Jamie Nicholson has done a masterful job of researching the historical circumstances that made the Derby the enthralling and significant event it is. The characters involved in establishing "the greatest two minutes in all of sports" and the sequence of events that gave rise to the Derby's enormous popularity are truly incredible.

You may never get to experience the thrill of entering the winner's circle and smelling the wonderful aroma that emanates from the garland of roses that signifies the greatest achievement in the sport of Thoroughbred racing, but this wonderful book will take you on a journey that gets you as close as any piece of writing possibly could.

Chris McCarron

Preface

In the interest of full disclosure, I feel compelled to mention that I am a Thoroughbred racing enthusiast and a supporter of the Thoroughbred industry. I do this to alert the reader to a potential for bias, and to claim a small amount of firsthand knowledge of the sport of Thoroughbred racing that supplements my research for this project.

I grew up on a Thoroughbred farm in Lexington, Kentucky, that was founded by my maternal grandfather in 1956. The farm was sold to Sheikh Mohammad bin Rashid al Maktoum, arguably the most powerful Thoroughbred owner of modern times, in 2001. I worked on the farm in the summers and some evenings and weekends during the school year from 1993 until its sale. I spent most of my time as a part of the maintenance crew; my responsibilities included mowing grass, repairing fences, baling hay, tending cattle, collecting garbage, and myriad other labor-intensive tasks upon which I look back ever more fondly with each passing year. I was also involved in some preparation of yearling horses for sale, and worked as groom at a few auctions, brushing horses and cleaning stalls, as I got older.

My wife's family is active in Thoroughbred racing and breeding, and many of my extended family members make their living in and around the Thoroughbred industry. In addition to my time on the family farm, my own work experience has included stints at an equine auction company, in a Thoroughbred advertising agency, in a horse insurance agency, and with a racehorse trainer.

I have watched the Kentucky Derby from practically every vantage point possible in Churchill Downs. I have witnessed the race while seated in a clubhouse box dressed in a suit and tie, and I have seen it standing amid the multitudes in the infield wearing no shirt at all. I have been seated at the starting gate and at the finish line. I have watched televised coverage of the Derby from other racetracks and from various living rooms, sometimes in the company of lifelong Kentuckians and sometimes with fascinated outlanders.

My earliest Derby memory is 1984, when my parents, who were traveling to Louisville that day, introduced my sister, a baby-sitter, and me to an old Derby party tradition of cutting up a Derby program's list of starters and placing all the names in a hat, to be drawn blindly before the race. This was in the days before color ink was used for race day programs, so a dark green page for the big race in an otherwise black-and-white program underscored the significance of the Derby. Claiborne Farm's dark bay colt Swale was the winner that day, under the guidance of jockey Laffit Pincay Jr. I suspect that I did not draw Swale's name in our prerace ceremony, as my recollections do not include who won the prize; had I been the winner, I believe that a memory of triumph would have stayed with me. I mention my first Derby memory to establish the point after which my historical objectivity might diminish. My analysis of more recent Derbies has inescapably been filtered through my own personal experiences and observations.

Introduction

The Unique Identity of Kentucky and Its Derby

What is it about the Kentucky Derby? Why does it thrill people who will not see another horse race all year, who otherwise pay no attention to an anachronistic sport whose heyday appears to be long past? Each year a quarter million people file into Churchill Downs in Louisville on Derby weekend, and hundreds of thousands more attend festivities around the city in the two weeks leading up to the big race. The Kentucky Derby is not the fastest, longest, or most monetarily valuable horse race in the United States. It was not the first race—or even the first derby—to be run in America. Each year it is only one of dozens of derbies contested throughout the world. Why, then, does the cultural phenomenon that is the Kentucky Derby annually capture the attention of millions, while most American racetracks struggle to survive in the face of steady declines in the popularity of horse racing?

The term *derby* generally signifies a race for three-year-old horses, and its origins go back to eighteenth-century England and Edward Stanley, twelfth Earl of Derby, who cofounded the Derby Stakes in 1780.[1] Thus, it is not the derby element of the Kentucky Derby that makes the event unique; rather, the traditions and imagery associated with the Kentuckian roots of the event are responsible for its distinct flavor. These include, most

1

notably, the singing of "My Old Kentucky Home," the blanket of roses ceremonially draped upon the winning horse, mint juleps, ladies dressed as "southern belles," and the wild cacophony of the infield that contrasts so markedly with the civility and refinement in the clubhouse. These aspects of the Kentucky Derby experience all have their roots in Kentucky's unique and ever-changing identity within American popular culture: it is Kentucky—and its associated history, imagery, and mythology—that gives the Kentucky Derby its distinct character and has allowed the event to remain culturally relevant despite myriad changes in American society since the race was first contested over 135 years ago. Throughout these years, regardless of what the prevailing mood of the nation has been, the quicksilver nature of Kentucky's place in the minds of Americans has attracted Derby fans to the Bluegrass State—and given them something to celebrate once they arrive.

Kentucky's special spot in American popular culture can be traced back to the 1784 publication of John Filson's *The Discovery, Settlement, and Present State of Kentucke*.[2] First published in Delaware, and eventually translated into French and German, *Kentucke* was popular on both sides of the Atlantic. Filson described the landscape, climate, and natural resources of what are now the central and eastern parts of the state. The book was an important (and self-serving) promotional tool, as Filson was a land speculator with sizeable Kentucky holdings. With his words, Filson painted a picture of a land of abundance blessed with bountiful wildlife, fertile soil, rich mineral deposits, and a pleasant climate. Filson's description of the area as a latter-day Eden ensured that Kentucky entered the American popular consciousness as an immensely attractive place, forming a foundation for the idea popularized in the nineteenth century that Kentucky was a uniquely suitable area for raising top-class race horses.[3]

It was the book's appendix—written by Filson to sound like an autobiographical sketch of early Kentucky settler Daniel Boone—that would have the most far-reaching impact on Kentucky's long-term identity, however.[4] Filson's Boone, a quasi-mythical—though very much historically "real"—character, was a living paradox: he was portrayed as both a rugged woodsman and a civilizing agent who tamed the wilderness and brought European values to the savage natives; he was an Indian fighter, yet a man who lived peacefully with the natives; he was both a trailblazer for civilization and an Enlightenment-era "Man of Nature" escaping from civilization. Filson's early descriptions of Boone firmly established the figure of the romantic American pioneer in the American imagination, forging aspects of Kentucky's identity that would eventually become crucial elements of the appeal of the Kentucky Derby: both the Kentucky hillbilly and the Kentucky colonel caricatures that would heavily influence Kentucky's place in twentieth-century American popular culture can be traced back to Filson's characterization of Boone.[5]

Filson's early descriptions of Kentucky and Boone created the notion that Kentucky was an untamed yet civilized place (a description that could apply to the modern Kentucky Derby, with its visible dichotomy between the uninhibited environment of the infield and the more refined, restrained air of the boxes and suites in the exclusive "Millionaires' Row" section of the clubhouse). Filson's Kentucky was a land of contradiction and paradox. During the antebellum era, the state attained a status as a place *in* the South, but not *of* the South. Kentucky was a slave state, but was widely believed to practice a more "benign" or "civilized" form of slavery than that in the deeper South. Proponents of that perception pointed to the relatively short growing seasons of Kentucky's staple crops, hemp and tobacco, which resulted in more "downtime" for laborers, including slaves.[6] This idea was popularized by novelist Harriet Beecher Stowe, who in *Uncle Tom's Cabin* described Kentucky as home to "perhaps the mildest form of the system of slavery."[7]

Stephen Collins Foster reinforced these images of antebellum Kentucky in his song "My Old Kentucky Home," first published in 1853. Though the lyrics were officially "sanitized" in 1986 by the Kentucky legislature, which replaced the word "darkies" with "people," the song originally referred to the sale of a slave downriver from his Kentucky home, where "the birds make music all the day." Foster may have been motivated to write the song after reading Stowe's novel, as an original draft of "My Old Kentucky Home" included the line "poor Uncle Tom goodnight."[8] Despite the references in "My Old Kentucky Home" and *Uncle Tom's Cabin* to the prevalence of the brutal southward-moving slave trade in Kentucky, the state managed to keep its reputation as a place where oxymoronic "benevolent slavery" existed. For reasons that will be examined later, the song has brought tears to the eyes of Derby-goers for almost a century during the annual prerace ceremonial performance as the equine contestants make their way onto the Churchill Downs racing surface.

Kentucky's reputation as unique among the states continued to grow immediately before and during the American Civil War. In the fiercely competitive presidential election of 1860, Kentucky voters rejected not one but two native sons, Abraham Lincoln and John Breckinridge; Tennessee's John Bell of the Constitutional Union Party carried the state. Though Kentucky was belligerently neutral at the beginning of the war, thousands of Kentuckians went to the killing fields on both sides of the conflict. The term "brother against brother" had significant meaning for many of Kentucky's soldiers during the Civil War. Thus, it was appropriate that the presidents of both the Union and the Confederacy were born in the Bluegrass State.

After the last shot in the Civil War was fired, Kentucky remained a place where northerners and foreigners could easily access "the South." Kentucky had been a slave state and remained a racially segregated society after emancipation, but the Commonwealth also retained its reputation of being more racially tolerant

4

and progressive than the deeper South. This reputation for relative racial harmony, born in the nineteenth century, would continue into the twentieth century and would prove to be an asset to promoters of the Kentucky Derby.

In the aftermath of the Civil War, Kentucky embodied a constellation of longings and fears that lay at the root of America's emergent national identity. In the American popular imagination, Kentucky was home to both the mountaineer of the eastern Kentucky highlands and the gentleman farmer of the central lowlands. The mountain folk were castigated in the print media as violent, lawless, ignorant, and dangerous people and simultaneously celebrated as a modern link to a racially pure American past. The Kentucky gentleman, on the other hand, was a more refined yet fearless and independent über-republican yeoman. It would not be until the backward, violent stereotype of the Kentucky hillbilly had been overshadowed in American popular culture by a neo-Confederate "Kentucky colonel" icon during the early twentieth century that the Derby would begin to emerge as a culturally significant event on a national level, when many Americans, faced with changing social structures and the uncertainty of modernity, would seek to access a simpler, more stable time that Kentucky seemed to represent. The Derby would give them an opportunity to experience some of the history, myth, and romance of "Old Kentucky" without having to venture too far out of their comfort zone geographically, culturally, or politically.[9]

There are few events in the world at which such conspicuous displays of wealth and luxury coexisting with hedonistic bacchanalia can be seen as at the Kentucky Derby. The relationship between the elite and the masses at the Derby has been part of its identity and attraction since the early years. The dichotomy between the drunken lawlessness in the Derby infield and the splendor and refinement in the clubhouse today mirrors the two elements of Kentucky's identity that helped give rise to the popularity of the event in the first place. Reminiscent of the earlier dichotomy between the Kentucky hillbilly and Kentucky colonel icons, this dual identity remains one of the defining aspects of the Kentucky Derby experience. Despite the overall decline in the popularity of horse racing in the United States, the Kentucky Derby remains one of the premier sporting events in America, and Kentucky continues to evoke sets of contradictory imagery in the minds of Americans. Born from this imagery, the Derby now plays a significant part in perpetuating it.

The modern Thoroughbred industry has much to learn from the story of the Kentucky Derby's rise, survival, and enduring prosperity as a new generation of industry leaders tries to return horse racing to its former place of prominence within American sports culture. Events like the Derby cannot simply be conjured up out of thin air, but elements of the attraction that have made the Derby successful can be exploited in other arenas. The Derby did not become a popular and transcendent event merely because it was promoted (as many have claimed). It was what was being promoted that made the difference, and made the Derby. The racetracks and race meets that have been able to survive and even thrive within the modern American sports landscape have been able to draw patrons from outside the ranks of hardcore horse racing fans. To appeal to "regular" folk, promoters of racing must be able to provide context for the sport—a reason for watching what would otherwise be a herd of pretty animals being ridden around a large oval.

The Kentucky Derby today exists as a kind of mediator between Kentucky's mythic past and modern society, as the pageantry of the Derby evokes elements of Kentucky's rich history. The Derby is not the only such mediator in American culture but, due to its popularity and visibility, it is certainly one of the most significant. The race's popularity and longevity can be at least partly attributed to the pageantry that helps Derby fans to experience Kentucky and to make meaning of themselves as Americans.

At its essence, the Kentucky Derby is a celebration of a place, enhanced by specific associated traditions, icons, and images—notably the mint julep, roses, hats, and "My Old Kentucky Home." Other transcendent sporting events like the Masters, Wimbledon, and the Tour de France follow this same model, as do successful American Thoroughbred race meets at Saratoga, Del Mar, and Keeneland. The Derby, then, is not unique as a celebration of the past, or of a place. But exactly what is being celebrated, experienced, and remembered at the Derby, and how that has changed over the course of its long history, is unique. The Derby is more than just a horse race. And that is the subject of this book.

1

Early Struggles and Foundations for Success

1875–1910

"Today will be historic in Kentucky annals as the first 'Derby Day' of what promises to be a long series of annual turf festivities of which we confidently expect our grandchildren, a hundred years hence, to celebrate in glorious rejoicings," the *Louisville Courier-Journal* boldly predicted on May 17, 1875.[1] That afternoon ten thousand curious and enthusiastic spectators filled the brand-new Louisville Jockey Club and Driving Park and witnessed history under a cloudless sky. Fashionable ladies and gentlemen from all parts of America were seated in the grandstand, and the clubhouse veranda was dotted with parasols, rocking chairs, and black waiters in white coats carrying trays of frosted silver cups. Wagons and carriages of all descriptions filled with locals from all walks of life were scattered across the infield. All had come to see the first running of the Kentucky Derby. The second of four races that afternoon, the inaugural Derby did not disappoint. Entered as a "rabbit" to set a fast pace for his favored stable mate, come-from-behind specialist Chesapeake, Aristides was sent to the lead early as planned by jockey Oliver Lewis, but saved enough energy to survive a late challenge from Volcano, thus achieving a surprising two-length victory. The crowd erupted in applause for the little red colt and his game jockey, who wore

Aristides, winner of the first Kentucky Derby, ridden by jockey Oliver Lewis, and owned by H. P. McGrath. (Keeneland Library, Lexington, Kentucky.)

the orange and green silks of winning owner H. P. McGrath as horse and rider made their way to the winner's circle—champions of the first Kentucky Derby.

Horse racing had been popular in Louisville since the late 1700s, but the city had been without organized Thoroughbred racing since the Woodlawn race course had closed five years earlier, a testament to the fact that while commercial breeding was already an established part of the state's agricultural economy, Kentucky was by no means the undisputed capital of the American Thoroughbred industry that it would later become. In fact, in the mid-1870s, much of Kentucky's identity to outsiders was based on its reputation as a hotbed of lawlessness and violence. Nine months before the first Kentucky Derby, the *New York Times* described the Commonwealth as "a land which produces more beautiful women, unrivaled horses, fine whisky, and blue grass than any other section of the universe." But, the *Times* continued, "Some classes of its inhabitants . . . think it no harm to kill a man or two yearly to keep their senses of honor keen and their weapons bright."[2]

For Meriwether Lewis Clark Jr., the first Derby marked the culmination of years of effort to create a world-class racecourse in Louisville. The series of events that led to the establishment of the Kentucky Derby was set in motion when the recently married twenty-six-year-old Clark (a grandson of famous American explorer William Clark and scion of one of Louisville's oldest families) traveled with his wife to Great Britain and continental Europe in 1872, where he was introduced to many leading members of the English and French racing establishments. He toured their top racing facilities and was particularly impressed with English racing. Upon his return to Kentucky, Clark led an effort to build an upscale facility in the mold of Epsom Downs, one of England's oldest and most famous racecourses, complete with a signature race modeled after the English Derby, a one-and-a-half-mile race for three-year-olds contested annually at Epsom. Clark convinced a group of 320 local sportsmen and business leaders to invest $100 apiece to fund the construction of a racetrack and grandstand for the Louisville Jockey Club and Driving Park Association, to be located on eighty acres of land owned by Clark's uncles Henry and John Churchill (with whom Clark had lived for part of his childhood after the death of his mother). Within a decade the track would be known colloquially as Churchill Downs, destined to become the most famous racetrack in America.[3]

M. L. "Lutie" Clark, a dapper and physically imposing man with slicked-down hair and a flower habitually in his lapel, imagined the Kentucky Derby as an event on a grand scale from the beginning. He did not live to see the full fruition of his vision, but from the very first running the event received attention from national print media and racing fans across the country.[4]

Only twenty-nine years old when the track opened, Clark had already acquired cosmopolitan tastes for food and drink, and was known for hosting lavish parties in the clubhouse apartment that served as his residence during race meets. He hoped that the Louisville track would become a place for the city's fashionable crowd to socialize, but he also offered free admission to the infield for all on Derby Day. Ladies were encouraged to attend the races but were segregated from the betting shed, which was considered an "inappropriate" environment for women. Clark wanted the track, the clubhouse, and the grounds to be well manicured and top class, even if that required expenditure of his personal wealth, which it often did. Clark's Derby night parties at Louisville's posh Pendennis Club were legendary: one year the dinner tables were arranged around an indoor pond filled with moss, ferns, a fountain, and live baby swans. Above all, Clark promoted the Kentucky Derby as a signature race and showcase for the racetrack.

Early journalistic prognostications for the Derby demonstrate that the race was special from its inception. To say that it reached lofty levels of popularity and cultural significance in the twentieth and twenty-first centuries from a starting point of complete national insignificance would be inaccurate, but the path toward the special place in American culture that the Derby eventually achieved was often bumpy and uneven. In an era when racing was conducted for the sake of sport as much as for profit, Churchill Downs struggled to survive financially in the early years, but the Derby was popular with race fans and high society, and its significance crossed state and regional boundaries. New York millionaire William B. Astor Jr. won the second Derby with a gelding named Vagrant he had purchased only weeks before. Among the ten rivals Vagrant defeated was Parole, owned by another New York millionaire, tobacco-manufacturing heir Pierre Lorillard IV (who would later become the first American owner to win the English Derby). In 1881 major New York owners Michael F. and Phillip J. Dwyer won the Derby with heavily favored Hindoo, one of the best horses of his era and part of the inaugural class of inductees at the National Racing Hall of Fame. The Dwyer brothers had been butchers in New York City before making a fortune in the meatpacking industry as suppliers of area restaurants and hotels. They would become major players in the eastern racing scene as racetrack operators and racehorse owners, though Mike Dwyer would also gain notoriety as one of the country's heaviest and most reckless gamblers.

The following year the Dwyer brothers owned another of America's top three-year-olds, Runnymede. Despite Lutie Clark's efforts to recruit the colt to the Derby, the Dwyers were hesitant because they had been frustrated the previous year by their inability to find a bookmaker in Louisville to take their bets on Hindoo. The brothers told Clark that they would return to the Derby only if Clark would provide bookmakers to service their bets. When Clark told the Dwyers that none existed in the city, the parties reached a compromise: the Dwyers would be allowed to bring their own bookies. After securing their bets with the bookies at odds of 4-5, the Dwyers watched Runnymede find clear running room late in the race only to be caught deep in the stretch by a lightly regarded gelding named Apollo, who prevailed at the wire by a half length, becoming the first, and to date only, horse to win the Derby without making a start as a two-year-old. The Dwyers lost their bets with their bookies, but Louisville race fans gained a new and popular gambling option, and bookmakers would remain a fixture at the Derby for the next quarter century.

Another prominent American attracted early on to the Kentucky Derby was Berry Wall, a New York bon vivant, who was at least indirectly responsible for the creation of the important connection between the Derby and roses. Early in 1883 Wall was in Lexington, Kentucky, visiting a friend, when he met leading Thoroughbred owner and breeder Jack Chinn, who invited Wall to his farm thirty miles away in Harrodsburg the following day. At the farm, Wall was captivated by Chinn's three-year-old colt Leonatus and asked to buy him. Chinn initially accepted, but quickly had second thoughts and cancelled the deal. Wall's disappointment did not prevent him from betting on Leonatus to win the Derby with anyone who would take his money in New York in the weeks leading up to the race. Wall attended the Derby as a guest of Clark. After Leonatus easily bested his six rivals to win the ninth Derby, Wall refused to divulge the exact amount of his winnings but acknowledged, "I have a lot of money to spend."[5] He did just that by sponsoring a dinner at the Pendennis Club for thirty couples and a subsequent gathering later that night at the Galt House Hotel for sixty couples. The lavish decorations at the parties included American Beauty roses which, developed in France under a different name, had made their way to the United States only three years earlier. No one in Kentucky had seen this type of rose before and they earned rave reviews. Clark was particularly impressed and began presenting the Derby's winning jockey with a bouquet of roses the following year, a tradition that would eventually evolve into the ceremonial blanket of roses worn by the winning horse today.

The Derby's allure for the rich and fashionable, local and national, helped it to gain a reputation by 1886 as "undoubtedly the greatest annual event of the American turf," according to the *New York Times*.[6] On Derby Day that year the *Courier-Journal* evinced considerable enthusiasm: "The widespread interest in the meeting has attracted people from all over the country, and the city will be crowded today. That there will be a crowd at the races goes without saying. Everybody goes to the Derby; it is a Kentucky, almost a national, institution, and people who do not know one horse from another for the remainder of the year feel an intense interest in the colt of the year."[7] Anticipation was high, with record attendance expected.

The 1886 Derby proved to be a high point from which its national significance would fall for close to a quarter century.

One of many threats to the Derby's stature stemmed from hostilities between gold-rush millionaire James Ben Ali Haggin and Churchill Downs officials that year. Haggin was born in Harrodsburg, Kentucky, in 1822, the grandson of an early Kentucky settler. He practiced law in Shelbyville before heading west in 1849, where he made a fortune in mining. His sizeable landholdings included part of the Anaconda copper mine in Montana, which he owned as a member of a partnership that included George Hearst, father of newspaper magnate William Randolph Hearst. At one time, Haggin's mine holdings were unsurpassed by any in the world. In 1880 he began a Thoroughbred operation in California that would soon become one of the largest and most successful in the country.

On Derby Day, 1886, Haggin became incensed at his inability to find a bookmaker to take a bet on his colt, Ben Ali, the favorite for that afternoon's big race. Track officials had locked out the bookmakers over a contract dispute. After watching Ben Ali take the Derby by a half length, Haggin announced that if the bookmakers were not welcomed back to the track, he would leave Churchill Downs and never return. This was no small threat, as Haggin was ridiculously wealthy and one of the world's leading owners of Thoroughbreds. The crisis seemed to have been averted when the bookies and track officials reached an agreement allowing for their return to business the following day. However, after harsh words were exchanged between the winning owner and a track official, Haggin left Louisville, vowing never to return to Churchill Downs and promising to see to it that his wealthy friends likewise boycotted the races.[8] Haggin purchased Elmendorf Farm outside Lexington in 1897, which served as home base for his world-class breeding operation, but true to his threat, he would never again start a horse in the Derby.

Though the fracas between Haggin and Churchill officials certainly did not enhance the Derby's reputation, the precise amount of damage it caused is difficult to measure, as major

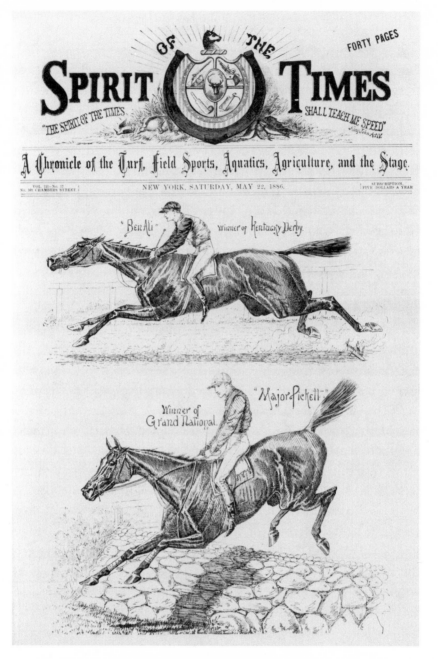

Ben Ali, *Spirit of the Times* cover art, 1886. Ben Ali won the Derby in 1886, but his owner, James Ben Ali Haggin, had a greater long-term impact on the race. Following a dispute over access to bookmakers, Haggin told Churchill Downs brass that he would no longer race at the track and that he would see to it that his fellow top eastern owners did likewise. (Keeneland Library, Lexington, Kentucky.)

eastern owners were more concerned with the increasingly lu-
crative and prestigious racing scene in and around New York
by that time anyway. Although major New York owners largely
stayed away, the Derby nevertheless attracted horses from across
the country for the remainder of the decade. In 1887 Elias Jackson "Lucky" Baldwin, founder of the original Santa Anita Park
racetrack on his Southern California ranch and nicknamed for
his uncanny success in various nineteenth-century mining ven-
tures, sent his colt Pendennis from California to start in the Derby. Though the horse finished last, the presence of Pendennis at
the Derby in 1887 shows that Haggin's boycott of the Derby did
not keep all the top national owners away from Louisville. In
fact, the winners of the four Derbies immediately after Haggin's
departure were won by non-Kentuckians. In 1888 Macbeth II
won the Derby for owner George V. Hankins, the "King of Chicago Gamblers." The following year a colt named Spokane, bred
and trained in Montana, narrowly nipped heavily favored Proc-
tor Knott at the finish line and was declared the winner after a
long deliberation by the placing judges (a decision that reportedly netted notorious outlaw Frank James a sizeable payoff on a
bet placed on the winner). In 1890 "Big" Ed Corrigan, a Kansas
City industrialist and Chicago racetrack operator, won the Derby
with Riley, a horse he owned and trained.

The appeal of the Kentucky Derby had never been based
solely upon its significance in the world of horse racing; thus,
the dearth of wealthy eastern owners would not necessarily have
caused a noticeable downturn in the popularity of the race. But
their absence, combined with the increasing popularity of new
races for three-year-olds like Chicago's American Derby and the
proliferation of racing in and around New York City, indicated
tough times ahead for the Kentucky Derby.

First run in 1884, the American Derby carried a much larger
purse than the Kentucky Derby and attracted higher-quality com-
petitors. The Kentucky Derby was soon eclipsed by its Chicago

rival in terms of significance and attention. By 1893, the American Derby was worth $50,000 to the winner, while the winner of the Kentucky Derby that year received less than $4,000. The American Derby's elevated purse that year was likely related to local enthusiasm over the enormous Columbian Exposition taking place in Chicago, but Chicago's Derby was regularly attracting better horses and offering higher purses.

By the early to mid-1890s, the size and quality of Derby fields had deteriorated to the point that the event had become a subject of ridicule by local and national journalists alike. The *Louisville Commercial* opined that the Kentucky Derby had degenerated into "a contest of dogs."[9] The *New York Times* reported that the Kentucky Derby had "lost all pretensions to greatness."[10] The absence of top national owners was obviously a main reason, but operational mismanagement, deteriorating facilities, and competition from races like the American Derby also contributed to the Derby's embarrassingly small fields, uncompetitive purses, and diminishing national prestige in the late 1880s and 1890s. The emergence of a mysterious disease that caused stillbirths in horses and decimated Bluegrass breeders' 1890 and 1891 foal crops only added to the dismal situation.[11] The Derby's decline was snowballing, and the nation's top three-year-olds—along with their rich, fashionable, and influential owners—were staying away.

Despite the decline in national prestige within racing circles, the Derby retained some of its cultural relevance, and still attracted large crowds by the standard of the day. National conventions were regularly held in Louisville at Derby time. In 1891, a year in which a Lexington newspaper called the four-horse race "a bum Derby," and the *New York Times* called it "farcical," a number of national conventions planned to convene in Louisville at Derby time.[12] The Scottish-American Convention, the National Convention of Elks, and the Kentucky Democratic State Convention all adjourned their meetings so that delegates could attend the Derby. Two years later a convention of the Republican League of Clubs, which drew representatives from across the country, held an abbreviated session on Derby Day so that the delegates could go to the races.

The following year, 1894, one important Derby competitor ceased operation. That fall, Chicago racing leaders reached a decision to discontinue racing at Washington Park, home of the American Derby, because of "the popular clamor against poolselling and the degeneration of racing from a harmless and high-class sport into a species of gambling."[13] Presumably betting in some form has been a part of horse racing since the animal was first domesticated, but in late-Victorian America there was a growing concern over the professionalization of gambling. Much of the "popular clamor" came from reform-minded adherents to the Social Gospel movement who sought to combat what they saw as the ill effects of the rise of urban-industrial society (including political corruption, saloons, gambling, and prostitution), which they believed threatened public morals and the Protestant work ethic. These reformers tended to be from the middle classes and sought social stability and regeneration through the eradication of vice.[14] Horse racing (especially the gambling element) represented a threat to social stability because it offered an opportunity for socioeconomic advance achieved without adhering to the traditional American notions of hard work and frugality. As is the case today, the top end of horse racing was dominated by the rich, but there was a measure of truth to the ancient racing adage that "all are equal on the turf and under it." Regardless of one's background or social status, anyone with the right horse (or a bit of money to bet on it) could defeat the wealthiest blueblood at the racetrack. A successful handicapper could, in theory, become quite wealthy without hard work or frugality. This offended the sensibilities of many reformers, including those who worked to rid their communities of horse racing in late-Victorian America.

The American Derby returned in 1897 after a three-year hiatus, but it would be contested and interrupted intermittently thereafter. It was held only once between 1905 and 1925. By the end of that period the Kentucky Derby, run every year on the same track, had become the most popular and most celebrated horse race in the nation. Whether the Kentucky Derby would have reached its lofty levels of popularity in the twentieth century without the demise of the American Derby is legitimately debatable, but the latter's disappearance unquestionably facilitated the Kentucky Derby's cultural ascension.

In August 1894 the debt-ridden Louisville Jockey Club was sold to a group of gamblers, bookies, and businessmen that called itself the New Louisville Jockey Club, led by "pool room" operators W. E. Applegate and William F. Schulte. The term *pool room* referred to halls where horse races were wagered upon in the form of "auction pools," in which the wagering rights to each horse in a given race were auctioned off, creating a pool of money that would be distributed to the bidder whose horse won the race after the "house" took its cut. (Pool rooms often included billiards tables, giving rise to the colloquial name of "pool" for games played on billiards tables.) M. L. Clark, the president and largest shareholder of the old Louisville Jockey Club, had not been paid his salary for more than two years. From the proceeds of the sale, the old group was able to pay all its creditors except for Clark, who declared, "I could wish nothing worse for my worst enemy than that he should become my successor and contend with all that I have contended with."[15] Clark and the old group had been criticized for the declining quality of racing in Louisville and the declining status of the racetrack among American horsemen. It seems that the old organization had been more interested in sport-for-sport's-sake than in turning a profit. This approach contributed significantly to the early success of the Derby but was not conducive to long-term viability for the racetrack or its signature event.

Despite his suggestions that he would be moving on to greener pastures, Clark was convinced by the new ownership group to remain a part of the Derby and of Churchill Downs as presiding judge, a significant post in the days before photo-finish cameras. Clark had an untarnished reputation for integrity and was known across the world of racing for his refusal to tolerate any semblance of dishonest race riding by jockeys, gambling-related conspiracy, or other racetrack chicanery. Clark's enthusiasm for enforcing rules did get him into trouble at times, however, and sometimes even led to gunplay: in one instance he was shot in the shoulder by a disgruntled horse owner named Thomas G. Moore, who claimed that he had been insulted by Clark when Clark refused to allow him to run horses at the Louisville Jockey Club track because Moore was in debt to the racetrack. Moore confronted Clark after the races at the Galt House Hotel in Louisville and demanded an apology. Clark refused, and both men drew pistols. Moore shot Clark in the shoulder, but Clark soon recovered. Moore was subsequently banned from the racetrack for one year for "his language and conduct on the track during the meeting." Descriptions and explanations of the events surrounding the altercation between Moore and Clark vary wildly. But Clark's reputation as a racing official who would not stand for underhandedness or even the appearance of it on the racetrack was solid.[16]

"I do not like a bone in Clark's body," one horseman proclaimed, "but he is the straightest turfman in the world, and is recognized as such all over the world. If I have to race for my life I would rather have Clark tap the drum and get in the judge's stand than any other man I know of."[17] Clark's firm stance against racetrack misbehavior helped to keep opponents of racing in Louisville at bay and had enabled Churchill Downs and the Kentucky Derby to survive their infancy. In an era when racetracks were perennial targets of various reform movements, Clark's reputation would have been invaluable to an ownership group that was heavily tied to professional gambling, the element of horse racing that its opponents most feared and detested.

The new ownership did its best to quiet the growing numbers of "progressive" reform-minded groups in Louisville that were opposed to horse racing, gambling, and drinking. In an attempt to assuage the fears of racing opponents, the New Louisville Jockey Club included the phrase "No improper characters admitted" in its spring 1896 print ads.[18] This phrase could be construed as either a warning or a marketing ploy, but regardless, it was a sign that the new ownership group was well aware of growing suspicion of the appropriateness of racing and gambling in America.

The new owners also made some much-needed upgrades to the grounds at Churchill Downs. They immediately embarked on a campaign of improvement to the racetrack's facilities that included the construction of a new grandstand on the opposite side of the track from the original structure, which had fallen into disrepair. The new location meant that patrons were no longer forced to look into the afternoon sun to view the races. Like the old building, it included a separate ladies' section situated so that women could enjoy the racing from comfortable seats that were a safe distance from the "unseemly" betting shed. The new grandstand, adorned with the now-iconic twin spires, was ready for Derby Day 1895, earning plaudits from press and patrons alike.[19]

Conspicuously absent from the new facility was a clubhouse. The old clubhouse was still standing, but it was now inaccessible from the grandstand on the opposite side of the track. Unlike the original Louisville Jockey Club organizers, the new group was not socially prominent in Louisville's exclusive circles. The New Louisville Jockey Club's background was in gambling. Schulte, Applegate, and the other investors were more concerned with providing easy access (for men) to the betting shed than they were with providing society types with a separate seating area.

The new ownership did listen to the long-standing complaints of horsemen, however, and as part of the track renovation, new world-class stable facilities were constructed. Additionally, the new group addressed the grumblings, heard from horsemen and journalists for years, about the Kentucky Derby's excessive distance. For the 1896 Derby, track officials shortened the race

The famous Churchill Downs twin spires, ca. 1903. Construction on the new grandstand began in 1894; it was ready for the 1895 spring meet. The colonnaded clubhouse to the left was added in 1903. (Keeneland Library, Lexington, Kentucky.)

to its present distance of a mile and one-fourth from its original one-and-a-half-mile length, a decision that paid immediate dividends. That year New York racetrack owner and notoriously heavy gambler Michael F. Dwyer (who along with his brother Phillip had owned 1881 winner Hindoo) again reached the Derby winner's circle when Ben Brush defeated seven rivals in a competitive race reminiscent of the Derby's early years. Ben Brush's victory ended a long string of unremarkable races and squelched much of the journalistic criticism of the event. After the race, a collar of roses was placed on Ben Brush, the first documented instance of that honor.

Things were looking up for the track and for its signature event, but less than three years later the Derby lost its founder and chief proponent. On April 22, 1899, Meriwether Lewis

Clark was found dead at the age of fifty-three from a self-inflicted gunshot wound in a Memphis hotel. His doctor reported that Clark had been suffering from "melancholia." There was some speculation that Clark may have experienced financial hardship in the aftermath of the economic depression that hit the United States beginning in 1893, but he had battled depression much of his life.[20]

Clark had dreamed that the Derby's significance would one day exceed that of any other horse race in the nation. In the Derby's early years he had predicted that one day the winner of the race would be worth more than the farm on which he was raised.[21] This seemingly preposterous prognostication had been fulfilled by the 1881 winner, Hindoo, and continues to be true today, with syndications of recent Derby winners for stud purposes (including Fusaichi Pegasus, Smarty Jones, and Big Brown in the past decade) reaching well into the tens of millions of dollars.

Clark had established the Kentucky Derby as a major date on the local social calendar and as a noteworthy event in the pages of the national sporting press. He had worked tirelessly, often without pay, to ensure that the Louisville Jockey Club was a respectable organization and an attractive destination. While his temper, arrogance, opulent lifestyle, and expensive habits of consumption may have kept Clark from being thoroughly embraced and celebrated by the public and the press in his lifetime, no one could dispute his crucial role in the development of the Derby.

Three years after Clark's death the New Louisville Jockey Club underwent a major change in management. Majority shareholder William Applegate maintained a significant interest in the business, but turned over operational control to a new group that included Louisville mayor Charles Granger and the man who would become the human face of the Kentucky Derby for almost fifty years, Martin J. "Matt" Winn. Applegate understood that the racetrack required new energy and focus if it were to survive. Unlike the prior group, the new management team was made up

Martin J. "Matt" Winn (right), the man more responsible than anyone for the Kentucky Derby's ultimate success, would later be called "Mr. Derby" by sportswriters. (Keeneland Library, Lexington, Kentucky.)

of socially prominent Louisvillians who were able to attract a wider group of spectators to the races than had their immediate predecessors. Thus began the most important period in the history of Churchill Downs and the Kentucky Derby.

Plans for a new clubhouse at Churchill Downs had been in the works before the 1902 shakeup, and they were quickly implemented. Today what is commonly referred to as the clubhouse is actually a sprawling conglomeration of luxury suites, box seats, and dining rooms, including a section favored by celebrities called Millionaires' Row, but it was once a freestanding building reserved for members of the Louisville Jockey Club and their guests. The cost of construction was partially offset by the sale of two hundred club memberships to leading Louisvillians

Churchill Downs clubhouse, ca. 1914. The new clubhouse opened to rave reviews in 1903, evoking the Old South with its white columns and wide veranda. (Photographic Archive, P_00408, Special Collections, University of Louisville, Louisville, Kentucky.)

for $100 apiece. The new clubhouse was designed in the Classical Revival style and included a wide veranda reminiscent of the Old South. The *Kentucky Irish-American* called it "a thing of beauty."[22] The attention paid by the press to the new facilities underscores the emphasis that the new group in charge of Churchill Downs placed upon marketing their product to general populations, including the socially prominent, rather than just to hardcore gamblers. This had been a major concern of Lutie Clark's, but the upper classes had received less attention from the group that immediately succeeded him. By reestablishing the Derby and Churchill Downs as a playground for the rich, Winn helped raise the stature of, and prospects for, both the event and the racetrack.

Matt Winn was born in a small house on Louisville's Fifth

Street, between Main Street and the Ohio River. His father, an Irish immigrant, owned a local grocery store. After attending Catholic grammar school and Bryant & Stratton business school, Winn began his professional life as a teenaged bookkeeper for a glass company. He later accepted a position as a traveling sales-man for a Louisville wholesale grocery company, affording him the chance to buy, sell, and barter his way across the Common-wealth for ten years. Then, in 1887, Winn's tailor approached him with a proposition: he needed capital to expand his clothing operation and a partner with sales experience. Winn accepted the offer of partnership and entered the clothing business, where he would remain until joining the administrative team at Churchill Downs in 1902.

In his tenure of almost half a century at Churchill Downs, there was quite simply no better promoter of the Derby than Matt Winn. "Colonel" Winn, as he was widely known, was a gregarious fellow and an aficionado of bourbon whiskey (though "never before noon") and cigars. Winn did not earn his colonel-ship from any military service. Kentucky colonel is an honorary title that has been bestowed upon thousands of men and women through the years. Isaac Shelby, then in his second stint as gov-ernor of Kentucky, granted the first Kentucky colonelship during the War of 1812. In its early years the colonelship carried some official duties and responsibility, but the title had been complete-ly honorary and ceremonial since the late 1800s.[23]

Winn was awarded his title by Kentucky governor J. C. W. Beckham while Winn was serving on Mayor Granger's Board of Public Safety in 1904. (Ironically, Beckham would lose a 1927 gubernatorial bid on a platform opposed to wagering on horse racing.)[24] The title bestowed on Winn by Beckham was a cru-cial element in the ultimate success of the Kentucky Derby. Winn was terribly proud of his title, and his name was practically nev-er printed or uttered without the "Colonel" prefix from that day forward. Notwithstanding the title's purely honorary signifi-cance, to Winn, the son of an immigrant grocer, it represented a symbolic statement of status. The title became an indispensable part of Winn's identity and persona, which Winn would eventually exploit masterfully in his promotion of the Derby.

Winn worked tirelessly to encourage top owners to bring their stock to Churchill Downs and to elicit favorable reviews of the Kentucky Derby from influential sportswriters. In doing so, Winn served as a living, breathing advertisement for Kentucky as a place where colonels sip juleps and smoke cigars on verandas. In his travels to promote the Derby, he was also promoting himself as an embodiment of a lifestyle—a lifestyle that could be enjoyed by those who came to the Kentucky Derby.

The legend of Matt Winn became an important part of Kentucky Derby mythology and lore. Winn claimed to have seen every Kentucky Derby in person, including the very first from the back of his father's grocer's cart in the Churchill Downs infield. He also claimed that he had saved the Derby in 1902 by forming the group that took over the struggling track. By his own account, Winn, then a merchant tailor and a gambler, was asked by Churchill Downs's secretary Charlie Price to buy the financially strapped racetrack.[25] According to his autobiography, Winn was at first shocked by the request. He told Price that he was nothing more than a tailor and did not know the first thing about running a racetrack. Price told Winn that if no buyer could be found, the racetrack would be forced to close, and there would be no more Kentucky Derbies. To this Winn claimed to have responded, "This is a rash and reckless thing you are asking me to do. I'd say no and make it stick for a thousand years if it involved anything but the Derby. But they mustn't stop running that race."[26] The tailor was able to raise the money from a group of his "close friends," including Mayor Granger, and Churchill Downs was purchased for $40,000. In reality, the majority owner of the racetrack, W. E. Applegate, was the driving force behind the deal that brought Winn and Granger to the racetrack, and Applegate retained a significant percentage of ownership.[27] But the facts do not make nearly as romantic a story as the one that Winn remembered about the reorganization that took place at Churchill Downs in 1902; Winn was as capable a self-promoter as he was a promoter of the Kentucky Derby.

Racing historian Joe Palmer made light of the larger-than-life persona that Winn created for himself and sold to the American public: "It is no longer possible to write anything new about Colonel Matt Winn," Palmer wrote, with tongue firmly in cheek. "He came into Kentucky through the Cumberland Gap (it is a baseless legend that he cut it himself) about 1770. After clearing the land of cane breaks and Indians, he gave his mind to further improvement and invented bourbon whiskey, the Thoroughbred horse, hickory-cured ham, and Stephen Foster. It was not until 1875 that he risked the combination of all these elements and produced the first Kentucky Derby."[28] Winn's contributions to the growth of the Kentucky Derby were undoubtedly immeasurable. But his almost legendary stature has largely worked to obscure exactly what those contributions were.

In 1908, the rise to power of an antigambling group in Louisville challenged the Derby's very existence and eventually afforded Winn the opportunity to change the face of Thoroughbred racing in America. Still stinging from fierce opposition from track president Charlie Grainger during election season, the new city hall group wasted no time in passing an ordinance that banned bookmakers (then the primary means of wagering on horse racing) from operating in Louisville. Reform groups had been a thorn in the side of Churchill Downs since at least 1877, when they opposed a proposal to make Derby Day a local holiday, but this threat was much more serious. The future of the racetrack, which relied heavily on licensing fees from bookies, was in immediate and serious jeopardy—the very survival of the Kentucky Derby was threatened. Track officials quickly scrambled to find some way around the new law, and the possibility of reinstituting the pari-mutuel (French for "bet among ourselves") wagering system was soon suggested. Older racing enthusiasts recalled that Lutie Clark had first encountered this then-revolutionary system of wagering (invented by Parisian Pierre Oller in 1865) while traveling in Europe prior to the founding of Churchill Downs. The pari-mutuel system created a pool of all money wagered on a given race. After the "house" took its cut, the pool would be split by those who had placed a wager on the winning horse in proportion to the amount wagered. Thus, the more money bet on a particular horse, the lower the odds and return would be for those who bet on that horse. The system removed the possibility of underhandedness on the part of human bookmakers, but required a complicated machine to calculate the figures.

Upon hearing of the plan to circumvent their antigambling law, city leaders reminded track officials of an old Kentucky state statute that banned "machine" gambling. The law was intended to prohibit machines that facilitated games like keno and faro, but by the letter of the law it appeared that pari-mutuel machines would be in violation. Fortunately for the future of horse racing, Winn and Grainger recalled that while Clark had promised to have a pari-mutuel system in place for the opening of the Louisville Jockey Club in 1875, it was not actually implemented until 1878. The pair discovered to their delight that in that three-year interim Clark had sought and acquired an exemption for pari-mutuel wagering in the form of an amendment to the machine gambling law, which allowed that system to operate until 1889, when pressure from bookmakers forced Clark to discontinue its use. Winn and Grainger quickly began an exhaustive search for the machines necessary to reimplement the system. They found one in a Churchill Downs storeroom and another in a Louisville pawnshop. Two more turned up, but they still needed additional machines to handle the Derby Day crowd. They found an unlikely savior in Phil Dwyer, who with his brother had been responsible for the introduction of bookmakers to Churchill Downs. Dwyer located two additional machines in New York City, where the pari-mutuel system had proven unpopular in the 1870s and had been abandoned.[29]

The *New York Times* reported that the on-site money bet on the Derby that year was less than half of what it usually was, but conceded that much of that difference could be attributed to the thunderstorm that dumped nearly three-fourths of an inch of rain on Louisville on Derby Day, creating "fetlock deep" mud on the track. Bettors who placed the minimum $5 wager (it would be lowered to $2 two years later) to win on Stone Street that wet day were rewarded with a $123.60 return on their investment.[30]

Later that year the Kentucky State Court of Appeals (then the highest court in the Commonwealth of Kentucky) held in *Grinstead v. Kirby* that pari-mutuel wagers were legal under Kentucky law, ensuring that Derby patrons would have an officially sanctioned means of backing their favorite horse in what, for many, would become an important part of the Derby experience. Unlike bookmakers, whose interest in the outcome of races could invite the appearance of (or actual) chicanery and corruption, the operators of pari-mutuel wagering had no rooting interest in the actual outcome of the races as the amount bet on each horse determined the odds for that horse. Also, the pari-mutuel system possessed a communal quality as winners collected from a pool created by all the punters. This slight distinction from a wager between two people in which there was one winner and one loser was significant to reformers, who objected to a winner "taking" from a loser.[31] This "sanitized" form of gambling would eventually be the path to the restoration of racing in many of the states that had abandoned it, and today is by far the most prominent method of gambling on American racing.

With the survival of racing in Louisville assured, Winn embarked on a quest to make the Kentucky Derby the most important race in the country. To accomplish this task, he would need all of his charm and charisma to win the support of racing's top owners, who were focusing their racing campaigns on the more prestigious and richer races in the East. In that endeavor Winn received some fortuitous help from a piece of legislation pushed by the governor of New York, the future chief justice of the U.S. Supreme Court, Charles Evans Hughes.

On June 11, 1908, the New York legislature passed the Hughes-supported Hart-Agnew bill (named for the bill's legislative sponsors), outlawing all gambling in New York. Though it did not specifically prohibit horse racing, this law eventually led to the blackout of the 1910 and 1911 racing seasons on the country's most important racing circuit which, in turn, forced eastern owners to find alternative locations to run their horses (some shipped their horses overseas) or to abandon the sport entirely. The Hart-Agnew law followed in the footsteps of other laws passed across the country that came close to effectively ending the sport of Thoroughbred racing in the United States. In 1906 Tennessee, once a major center of Thoroughbred racing, outlawed gambling on the sport. States across the South and across the country soon followed suit. Opponents of the sport claimed that racing had become tainted by the influence of gamblers from the North. While it may have been acceptable for gentlemen to wager on the outcome of sporting events, professional gamblers were seen as a different element entirely.

In 1897 there had been 314 racetracks operating in the United States and 41 in Canada. By 1908 the number of active racetracks in the United States and Canada had fallen to 31.[32] After the wave of reform that hit the sport in the early 1900s, racing would not reach its preform levels of popularity until the 1930s, when many states began to approve pari-mutuel racing in order to increase tax revenues during the Great Depression. This general decline in American racing at the beginning of the twentieth century made the survival of racing at Churchill Downs in that era all the more significant.

As the antigambling movement was sweeping the nation in the late nineteenth and early twentieth century, another dramatic change was permanently altering the face of American Thoroughbred racing—the disappearance of black jockeys from the sport. In the early days of Churchill Downs and the Kentucky Derby, blacks were annually among the leading jockeys and trainers. In the first Kentucky Derby, thirteen of the fifteen riders were black, including the winning jockey, Oliver Lewis. But by the early 1900s black riders had all but disappeared, not only from the Kentucky Derby but from major American racing as a whole. In 1975, ninety-six-year-old trainer Nate Cantrell recalled the end of the era of black dominance in American racing. "In the old days, if you ran twelve horses, from six to eight of the jockeys were always black. And it remained that way until a lot of money got in the game. The white men then, like they do now and like they've always been, wanted his people to have, not only the money, but also the reputation."[33]

In the early days of American racing, particularly in the South, many jockeys had been slaves. After emancipation, many of these continued to serve their former masters in the same capacity. Relationships between white owners and their black trainers and jockeys in the years immediately after the Civil War continued to have undertones of a master-slave relationship. While jockeys were seen as mere tools of their owners, not successful athletes in their own right, white supremacy was not threatened. However, by the turn of the century, jockeys were becoming relatively rich and famous. There was widespread suspicion about professional athletes in general in this era as it became increasingly possible to make a good living in the realm of sport that had previously belonged only to those with disposable time and money. Having the leisure time to devote to sport was once an indicator of elevated social status. Professional athletes turned that system on its head. Black professional athletes were doubly unacceptable in this environment.

Black jockeys won half of the first sixteen Derbies, and fifteen of the first twenty-eight. Both Oliver Lewis and Ansel

Edward D. "Brown Dick" Brown, ca. 1900. One of the top horsemen of his era, Brown trained 1877 Derby winner Baden-Baden. (Keeneland Library, Lexington, Kentucky.)

Williams, the jockey and trainer of the first Derby winner Aristides, were black. Aristides was owned by the flamboyant H. Price McGrath, a tailor who had made a fortune in questionable gambling enterprises from New Orleans to New York, which afforded him the opportunity to enter the world of racing on a large scale. He wore large white hats and loud red neckties, and was fond of referring to "his darkies" as though they were property. In 1877 a black jockey-trainer tandem again found themselves in the Derby winner's circle after Billy Walker guided Baden-Baden to victory for trainer Ed "Brown Dick" Brown. Brown was one of the most successful trainers in the country and famous for his expensive suits and large bankrolls. Walker was one of the nation's top jockeys during the 1870s. The year he won the Derby aboard Baden-Baden, the U.S. Congress adjourned to watch Walker race in Baltimore aboard top horse Ten Broeck.

Ten Broeck the horse was named for Richard Ten Broeck the famous Kentucky breeder and father-in-law of Lutie Clark. The horse was also immortalized in a famous Kentucky folk song, "Molly and Tenbrooks." On July 4, 1878, Ten Broeck and Walker were part of one of the most famous match races in American history when they took on a filly from California named Mollie McCarthy at Churchill Downs. Walker and his horse won the race, but Clark had heard a rumor prior to the start that Walker planned to "throw" the race. Clark warned Walker: "You will be watched the whole way, and if you do not ride to win, a rope will be put about your neck, and you will be hung to that tree yonder and I will help to do it."[34]

During the 1880s Isaac Burns Murphy was the most famous rider in America. Despite his skin color, he was widely respected by race fans and horsemen for his skill in the saddle. In 1884, the same year Moses Fleetwood Walker became the last African American to play in a major league baseball game until Jackie Robinson, a newspaper report of Isaac Murphy's first Derby aboard Buchanan called his riding "admirable."[35] The report of Murphy's winning ride in the 1890 Derby aboard Riley fell beneath the headline "The Colored Archer," a reference to a famous white English rider Fred Archer. The article contained a handsome illustration of the jockey, and credited him with being the "greatest judge of pace this country ever saw." But the article

Isaac Burns Murphy, ca. 1890. Murphy, one of the greatest riders in American history, was the first jockey to win three Kentucky Derbies. (Hemment Collection, Keeneland Library, Lexington, Kentucky.)

also credited the mistress of the central Kentucky farm on which Murphy was raised for instilling him with "good breeding and fine moral character." In an effort to show that the large salary Murphy earned did not make him a threat to the racial order of white-dominated American society, the same article explained that Murphy had "always been very grateful to his benefactors," that he was "saving in his habits," and that he "spends his leisure hours in reading and studying."[36] Murphy's public image would stand in marked contrast to that of the twentieth century's first black superstar athlete, champion boxer Jack Johnson, whose conspicuous consumption, braggadocio, and tendency to associate with white women scandalized the nation and eventually resulted in Johnson's flight to Europe to escape trumped-up criminal charges.

In 1891 Murphy became the first jockey to capture successive Kentucky Derbies. This was Murphy's third victory in the Derby, a feat that would not be matched until 1930, when Earl Sande captured his third Derby aboard Triple Crown champion Gallant Fox. But Murphy's career quickly went downhill after his last Derby victory. He battled weight problems and was widely believed to have struggled with alcoholism. Murphy died in 1896 at the age of thirty-four or thirty-five. More than five hundred people attended his Lexington funeral service, but his place in popular memory has been inconsistent since then.

In the year of Murphy's death a black jockey named Willie Simms won his first Kentucky Derby aboard Ben Brush. Simms, like Murphy a posthumous inductee into the National Thoroughbred Racing Hall of Fame, won two Kentucky Derbies in the 1890s and was applauded by the sporting press both for his prowess in the saddle and his deferential demeanor. Following one of the greatest rides in Derby history, which gave Simms his second Derby victory aboard Plaudit in 1898 by a whisker's margin, the jockey told reporters, "There is not much to say about it, and I suppose the people in the stand who are more familiar with racing can tell more about the race than I can."[37] It would be unfathomable for a modern athlete to suggest that any spectator might know more about a performance than the athlete him- or herself, but this says much about the environment in which Simms and other black jockeys existed in the late 1800s. There was no mention of the skin color or race of the winning jockey and trainer in the coverage of the first Kentucky Derby, but by the end of the nineteenth century, "blackness" had become more significant. While riders like Murphy and Simms were celebrat-

Willie Simms, ca. 1894. Simms won two Kentucky Derbies, in 1896 (Ben Brush) and in 1898 (Plaudit). (Hemment Collection, Keeneland Library, Lexington, Kentucky.)

ed as outstanding jockeys, they also won approval for remaining within their "place" as black Americans.

The last great black jockey to ride in the United States, Jimmy Winkfield, was also the last black jockey to win the Kentucky Derby, a feat he accomplished in 1901 and 1902. In 1901 Winkfield, called "a little chocolate colored negro" by the *Courier-Journal*, won the Derby aboard His Eminence, but was replaced as the horse's rider later that summer in favor of a white jockey.[38] In 1902 Winkfield became the second jockey (joining Isaac Murphy) to win consecutive Kentucky Derbies. Described that year

Jimmy Winkfield, winner of back-to-back Kentucky Derbies in 1901 and 1902, and the last black jockey to win the race. (Keeneland Library, Lexington, Kentucky.)

by the *Courier-Journal* as "black as the ace of spades," Winkfield won aboard Alan-a-Dale, a horse bred, owned, and trained by a great-grandson of famous Kentucky statesman Henry Clay.[39] Winkfield himself also had connections to the "Great Compromiser," as his mother, Victoria, was descended from slaves owned by Henry Clay.

In the weeks leading up to the 1903 Derby, Winkfield was still considered one of racing's top national riders. Journalistic descriptions, however, demonstrated that this title would have to be accompanied by an asterisk. Local press reports described

Winkfield as "a colored boy, but one of the great race riders of the world."[40] Jockeys had not always been given so much individual attention in the press. But by the turn of the century, as riders were receiving more fame and money, black jockeys were being forced out of American racing. The year 1903 proved to be Winkfield's final Kentucky Derby. Later that year he agreed to ride for one of the nation's top owners and trainers, John E. Madden, master of Hamburg Place outside of Lexington, Kentucky, in what was then the nation's richest race, the Futurity at Sheepshead Bay in New York. Winkfield, however, accepted a $3,000 offer from another owner to break his contract with Madden, who had won the 1898 Derby as the owner and trainer of Plaudit and would later breed five Derby champions. Upon learning of this breach of contract, Madden told the rider that he would see to it that Winkfield would not ride for anyone in the United States again. While that threat did not entirely pan out, Winkfield's offers for mounts did fall drastically and he was forced to leave the country to ply his trade.[41]

Though black jockeys became increasingly rare in American racing in the early 1900s, blacks were still employed in large numbers as grooms and stable hands at racetracks and breeding farms. Grooms did not receive public attention or adulation like top jockeys or trainers did, remaining in the background and performing subservient roles. Black grooms and exercise riders fit nicely within traditional racial hierarchies, and were often described as merely part of the Derby scenery by journalists. Black jockeys' successes in the Derby in the event's first quarter century were realized at a time when Churchill Downs leaders were often struggling to keep the track and the Derby in operation. But by the time the Derby and Churchill Downs reached solid footing, black jockeys would not be there to share the spotlight.

In 1911 jockey Jess Conley, a black rider, would finish third in the Kentucky Derby aboard Colston. The horse was named for his owner, a black former jockey named Raleigh Colston.

The *Louisville Herald* reported that "Colston carried the dollar of every dusky hued spectator in the city. Had Colston won there would sure have been some pork chop feasts in town today."[42] After Colson, only one black jockey would ride in the Kentucky Derby until Marlon St. Julian finished ninth aboard Curule in 2000, the exception being Henry King's tenth-place finish aboard Hal Price Headley's Planet in 1921. In 1930 the *Baltimore Afro-American* reported that there were "fewer than half a dozen" black jockeys riding in the United States.[43] Top jockeys who in the 1870s and 1880s had been called simply "riders" or "jockeys" in newspaper reports were by the turn of the century "black jockeys." Soon they would be forgotten almost altogether for decades, only briefly remembered in obituaries or obscure articles that would recall a strange time when jockeys were not all white in the United States.

Over the years writers and historians have suggested several causes for the disappearance of black jockeys. Many have argued that the migration of blacks to the industrial North in the twentieth century removed blacks from regular exposure to horses. One old-timer horseman explained that black jockeys had simply gone out of use, "like the old sidebar buggy of that period."[44] In fact, black riders were forced out of the sport by jealous white jockeys and bigoted owners and trainers in an increasingly racially biased American society whose court system had given official sanction to various Jim Crow laws by the end of the nineteenth century. As the Derby became increasingly popular on a national scale in the twentieth century, blacks still played indispensable roles in the lives of racehorses and the sport of horse racing. But grooms, hot-walkers, and stable hands operated far from the spotlight that would shine ever brighter on top athletes, including jockeys.

As the increasingly white Derby was wallowing in short fields and mediocre performances on the racetrack at the turn of the century, Kentucky's reputation in the national press was not far-ing much better. Stories about violence and lawlessness in the Bluegrass State were pervasive in national print media, which did not help to attract either people or horses to the Derby. In the aftermath of the Civil War, and in the presence of growing nationalism at home and abroad, Americans in the late nineteenth century wanted to know what made their country unique. In this environment, "local color" books and articles became fashionable with American audiences. Eastern Kentucky became a favorite topic for writers in this emergent genre. Tales of violence and "feuds" in mountainous eastern Kentucky fit well into the popular notion that Kentucky was different. Stories of the Hatfield-McCoy feud, waged on the border between Kentucky and West Virginia, were especially popular with late nineteenth-century audiences.

Feuds and politically motivated violence in the region in the late 1800s were reported zealously from the Breathitt County seat of Jackson, described by one reporter as "a miserable town in the heart of the hills."[45] Writers were generally content to give their eager readers explanations of the violence that bordered on the absurd (including a fight over a watermelon, lingering resentment over the results of the Civil War, and slanderous remarks about a relative) rather than attempt to arrive at any real understanding of the causes of the violence.[46] In almost every case, reports of the mountains included tacit assumptions that the violent and lawless mountaineers could not be explained in a way that readers could understand. These were people who were assumed to be different by their very nature, and certainly distinguishable from (though related to) their central Kentucky lowland brethren. But this distinction existed more in perception than in reality, as national newspapers covered violence occurring across the state at the dawn of the twentieth century.

In 1900 Kentucky became (and remains) the only state to have a sitting governor assassinated. On January 30, William Goebel was shot outside the state capitol building in Frankfort where the state legislature was deliberating over the results of a contested gubernatorial election that, according to the certification of the Board of Election Commissioners, had been won by Republican William S. Taylor by scarcely two thousand votes. Civil war seemed imminent when Taylor called in the state militia and ordered the legislature to reconvene more than one hundred miles away in London, located in the southern part of the state. However, the legislative committee called upon to investigate the election invalidated enough "illegal" Republican votes to declare Goebel the rightful winner. Goebel was sworn in as governor before he died, and eventually court decisions upheld the legitimacy of the Democratic legislature's findings. Goebel's death created deep fissures in Kentucky politics for decades to come and reaffirmed Kentucky's national reputation as a hotbed of lawlessness and violence.

Kentucky violence, and coverage of it by national newspapers, did not end with the Goebel assassination. The feuds of eastern Kentucky that had fascinated Americans in the late nineteenth century continued into the twentieth. In 1904 the *New York Times* ran a lengthy article beneath the headline "Kentucky's Reign of Terror and Murder: A Tale of Savage Personal Warfare Unparalleled in the History of Civilized Communities."[47] The article described the bloodshed in Breathitt County, Kentucky, over the previous two years and previewed further anticipated violence. Five years later, in 1909, the same newspaper again visited Jackson, the Breathitt County seat, claiming, "Breathitt County [is] again a battlefield: Election night starts a new feud in Jackson with an outbreak of violence reviving old feudal days and calling out troops."[48] Again the *Times* described "Bloody Breathitt" in a way that made its inhabitants seem like crazed maniacs. The previous summer the newspaper had reported calls coming from central Kentucky to "abolish" the county entirely.[49]

The western part of Kentucky also had its share of well-publicized violence in the first years of the twentieth century. At that time tobacco farmers, particularly those in the "Black Patch" region of western Kentucky and Tennessee (so named because of the "dark-fired" tobacco grown in the region), were struggling to survive. The American Tobacco Corporation, owned by James Buchannan Duke, had obtained a virtual monopoly on the American tobacco market, driving prices paid to farmers to critically low levels. In response, farmers in the Black Patch organized a cooperative called the Planters' Protective Association, with the goal of pooling tobacco crops to achieve higher prices.[50]

Only about a third of the Black Patch growers joined the association, and the American Tobacco Company tried to cripple the Protective Association by offering nonmembers higher prices for their crop. The area soon turned violent as vigilante groups of Night Riders attempted to intimidate growers not participating in the association with barn burnings, whippings, beatings, and even murder. Eventually the violence spread beyond the group's original goal, and vigilantes began to target personal enemies and blacks. In 1907 the Planters' Protective Association officially repudiated the Night Riders. Kentucky governor A. E. Willson dispatched troops to calm the region, and the violence subsided by 1909.

During the early 1900s, these reports of violence in the national press did not paint an appealing picture of the state and did not encourage tourism to the area which, in the short run, had negative consequences for Kentucky and the Derby. Had popular memory of Kentucky as a lawless and ultra-violent land not faded, it might have been quite difficult for event promoters to convince travelers or horsemen to visit Kentucky. However, once the reports of violence in Kentucky abated, residual interest in tales of mountain feuds remained, ensuring that Kentucky remained a unique and interesting place in potential visitors' minds. The phenomenon is not unlike what has happened in recent years to the tourism industries of Vietnam, Northern Ireland, and the Balkans. Closer to home, the "Wild West" was

"Kentucky's Fame" postcard, ca. 1910. This postcard depicts some of the imagery most readily associated with Kentucky at the time, including a Kentucky "belle," a group of Night Riders crossing a tobacco field, a pistol, a Thoroughbred race-horse, and a bottle of bourbon. Though Kentucky's reputation for violence would dissipate, the Commonwealth would continue to be known for its racehorses, beautiful women, and bourbon whiskey. (Kramer Art Company Postcard Proofs, 199PH10.46, Kentucky Historical Society, Frankfort.)

not a tourist destination when guns were actually blazing, but crowds later flocked to Buffalo Bill's Wild West show in the eastern United States and across Europe, helping to pave the way for a tourism industry in the American West. The same was true in Kentucky.

As tales of Kentucky violence disappeared from the pages of American newspapers, the memory of the bloodshed quickly joined the reservoir of myth and legend that had originally helped make Kentucky unique in the minds of Americans. This notion was evident in a postcard produced in Cincinnati in 1910, the year after the end of the Tobacco Wars. The card contained a collage of images, including a Night Rider, a pistol, a bottle of bourbon, a "Kentucky Belle," and a racehorse, arranged beneath the title "Kentucky's Fame."[51] In the course of the following decade, the bourbon, the horse, and the belle would remain major icons associated with Kentucky. The Kentucky Night Rider would take his place among the alluring imagery associated with a legendary past that gave the state its distinct identity, and that imagery would soon help to make the Kentucky Derby the most popular sporting event in the country.

As the first decade of the twentieth century gave way to the second, Kentucky's reputation for violence would be eclipsed in American culture by a growing association between Kentucky and the memory of the Old South. This shift made Kentucky and the Derby more attractive to Americans at a time when the Old South was being remembered and celebrated (by whites) as a romantic time and place that was a model for racial, social, and gendered order in an ever-more-complicated modern world. This shift in the popular perception of Kentucky was another element in the confluence of events and circumstances that would eventually allow the Derby to take its place in the American pantheon of sporting events and, in time, become America's greatest sports spectacle.

2

The "Southern" Path to National Prominence

1910–1930

On the heels of the reintroduction of the pari-mutuel machines in 1908, Matt Winn again took a page from the book of M. L. Clark and returned the free infield policy to Churchill Downs on Derby Day in 1910. It was a fitting start to what would be the most important two decades of growth in the Derby's history. The "free field" had been an important part of the Derby's charm and identity in the early years but had been discontinued by the turn of the century in a shortsighted attempt to increase revenue. In the early years, the infield possessed a country fair atmosphere on Derby Day. Spectators could drive their buggies and wagons right into the middle of the racecourse and be part of a gathering that the *Courier-Journal* had described as "a regular Fifteenth-amendment crowd, for everybody was there, without regard to age, color, sex, or previous condition of servitude."[1]

Though the crowds in the free infield were small and tame by modern standards, they were a precursor to the unique infield environment that would begin to take its modern shape and feel in the 1960s, eventually earning a reputation as a world-class site of unbridled revelry. Winn himself would put the free infield policy on permanent hiatus in 1920 (a decision announced the year before), when the Derby's status as a major sporting extravaganza was more secure and demand for tickets was too high to justify free admission. But during the 1910s crowds filled the free infield on Derby Day, creating a festival atmosphere that connoted a significance of the race that transcended the world of horse racing. The 1910 crowd witnessed a front-running victory by lukewarm favorite Donau for his owner William Gerst of Nashville. Besides his win in the Derby, Donau was best known for making a scarcely fathomable forty-one starts as a two-year-old and for a disagreeable temperament that once manifested itself in a starting line tantrum that ended with Donau lying in the dirt, refusing to budge.

In 1912, with American racing decimated by antigambling laws, the *Daily Racing Form* declared that "there is no disputing the preeminence of the Kentucky Derby."[2] The *Kentucky New Era* proclaimed that the Derby stood "virtually alone as the sole survivor of the great classics of the American turf."[3] The following year its position would be further strengthened when the English Jockey Club passed the Jersey Act, named for its sponsor Victor Child Villiers, seventh Earl of Jersey, that effectively disqualified horses bred in the United States from being recognized as "pure" Thoroughbreds.[4]

In the early 1900s England had become a popular destination for wealthy American racehorse owners like James Ben Ali Haggin as racing and gambling became increasingly unwelcome in a growing number of American jurisdictions. The English did not appreciate the influx of new horses, which caused the supply of racehorses to outpace demand and led to a drop in the prices of English bloodstock. English authorities addressed the issue by raising questions about the American horses' purity of blood. The condescension toward American stock in England, combined with the onset of World War I soon thereafter, made European racing an unattractive option for most American owners. The Kentucky Derby was an indirect beneficiary of this turn of events as it was one of the few high-profile races in America

Derby postcard, ca. 1913. (Postcard Collection, KUAV2008MS016-08-0139, University of Kentucky Archives, Lexington.)

that had survived the reform movements aimed at eliminating gambling and horse racing across the country. The Jersey Act would be modified in 1949 to recognize American Thorough-breds. But by that time, American racing in general—and the Kentucky Derby specifically—were on much firmer footing than they had been in 1913.

As the Jersey Act was being finalized in England, long-shot Donerail won the Kentucky Derby in track-record time. Pari-mutuel wagering was still something of a novelty at that time, having been reintroduced to Churchill Downs only five years earlier. A $2 win ticket on Donerail paid the princely sum of $184.90, a figure that made headlines around the country and is still a record payout for the Derby. One of the thousands in attendance that day for the first time was August Belmont Jr., who watched the race with Kentucky governor James B. McCreary. Among his many accomplishments, Belmont was the chairman of the powerful Jockey Club, a founder of Belmont Park in New York, a primary financier of the construction of the New York City subway system, and a major Thoroughbred owner and breeder. Belmont's presence helped to resurrect and reaffirm the status of the race, which had still not yet completely recovered from its decline in the 1890s despite the significant signs of improvement and a brighter outlook in the face of serious decline in competition from other racing jurisdictions. Eastern racing's elite had long been skeptical about the quality of racing west of the Hudson River, but many joined Belmont in attendance the following year.

In 1914 the track record was again lowered at the Derby, this time by a gelding named Old Rosebud. The winning owner that year was Hamilton Applegate, the son of principal Churchill Downs stockholder W. E. Applegate and himself a Churchill Downs board member and director. The record-breaking colt was named after a brand of whiskey produced by Applegate and Sons distillery, which was also owned by the Applegate family. Old Rosebud paid only $3.40 for a $2 bet, but he proved to be a very talented runner over the course of his long career, winning half of his eighty lifetime starts. His victory was well covered by the national press, increasing the national exposure for Louisville's race. The *New York Times* reported that the 1914 Derby "was witnessed by one of the largest crowds that ever attended the event, including many society folk from neighboring cities, and leaders in turf circles from all over the country."[5] The *Daily Racing Form* observed that the "visiting easterners" were "especially numerous."[6]

The "leaders in turf circles" who were part of the 1914 Derby crowd returned to Louisville in 1915, some choosing to begin their racing seasons in Louisville for the first time. That year a talented filly named Regret became the first female to win the Derby, beating a top field of three-year-olds in wire-to-wire fashion for leading owner and multimillionaire Harry P. Whitney. "I do not care if she never wins another race, nor if she never starts in another race. She has won the greatest race in America and I

(*Above*) Regret, the first filly to win the Kentucky Derby, ridden by jockey Joe Notter. (Cook Collection, Keeneland Library, Lexington, Kentucky.)

(*Below*) Harry P. Whitney (left) twice owned the winner of the Derby: Regret (1915) and Whiskery (1927). (Keeneland Library, Lexington, Kentucky.)

am satisfied," Whitney told reporters and well-wishers after the race.[7] "The glory of winning this event is big enough, and Regret can retire to the New Jersey farm any time now."[8] Whitney, the dashing eldest son of wealthy former secretary of the navy William C. Whitney, had inherited fabulous amounts of money from both his father and his uncle, Colonel Oliver Hazard Payne. Whitney was married to artist and socialite Gertrude Vanderbilt and was an avid sportsman and a noted philanthropist. Because of his high national profile and celebrity status, Whitney's victory in the Derby only added to the national publicity that the race had received during the two previous years.

The year after Regret's historic win, Churchill Downs directors announced that they would raise the purse of the track's signature race to $15,000 for the 1917 running. This move was partially facilitated by renewed support of the Derby by eastern horsemen. The first group of owners and horses to compete for the richer purse was the most geographically diverse the event had ever attracted. With an interruption of European racing during the Great War, many American and European owners returned their stock to the United States, and some found their way to Churchill Downs in the spring. One of the international horses at the 1917 Derby was Omar Khayyam, named after an eleventh-century Persian poet and mathematician. Foaled in England and shipped to the United States as a yearling, Omar Khayyam rallied from well off the pace to catch favored Ticket in the homestretch, becoming the first foreign-born horse to wear the Derby roses.

Prior to the 1918 Derby, as the United States was in its second year of involvement in World War I, there was some question of the propriety of conducting a race meeting in a time of war. Colonel Winn was friendly with President Woodrow Wilson's personal physician, Admiral Cary Travers Grayson, who assured Winn that the president supported the continuance of racing. Armed with that information, Winn was emboldened to stand up to antiracing journalists and Kentucky governor Au-

Exterminator, with jockey Albert Johnson. Known as "Old Bones" to his fans, Exterminator won the 1918 Kentucky Derby. Matt Winn called him the greatest Thoroughbred he ever saw. (Cook Collection, Keeneland Library, Lexington, Kentucky.)

gustus Owsley Stanley, who had voiced his own concerns about wartime racing. In an attempt to gain some positive press, Colonel Winn promised to donate 10 percent of the proceeds from the 1918 meeting to the Red Cross. That spring Churchill Downs harvested one thousand bushels of potatoes in the infield to donate to the American war effort.

Previews of the 1918 Derby appeared in newspapers across the country, many of which assured readers that patriotic displays would be part of the Derby event that year. "Patriotism will be the keynote of the opening of the meeting, and a number of exercises of a military and patriotic nature have been arranged that will be in keeping with the times," the *Thoroughbred Record* reported.[9] That afternoon a chestnut gelding named Exterminator put on a masterful performance in the muddy going. Exterminator, later affectionately known as Old Bones by his many followers, went on to win fifty of his ninety-nine career starts.[10] He was successful at distances from five and a half furlongs to two and one-fourth miles (a furlong is one-eighth of a mile), and became one of the most popular racehorses ever to compete in the United States. Some of Exterminator's popularity may be attributed to his humble origins and surprising rise to prominence in the 1918 Derby.

Exterminator's owner, Willis Kilmer, made his fortune in the patent medicine industry as head of marketing and sales for a company that manufactured Kilmer's uncle's invention, "Swamp Root," a concoction of alcohol and the extracts of leaves and herbs that purportedly promotes kidney and liver function and is still manufactured today. Kilmer was looked down upon at first by many in the elite circles of American racing but soon became more accepted, in part because of his willingness to throw lavish parties. Exterminator, however, very nearly did not run in the Derby at all. In the months leading up to the 1918 Derby, Kilmer's best hope for victory seemed to lie with Sun Briar, champion two-year-old of 1917 and early favorite for the Kentucky Derby in 1918. But Kilmer's confidence in Sun Briar dropped after a poor showing at the Kentucky Association track in Lexington in the spring of 1918. Kilmer then bought Exterminator, a long shot for the Derby who had a propensity for fast morning workouts, to serve as a sparring partner for Sun Briar. Sun Briar failed to progress to Kilmer's satisfaction as the big race neared, and it looked like his Derby hopes would not be realized. But Matt Winn encouraged Kilmer to instead enter Exterminator, the workhorse. Exterminator was the longest shot in the field but won convincingly. Colonel Winn never hesitated to call Exterminator the best horse he had ever seen, nor was he shy in reminding people of his involvement in Exterminator's career.

In the summer after Exterminator's Derby victory, Winn issued a statement declaring that geldings (like Exterminator)

Willis Sharpe Kilmer, owner of Exterminator and promoter of the patent medicine Swamp Root. (Cook Collection, Keeneland Library, Lexington, Kentucky.)

would no longer be eligible to compete in the Derby.[11] Though the military role of horses had significantly declined with the advent of modern warfare, one purported justification of horse racing was to help determine superior genes that could be used to strengthen the breed and thereby improve a nation's military capability. Two months after the announcement, however, the Armistice was signed, ending the fighting in Europe, and the antigelding policy was never actually implemented at the Derby.

Commander J. K. L. Ross (right) and H. G. Bedwell, the owner and train-er, respectively, of Sir Barton, at Saratoga Race Course, ca. 1918. (Cook Collection, Keeneland Library, Lexington, Kentucky.)

The following year, 1919, Sir Barton became the first horse to capture both the Kentucky Derby and the Preakness Stakes, then went on to win the Belmont Stakes to complete what would later be called the American Triple Crown (the modern order

Sir Barton, the first horse to capture the American Triple Crown, with jockey Earl Sande. (Cook Collection, Keeneland Library, Lexington, Kentucky.)

and distances of the three races would not be firmly established until the 1930s). Sir Barton's owner, Commander J. K. L. Ross from Canada, had inherited millions of dollars from his father, who had founded the Canadian Pacific Railway in partnership. Ross was well known for his large wagers, including one on the outcome of the 1919 Derby for $50,000 with Arnold Rothstein, himself notorious for his role in the infamous Black Sox scandal, in which Chicago players were alleged to have accepted money to "throw" the World Series, that took place later that fall.[12] The 1919 Derby was run before what the *New York Times* (yet again) called the largest crowd ever assembled at Churchill Downs, estimated at fifty thousand. Estimates of the 1916 Derby had run as high as sixty thousand, but Churchill Downs brass never shied away from the term "record crowd." As national interest in the Derby continued to grow, the crowds would continue to set records.

Sir Barton was the fourth future Hall of Famer to win the Derby in six years, topping a remarkable string of successes for Winn and Churchill Downs. Sir Barton was inducted into the National Racing Hall of Fame in 1957 along with Regret and Exterminator. They would be joined by Old Rosebud the following year. These victories by top-class horses in the 1910s helped to raise the Derby's stature within American racing and American sport.

In reviewing Sir Barton's 1919 Derby, journalists employed poetic imagery and flowery language that had been absent during wartime. The Derby was fortunate to be hitting its stride at a time when the craft of professional sportswriting was coming into its own. Journalists were eager to celebrate a new culture of leisure that stood in marked contrast to the most destructive war in the history of humankind. They declared the dawn of a golden age of American sports. One particularly verbose reporter for the *Chicago Tribune* described the Derby that year as "a gay festival upon a fair Kentucky landscape after a blithe renewal of an epic tradition which is sacred to this picturesque soil of Daniel Boone, pretty women, and Henry Watterson." The host city of Louisville, the writer rhapsodized, had "wide old historic streets, a monument to its Confederate dead, habits strange and pleasant to the invader from the north, and men and women who sacrifice their comfort to make you happy."[13] A Lexington journalist reported, "The Kentucky Derby, all the romance, the rich flavor of tradition and the far-famed glamour the name implies, were more than realized today when the biggest crowd on record appeared at Churchill Downs. It was Kentucky's big day and the Kentuckians were there to demonstrate their state pride. And from every section of the country the clans had gathered to become Kentuckians temporarily."[14] By the end of the 1910s Kentucky and the Derby had become something that Americans wished to experience, and patrons of the Derby were more than mere witnesses to a sporting event. They "became" Kentuckians for a day.

A crowd of sixty thousand was on hand at Churchill Downs for the forty-sixth running of the Kentucky Derby on May 8, 1920. The "mass of humanity" in the stands saw an undersized brown gelding named Paul Jones break sharply from post position 2 and take an early lead as the field passed by the grandstand for the first time on a racetrack still slow and drying out from the previous day's rain. Held under restraint by jockey Ted Rice down the backstretch, Paul Jones was turned loose as the pair came out of the final turn toward the finish line, gamely holding off a determined rally by Harry P. Whitney's Upset in the homestretch to win by a head in a dramatic finish. It was a record-setting day at Churchill Downs: new Derby marks were established for field size, attendance, purse (prize money), and wagering handle. The *New York Times* called the race "the greatest Derby ever run."[15] After the trophy presentation, winning owner Ral Parr declared, "It is a grand and glorious feeling to be able to say that your horse won the Kentucky Derby, the most famous race in America, and I am certainly feeling that way right now. We found plenty of Southern hospitality during our stay and I shall always cherish the memories of this visit to Louisville."[16]

The city of Louisville had been inundated with racing fans all week. As many as twelve special Derby trains arrived from Chicago alone. The visitors overwhelmed the city's infrastructure of accommodations; many people had to sleep as best they could in hotel hallways and lobbies. Some hired taxies to drive them around all night, and some decided to forego sleep altogether in favor of establishing a place at the front of the admission line at the racetrack. This scramble to find a bed in Louisville during Derby Week would soon become as much a part of the tradition as roses and mint juleps.

Man o' War working out. Widely considered to be the best American racehorse of the twentieth century, Man o' War famously bypassed the 1920 Kentucky Derby. (Cook Collection, Keeneland Library, Lexington, Kentucky.)

One person who was not in Louisville that week, however, was Samuel D. Riddle, owner of Man o' War, the most celebrated three-year-old colt in America. Man o' War would eventually join the pantheon of 1920s American sports icons that included Babe Ruth, Jack Dempsey, Red Grange, Bill Tilden, and Bobby Jones, but he would do so without running in the Kentucky Derby. Riddle chose to begin Man o' War's racing season in the Preakness Stakes in Maryland, held that year ten days after the Derby and run over a distance of one and one-eighth miles. Riddle's decision to avoid the Derby that year was partially based on his belief that May was too early to ask a three-year-old to travel the Derby's one and one-fourth mile distance. Also, the horse was stabled in Maryland for the winter, requiring a long and possibly dangerous train trip to Louisville. Sir Barton had won the Preakness only four days after winning the Kentucky Derby, but

Riddle had his sights set on prestigious New York races later in the summer and wanted to make sure his horse would be fresh for a full campaign.

Man o' War won the Preakness and the Belmont Stakes on his way to an undefeated three-year-old season in 1920. He is generally accepted among racing historians as the greatest American Thoroughbred of the twentieth century, and among the most outstanding equine athletes of any time or place. After his retirement from racing, he attracted over fifty thousand visitors each year to Faraway Farm outside Lexington, Kentucky. Man o' War's twenty-first birthday party was broadcast to a national radio audience, and his funeral drew a crowd of thousands. Riddle's decision not to run a top-class three-year-old in the Kentucky Derby was newsworthy in 1920, but by the 1930s that decision would be *unfathomable;* seventeen years later, when Riddle owned a top-class three-year-old son of Man o' War named War Admiral, the decision to run him in the Kentucky Derby would be an easy one.

By 1920 the Derby had made great strides from relatively humble beginnings. The large crowds and journalistic fanfare that the Kentucky Derby attracted despite Man o' War's absence were testament to the fact that it was already more than just a horse race—it was a celebration of Kentucky, a place and an idea with deeply rooted historical and cultural meaning for Americans. But the fact that it was possible for the owner of America's greatest racehorse to choose not to run in the Derby shows that the event was still growing in terms of popularity and cultural cachet on its way to becoming America's greatest sports spectacle.

In the 1920s the rapidly moving and changing American cultural landscape included waves of restriction and rebellion in a conflicted atmosphere that produced jazz, flappers, women's suffrage, and bathtub gin—as well as Prohibition, the Scopes Monkey Trial, and the resurgence of the Ku Klux Klan. In the Roaring Twenties, Kentucky was a destination of escape from the realities and complexities of modern life for an apprehensive population that elected Warren G. Harding president on his campaign promise of a "return to normalcy" after an internationally and domestically active Wilson administration and World War I.[17] In an era of increasing commercialization and commodification in which President Coolidge famously declared that "the business of America is business," the Derby itself was becoming a consumable commodity as an experience. A journalist's description of the Derby as the "best advertisement [Kentucky] ever had" underscored that process.[18]

In 1921 "Colonel" Edward Riley Bradley won his first of four Derbies as an owner when his colt Behave Yourself caught another Bradley-owned colt, Black Servant, in the stretch, but because of a sizeable wager he had riding on Black Servant to win, Bradley had mixed emotions over the outcome.[19] Colonel Bradley had been a successful bookmaker in Hot Springs, Arkansas, and Memphis before opening a casino resort in Palm Beach, Florida, called the Beach Club. The club's charter allowed Bradley to operate "such games of amusement as the managers and members may from time to time agree on," which reportedly netted Bradley in excess of $1 million annually.[20] Acting on his physician's advice to work less and spend more time outdoors, in 1906 Bradley had purchased the tract of land outside Lexington, Kentucky, that would become Idle Hour Stock Farm, one of the most famous and successful American Thoroughbred breeding operations of the early twentieth century. The rolling hills, white fences, and grand mansion at Idle Hour embodied the archetypical Kentucky horse farm as imagined by outsiders.

While Behave Yourself and Black Servant were being lauded on the track, the black servants back at the farm were also celebrating. The *New York Times* reported that "every man and woman, white and colored, on Idle Hour Stock Farm received a bonus for ER Bradley's success in [the] Derby."[21] The irony of a patronizing story about black employees celebrating the success

Colonel Edward Riley Bradley, center, at Hialeah Race Track in south Florida, ca. 1928, won four Kentucky Derbies as an owner. (Keeneland Library, Lexington, Kentucky.)

of a pair of horses named Black Servant and Behave Yourself seems to have been lost on the press. The image of happy black workers back at the farm while the white owners were at the races reinforced the link between the Derby and the plantation-like horse farms of central Kentucky owned by goateed Kentucky colonels that evoked the romance of the Old South for many Americans. The appeal of these images was very much a part of the Derby popularity in its age of ascent.

Because of its allusions to idyllic plantation scenes and simpler times, Stephen Collins Foster's "My Old Kentucky Home" served as an appropriate anthem for the Derby as an antidote to the complicated, modern world of the 1920s. The first published reports of the playing of "My Old Kentucky Home" at the Kentucky Derby appeared in 1921.[22] By the end of the decade, Colonel Winn had replaced "The Star-Spangled Banner" with "My

Idle Hour Farm, owned by E. R. Bradley, outside Lexington, Kentucky, ca. 1926. (Keeneland Library, Lexington, Kentucky.)

Old Kentucky Home" as the song to be played as the Derby contestants made their way onto the racetrack. It soon became one of the most recognized traditions associated with the event, part of the emotional experience of the Kentucky Derby. As early as the 1930s, journalists covering the race were conveying an incorrect assumption that the song had been a part of Derby tradition since the very beginning.[23]

The Commonwealth of Kentucky was also involved in the creation and promotion of the Old South imagery that had become associated with the state and with the Derby. In 1921 the descendants of its antebellum owners sold Federal Hill, the mansion and property in Bardstown, Kentucky, that was purported to be the source of inspiration for Stephen Foster's "My Old Kentucky Home" to the Commonwealth of Kentucky. There is no real evidence that Foster ever actually laid eyes on his relatives' estate, but Federal Hill was opened as a state historical shrine in 1923 before being taken over by the Kentucky Division of State Parks in 1936.[24]

The house and property that constitute "My Old Kentucky Home" in Bardstown quickly became a major tourist attraction,

"My Old Kentucky Home." The Federal Hill mansion in Bardstown, Kentucky, was, according to legend, the inspiration for Stephen Foster's ballad "My Old Kentucky Home." The house and surrounding acreage became a state park in the 1920s, but there is no evidence that Foster ever visited Federal Hill, which was built and owned by his relatives. (Kentucky Historical Society, Frankfort.)

and Foster's song by the same name has been Kentucky's official state song since 1928.[25] The adoption of the song and associated imagery by the Kentucky Derby and the Commonwealth reflects the attractiveness of the "good old days" to Kentuckians and to the tourists who continue to patronize the Derby and Federal Hill in Bardstown.[26]

The playing of Foster's ode to bygone times as a prelude to the big race reminded spectators that they were witnesses to something special. Similarly, the long tradition of Kentucky governors' attendance at the Derby and participation in postrace ceremonies added political gravity to the event and strengthened the bond between Kentucky and its Derby. In 1922 Governor Edwin

P. Morrow presented winning owner Benjamin Block with a gold service tray after Block's colt Morvich justified his support from the bettors that made him the post-time favorite, taking control of the race soon after the start and cruising to a length-and-a-half victory over E. R. Bradley's Bet Mosie. Morrow took the opportunity at the trophy presentation to wax poetic about the Commonwealth: "Kentucky has always recognized and honored courage, courage in men and women, and courage in the Thoroughbred," he declared. "Today before the beauty and chivalry of Kentucky, courage was the quality which won the Kentucky Derby."[27] (Morrow himself knew something about courage as he was a vocal opponent of lynching and violence against blacks. In 1920 he summoned the National Guard to protect Will Lockett, a black man on trial for the murder of a white child, from a large lynch mob in Lexington.) Block, a New Yorker, happily accepted the trophy, exclaiming, "Next to the thrill and satisfaction afforded me by winning the Derby, I feel gratification in having met and come to know Kentucky and Kentuckians. They have fully justified everything that I have always heard of southern hospitality."[28] Block then attempted to summarize the significance of his Derby win, declaring, "It is the greatest day of my life. I feel too deeply to talk about it. My horse has won other races, but there is only one Kentucky Derby. Morvich could bring to me, or to himself, no greater honor."[29] Block concluded his acceptance by acknowledging the particular kindness and hospitality of Colonel Winn, a professional dispenser of the stuff, whose "title" alone evoked images of the Old South with all its charm and allure.

That year the *New York Times* reported that the Derby Day migration toward the racetrack in Louisville began very early in the morning ("in large part the municipality overlooked entirely the little formality of retiring for the night") as "old-time hacks with drivers of varying hues ranging between ebony and chrome yellow, were bustling and busy at what appeared [to be] uncanny hours."[30] In the face of increased urbanization, modernization, tensions between races, classes, and genders, and uncertainty on the international political stage, many Americans wished to experience what Kentucky seemed to have. The Derby and the festival atmosphere that surrounded it gave travelers an opportunity to escape by becoming Kentuckians for a day. In Kentucky, Americans could access, either personally or vicariously, a taste of the Old South without having to travel to the geographically and culturally distant Deep South. The Derby gave Americans a chance to experience a quasi–theme park version of a bygone era. In the 1920s the Derby was a destination where blacks were literally at the service of whites and women resembled the southern belles of yesteryear—at a time when traditional gender roles and racial hierarchies were being challenged in reality.

Colonel Matt Winn did his own part to maintain the connection between the Derby and the "good old days" in the minds of potential Derby patrons. Winn employed, in his words, a "long line of colored boys" as valets, who accompanied him on his travels around the country.[31] Most of the attention Winn gives his servants in his memoirs comes in the form of derogatory or condescending anecdotes. In one story the colonel recalls a trip he made to a Miami racetrack in 1925. Winn and his traveling companion found themselves inconvenienced when the hotel wouldn't allow their black servants to enter the premises. "The following day, when Butler's Negro valet and mine tried to get to our quarters in the hotel to serve us, they were barred. This promised to handicap us; we had taken along some Kentucky ham, and other Kentucky products, and had expected the boys to cook in our quarters and act as waiters while we entertained for some friends. The colored boys were needed to fit into our plans, but the room clerk ruled them out."[32] All ended well for Winn and his companion when strings were pulled, allowing the "colored boys" to prepare and serve the meal as planned.

Though black jockeys had all but disappeared from racing by the 1910s, black grooms and stable hands were still quite common. Journalists regularly referred to the black stable crews in their coverage of the Derby, but the "help" did not receive the praise or accolades that white trainers and jockeys did. Stories of happy black employees celebrating Derby victories in the 1920s reinforced the image of the happy servile Negro of the Old South. Americans had long understood Kentucky to be more racially tolerant and less volatile than the "Deep" South, and these feel-good stories about black servants and employees at Derby time validated those assumptions for those who wanted to believe.

In Louisville, whites prided themselves on a "cordial" relationship between whites and blacks in their city. As evidence, whites in Louisville could point to the fact that in their city blacks were not denied the right to vote, streetcars were not segregated, and serious race-related violence was relatively rare.[33] According to historian George C. Wright, these assertions were, strictly speaking, accurate, though the difference in oppression was only a matter of degree in comparison to what blacks faced in the deeper South.[34] Despite the reality, the longtime perception of the existence of a harmonious relationship between whites and blacks in Louisville and Kentucky created a more attractive environment for people traveling to, or imagining, the Kentucky Derby. This perception allowed Americans to envision Kentucky as a romantic place that embodied the most appealing elements of the Old South, and to ignore the sinister realities and legacies of slavery.

The process by which Kentucky "became" a pseudo-Confederate state after the fact is neither short nor simple. But it is an integral element of the Derby's growth in popularity in the first part of the twentieth century, so it must be explained. The explanation requires a brief abandonment of chronological narrative and a return to the nineteenth-century roots of Kentucky's "southern turn."

Historically, Kentucky was very much a "slave state," as it was home to approximately 225,000 slaves at the dawn of the Civil War, and slavery remained legal there until the ratification of the Thirteenth Amendment in 1865. Kentucky remained in the Union, however, never joining the Confederacy. During the Civil War, Kentucky flaunted a position of "belligerent neutrality."[35] Kentucky sent two to three times as many men to fight in Union blue than in Confederate gray, but by the turn of the century Kentucky had become decidedly pro-Confederacy in its collective memory, and honored its Confederate dead with memorials and statues across the state.

One of the earliest indications of the desire on the part of prominent Louisvillians to pursue and embrace a southern identity for their city was the decision to organize and host the Great Southern Exposition, which opened in 1883. In August of that year the nation turned its attention to Louisville when President Chester A. Arthur addressed the crowd gathered for the exposition's opening ceremony. The expo combined elements of trade shows, museums, and world's fairs and contained over fifteen hundred exhibits, including a miniature southern plantation. In organizing the event, Louisville business leaders, including Louisville Jockey Club president M. L. Clark, hoped to promote their city's industrial and commercial capabilities and achievements, thus placing Louisville among the world's great cities.[36]

The fact that city leaders chose to call their event the Great *Southern* Exposition reflects Louisville's wish to tie itself to a push for a "New South," which advocates hoped would be part of a growing national economy based upon industrialization and commerce. One of the leading proponents of the New South was Henry Watterson, a former Confederate officer and editor of the *Louisville Courier-Journal* from 1868 to 1919.[37] During this period Watterson was among the most nationally visible Kentuckians. Watterson's impassioned and articulate advocacy for the New South helped to convince the rest of the nation that Kentucky was indeed a southern state. His criticism of racism and violence suggested that Kentucky was a relatively moderate and progressive southern state, and his championing of the idea of a New South helped to further sectional healing as businessmen from all regions united around a goal of economic prosperity. Watterson's vision of a Louisville-led New South that would integrate itself into the growing national economy helped to reduce sectional tensions at the same time as it helped to raise Louisville's national profile.

In an 1894 speech that reflected the budding desire of many Americans to put the Civil War behind them and unite behind a new spirit of nationalism and industrial strength, Watterson addressed the Grand Army of the Republic (GAR), a fraternal order whose membership consisted of ex-Union soldiers, at its annual encampment reunion in Pittsburgh. He spoke of sectional reconciliation and of a common bond among all who had fought in the Civil War in proposing that the group's convention be held in Louisville the following year.

> Candor compels me to say that there was a time when our people did not want to see you. There was a time, when, without any invitation whatever, either written or verbal, without so much as a suggestion of welcome, you insisted upon giving us the honor of your company, and, as it turned out, when we were but ill-prepared to receive you. It [would be] a pity, now that we are prepared, now that the lid is off the pot and the latch-string hangs outside the door, you should refuse us the happiness of entertaining you, of receiving you.
>
> Whatever regrets may linger in any bosom, no one of us has any reason to blush for the events of the greatest combat known to human annals. There was never a war where there was so little of public wrong, so much of private generosity: never a war whose verdict was so decisive, whose consequences have been so beneficent. Thank God, the flag you will find there is our flag, as well as your flag: the flag of a united people and a glorious Republic, to freemen all over the world at once a symbol and a pledge.
>
> Oh long may it wave
> O'er the land of the free and the home of the brave.[38]

Watterson's speech brought tears to his own eyes, and elicited cheers from his enthusiastic audience. More important, he was successful in convincing the GAR to come to Louisville; the following year's encampment in 1895 remains the largest convention ever held in the city.[39] Ironically, this meeting of ex-Union soldiers helped to solidify Louisville's pseudo-Confederate identity as much as hosting the Southern Exposition had in the 1880s. Newspapers across the nation covered the encampment and lauded the southerners in Louisville who graciously welcomed their northern brothers in an environment of reconciliation and understanding. On the day before the festivities were set to begin, the *New York Times* reported that the "cherished plan of having the veterans of the Blue and the Gray meet for once in good fellowship on Southern soil, and together eat of the fruits of peace and good will that have ripened through three decades that have passed since the stirring days of the sixties, is on the eve of realization, and gorgeously has Louisville arrayed herself for the occasion."[40]

The encampment had been held in Baltimore, a city with just as much claim to southern status as Louisville, in 1882. But the *Times* made no mention of the South in its coverage of the Baltimore encampment that year.[41] This discrepancy reveals both a successful effort by Louisvillians and other Kentuckians to transform their city and state into one with a Confederate past, and the changing conditions in American culture and society taking shape by the 1890s.

In 1895 a large monument honoring Confederate soldiers was erected on Louisville's busy Third Street. Though the Union cause was the "home team" and the "winning team," no similar monument honoring the forces that fought for the United States of America in the Civil War Union would be built in the Falls City, once a center of Union sympathy and strength, for almost two decades. In 1902 the Kentucky state legislature established a Confederate Home for Southern Veterans and appropriated funds to create a monument commemorating the Confederate dead in the battlefield at Perryville. No monument to the Union dead would be built until 1928 after Congress appropriated money for the project. In 1910 Kentucky's General Assembly gave the Daughters of the Confederacy money to finish a statue of General John Hunt Morgan, a Confederate pillager and raider from the Bluegrass State. More than ten thousand people attended its unveiling the following year, and the statue remains in its place of prominence on Lexington's old courthouse lawn.

By the early twentieth century the wounds of the Civil War were healing as (white) Americans were uniting behind visions of white supremacy, a growing national economy, and a fledgling American empire. They blamed "the race problem" for the Civil War and celebrated the memory of the Old South as a place where "American" attributes like republicanism and self-sufficiency were valued.[42] The Derby was a beneficiary of this new interest in the South and in sectional reconciliation as Kentuckians embraced a new Confederate identity for their state, making Louisville and the Kentucky Derby more attractive to visitors. In the turn-of-the-century environment of Social Darwinism and the White Man's Burden, southern sins no longer seemed so egregious to the rest of the nation as they had immediately after the Civil War. Southerners no longer felt the need to justify past action as the rest of the country began to celebrate the old Confederacy as a welcome part of a collective American national memory.

At the turn of the century two of the United States' most popular writers, Kentucky natives James Lane Allen and John Fox Jr., were shifting their attention from the Kentucky highlands to the increasingly chic central Kentucky bluegrass region, where horse farms resembled the great southern plantations of yesteryear. In 1903 Fox's *The Little Shepherd of Kingdom Come*, the story of an antebellum Kentucky mountain boy named Chad who enters a new world when he joins a party that floats down the Kentucky River and into the bluegrass, became an imme-

CONFEDERATE MONUMENT, THIRD AVE.,
LOUISVILLE, KY.

(*Above*) Confederate
monument in a Union
city, Third Street,
Louisville (Postcard
Collection, KUKA-
V2008MS016-08-209,
University of Kentucky
Archives, Lexington.)

(*Right*) General John
Hunt Morgan memo-
rial, old courthouse
lawn, Lexington. This
statue, unveiled in 1911,
exemplifies the Con-
federate identity Ken-
tucky embraced in the
early twentieth century.
(Courtesy of Maryjean
Wall.)

diate best seller upon publication and would remain popular with American readers through the 1930s. It would be adapted for the stage and was made into a Hollywood motion picture at least three times. The novel essentially worked as an examination of Kentucky society on two fronts. Highland and lowland Kentucky are compared in the first half of the novel as the protagonist is caught between two worlds in his thoughts and sentiments. In the novel's second part Fox examines Kentucky's role as a border state in the Civil War, as Chad is forced to choose on which side he will fight.

Fox portrays Kentucky as romantic, alluring, and unique— a land of contrast and contradiction. He describes mountain society as backward, isolated, and quaint while depicting the bluegrass as a land of refinement, social stratification, chivalry, horses, virtues, and vices. Chad's two love interests, one a simple mountain girl and the other a Confederate officer's daughter and bluegrass belle, represent these two societies. Ultimately Chad is unable to choose between them, but he does not return to the mountains. Instead he heads west, still the guardian (or shepherd) of a spirit of individualism and freedom that was his inheritance from his pioneer forefathers.

The novel, stage play, and film versions of *The Little Shepherd of Kingdom Come* were immensely popular in the early twentieth century. They captured much of the essence of Kentucky as it was perceived by outsiders at that time. Even though Louisville had no real connection to the mountainous region, and did not resemble the agrarian and genteel bluegrass region as described by Fox, it was home to the Kentucky Derby. As such, Louisville and the Derby inherited all the romance and mythology that had become associated with the state as a whole, particularly once Kentucky's perceived connection to the Old South began to outshine its connection to backward, feud-prone mountaineers.

Another best-selling book that followed the trend toward

a shift in attention from Appalachian Kentucky to the central Kentucky bluegrass region in American popular culture was *In Old Kentucky,* published in 1910. This was an adaptation of a wildly popular musical melodrama by the same title written by Charles T. Dazey. The story follows a mountain girl, Madge, who falls in love with a young bluegrass gentleman, Frank Layton, who is visiting the mountains to check on some property he owns there. The tale reaches its climax when Madge travels to Lexington to warn Layton that he is in danger of being killed by a rival for her affection. While there, Madge anonymously takes the place of a drunken jockey to ride Layton's horse to victory in the big race of the Lexington meet. Along the way readers become familiar with Layton's loyal black servant, Uncle Neb, who reverently refers to Layton as Marse Frank, and an older friend named Colonel Sandusky Doolittle, a caricature of a Kentucky gentleman who drinks mint juleps and smokes cigars all day. The musical version of the book, according to one review, featured "Negroes who can dance, a pickaninny band that can make considerable noise and a dusky little conductor who can swing the baton with the best of them."[43] Both the book and the play were hugely successful and further reinforced the notion that Kentucky was a timeless bastion of chivalry, manners, refinement, and benevolent black servitude.

Like *The Little Shepherd of Kingdom Come, In Old Kentucky* includes a main character who leaves the mountains for the central Kentucky lowlands. These characters mirrored the larger trend in American culture in the early 1900s, when Kentucky "became" southern, national attention moved away from "backward" Kentucky highlanders, and Americans embraced sectional reconciliation and celebrated Confederate memory. In this environment the idea of a place like the fictional lowland Kentucky, where there were charming and chivalrous Kentucky colonels, beautiful bluegrass belles, and singing black servants, was an attractive one as the Kentucky Derby became a destination for people who wanted to experience such a place for themselves.

Kentucky maintained its reputation as a place of romance, contradiction, and intrigue as the Derby's popularity and reputation grew exponentially in the early twentieth century. As Churchill Downs and the city of Louisville prepared to celebrate the Golden Jubilee Derby in the spring of 1924, the entire state was readying for a two-week statewide homecoming celebration to mark the 150th anniversary of the founding of the first permanent settlement in Kentucky, at Harrodsburg. Enthusiasm and state pride were at an all-time high, and one hundred thousand expatriates were expected to return to the bluegrass for the celebration. A *New York Times* article explained the appeal: "Kentucky has personality. No other of these United States has such individuality. No other has the distinct savor, the racy flavor, of what was once the dark and bloody ground. Kentucky is the only state that is an entity aside from its climate, geography, products or population."[44] It was this belief that made the Derby an attractive destination for people, who by the 1920s were traveling to Louisville by plane, train, and automobile. A Chicago journalist's description of that year's event as a place where "colored boys with golden horseshoes about their necks gave advice to modish beauties with diamonds around their throats," and where "arrogant feminists grew meek and humble" provides some insight into which elements of Kentucky's "individuality" outsiders found attractive at the Derby.[45]

Attendance predictions for the fiftieth running of the Derby ran as high as 160,000. Though the actual number of attendees was less than half that, those in attendance saw favorite Black Gold put away his rivals in the final seventy yards, becoming the first recipient of a gold winner's trophy, which has been awarded ever since. In the aftermath of Black Gold's impressive Derby score, a fantastic (and factually improbable) backstory of the win-

Postcard advertising special Derby trains on the Illinois Central Railroad. By the 1920s dozens of special trains, particularly from the Midwest and Northeast, annually invaded Louisville at Derby time. (Postcard Collection, KUKAV2008MS016-08-0136, University of Kentucky Archives, Lexington.)

ning horse and owner circulated around the country and would eventually be made into a major Hollywood motion picture.[46]

That story began with Oklahomans Al and Rosa Hoots (she an Osage Indian), who owned a mare named Useeit. On February 22, 1916, Useeit was entered in a selling race (the precursor to modern claiming races), in which the horses in the race could be purchased, in Juarez, Mexico. After the race Useeit was purchased, but Mr. Hoots decided that he was unwilling to part with his mare. Stories differ about how it was accomplished, but either under the cover of darkness or with the help of a rifle Hoots took his mare and went home to Oklahoma. Hoots was subsequently banned from the turf for life along with Useeit. But the mare was eventually reinstated to the Thoroughbred registry for breeding purposes, perhaps with the help of Colonel E. R. Bradley, who had been impressed by the mare on the racetrack and offered Hoots a breeding right to one of his top stallions, Black Toney. Hoots asked his wife on his deathbed to promise to someday breed Useeit to Black Toney. The mating took place in 1920, and the result was a colt that would be named Black Gold.[47]

A writer for the *New Orleans States* popularized this legend when he wrote that "before he died, old man Hoots whispered in Useeit's ear, 'A son of yours will perpetuate the name of the gamest pony that ever looked through a bridle, and I will ride him and I will look after him; I will pet him as I have petted you. The love I have given you will send him to the races, and everybody will say, "Useeit has sent a champion back on the turf." ' "[48]

Though there is no more than anecdotal evidence to support any claims of supernatural phenomena surrounding the life of Hoots and Black Gold, this legend only enhanced the popularity of the Derby and the romance that surrounded it. With each running, the Derby was becoming more entrenched in the American popular culture and popular consciousness. As an increasing number of Americans found themselves with disposable income and the means to travel, the Derby was an increasingly alluring destination for American tourists and sports enthusiasts alike.

For the first fifty years, a person who did not travel to Louisville for the Derby could only read about the race. Thanks to the technology of radio, that would change in 1925, the year descriptions of the race were broadcast to a network radio audience for the first time. The excitement of the Derby now became more immediate. "We are radiocasting to you, for the first time in history, the running of the Kentucky Derby," WHAS announcer Credo Harris blared across the airwaves. "And from this dizzying place [inside one of the cupolas atop the grandstand] we get a picture not only of the track and of the big race that is to come, but of the country for miles in every direction. We are going to see if, for a little while, we can let our eyes be your eyes, and translate the picture from here into your own imagination."[49]

In a broadcast three years later, Harris invited his listeners to "wind up your imaginations and come with me in fancy. Close your eyes and try to think that you are now at my side;

Automobiles in Churchill Downs parking lot, Derby Day, 1927. By the 1920s Derby fans flocked to Churchill Downs in planes, trains, and automobiles. (Photographic Archive, 1994.18.0858, Special Collections, University of Louisville, Louisville, Kentucky.)

hearing what I hear, seeing what I see. . . . Close your eyes and step with me into a land of unreality."[50] His words were heard as far away as Toronto and Dallas, and reached as many as 6 million listeners.[51] After laying three hundred miles of wire, Chicago station WGN began a four-hour broadcast from the Derby with a duo from the Pullman Porters' Quartet singing "My Old Kentucky Home" as part of a "special program to lend atmosphere to the race." The radiocast also included "an appropriate program of Southern songs and sidelights."[52] By 1929 the race would be broadcast nationwide by the National Broadcast Company, and two years later it would be picked up by the BBC in London. The popularity of the Kentucky Derby grew along with the technology that allowed audiences thousands of miles away from Churchill Downs to participate in the Derby experience.

The fact that the announcer described the "country for

miles in every direction"—not just the racetrack—is significant as it demonstrates that there was more to the experience of the Derby than just the horse race taking place. Listeners, it was assumed, wanted to imagine *Kentucky* (and not just the horse race) when they tuned in to a broadcast. Similarly, as continues to be the case today, coverage in newspaper reports of the Derby focused as much on the extracurricular goings-on at the Derby as on the equine athletes.

Colonel Matt Winn helped to fuel the enthusiasm of journalists, announcers, and spectators at the Derby every year. "All Kentucky Derby attendance records were surpassed today," Winn would annually declare. "Churchill Downs never held as great a crowd. They came from the four corners of the earth, well-dressed, orderly, enthusiastic lovers of the Thoroughbred . . . bearing testimony by their presence that the Kentucky Derby is the outstanding sporting event of America."[53] Churchill Downs would not release official attendance figures until the 1970s, by which time the real number could substantiate the annual claim of "100,000" Derby spectators. Winn was never hesitant to exaggerate in his promotional efforts, but by the end of the 1920s the Derby had indeed transcended the realm of horse racing and the world of sport to become a part of the cultural fabric of the United States.

The final Derby of the Roaring Twenties was won by Clyde Van Dusen, a diminutive gelding named by his owner for the horse's trainer (a former jockey). Clyde the horse was a son of the great Man o' War, who had famously bypassed the Derby in 1920. Clyde took the lead early in the race from post position 20 and held on for the win on the rain-soaked track, becoming the seventh gelding to win Churchill Downs's great race (and the last of the twentieth century).

There were plenty of attractive storylines for that year's Derby, but one Louisville journalist chose to write about "four Negro servants and two little pickaninnies" back at the winning

owners' farm who listened to the coverage of the Derby on the radio while "all the white folks" were at Churchill Downs. "With
a grin reaching from one of his black ears to the other," the foreman described to the writer how the farm workers had prayed
for rain that day because Clyde Van Dusen preferred a wet track.
"Yes suh, yes suh," the foreman explained to the reporter, "the
boss called up this mawnin' and I tole him that we was a prayin'
for that hoss, but mostly we wuz a prayin' for rain because . . .
the mo rain, the mo mud and the mo mud the mo fast dat hoss
can travel."[54] The scene back at the farm was part of the press
coverage of the event because it fit the image of Old Kentucky
that had become part of the Derby's identity. The idea that Kentucky was home to horse farms that resembled old southern plantations, complete with a black labor force and presided over by a
Kentucky colonel, was part of the allure of the state and the Derby itself for national audiences.

The Kentucky Derby had become a celebration of the present and the past: at once an event that appealed to current tastes
and one that leaned on a contrived set of past symbols and images for its relevance. In attending, reading about, or listening to
the Derby, people were able to become a part of the history of the
horse race and of a lifestyle and culture that seemed to be in danger of slipping away in the march toward modernity. During the
early twentieth century the Kentucky Derby climbed to a place
of prominence in American sport and American culture. This ascension was aided by a reservoir of myth, legend, and romance
that had been associated with the state since the first reports of
pioneers were published in the eighteenth century. By the time of
the stock market crash that signaled the onset of the Great Depression, the Derby itself had become an important part of the
state's identity. But the depression and war that would engulf and
dominate American society for the next decade and a half would
change the cultural landscape of the nation and threaten the very
survival of the Derby.

3

Conflict at the Derby in the Great Depression

1930–1940

During the 1930s, the Derby continued to draw patrons to Louisville from across the country. While it retained its place among the most popular festivals on the American sports calendar, the Derby was not immune to the changing cultural conditions brought about by the Great Depression. Once celebrated as a cheerful place where the masses and society swells interacted amicably, Churchill Downs became a tense environment increasingly marred by conflicts between guards and patrons. But even in the worst economic environment in the nation's history, both the rich and the regular folk continued to flock to the famous racetrack on Derby Day as the Derby continued its growth in national prestige and stature, securing its place as the greatest American horse race at a time when sports provided distraction and diversion for a society under unprecedented economic strain.

As portrayed in national print media, the conflicts and violence at the Derby in the 1930s would reinforce Kentucky's dualistic identity in the American collective imagination that dated back to the first published portrayal of Daniel Boone 150 years earlier. During the Depression, newspapers described fashionable Derby-goers in language that evoked images of Kentucky colonels and belles reminiscent of the Old South while reports of lawlessness in the Derby infield brought to mind the gone-but-not-forgotten tales of feuds and violence in rural Kentucky that had captivated American readers in the late nineteenth and early twentieth centuries. The contradictory images that emerged from the Kentucky Derby in the 1930s reinforced the long-held yet paradoxical notion that Kentucky was home to both lawlessness and refinement. Kentucky's reputation as an unusual and alluring place continued to grow during the Great Depression, which in turn further secured the Derby's prominent place in American popular culture.

From the beginning the Derby's infield, with its wide range of people, helped to contribute to a carnival atmosphere that was interesting and appealing even to those who were not necessarily followers of horse racing. At the same time the presence of high society gave the event an aura of significance and helped to attract "regular folks" to the event in large numbers. Early Derby journalists praised the crowds as representative of an idealized American society in which people could comfortably mix regardless of social station. This amicable mélange of humanity continued to be celebrated in newspapers and to attract Derby visitors well into the twentieth century. In the 1920s the *Chicago Tribune* had described the Derby crowd as "the great human family in happy holiday mood, all class distinctions lost in the camaraderie which causes millionaires to talk with stable boys, to exchange opinions on the chances of the horses, and to feel, for the day at least, a brotherhood not known in any other sport." The Derby was a place where "millionaire horsemen and society leaders mingled with the great, jostling, good natured crowd."[1] The *New York Times* claimed that the Derby "thrilled millionaires in the clubhouse boxes no less than the ragamuffins clinging to stable roofs and trees."[2]

The Derby had attracted America's rich and powerful for years, including leaders of business, politics, stage, screen, and athletics. But no one drew more attention in the early years of celebrity worship at the Derby than Edward Stanley, the seventeenth Earl of Derby, who attended the event in 1930. As the birthplace of Thoroughbred racing, Great Britain was the guardian of the sport's history. Lord Derby's attendance thus reinforced Americans' belief that the Kentucky Derby was a major event worthy of worldwide attention, lending the Derby and American racing increased stature. Lord Derby's postrace comments were broadcast by NBC radio to a national audience. He engaged in good-natured debate over the correct pronunciation of the race (*durby* or *dahrby*), and praised Kentucky's version as "fine stuff."[3]

While Lord Derby's presence at the 1930 Derby made headlines, the performance on that rainy afternoon by Gallant Fox was impressive in its own right as he seized the lead at the top of the backstretch and never relinquished it, winning easily by two lengths. Winning jockey Earl Sande had won the Kentucky Derby twice previously, in 1923 and 1925. He had largely retired from the sport but, hit hard by the stock market crash of 1929, he was amenable to an invitation from Gallant Fox's owner William Woodward Sr. to return to riding. Sande's three Derby wins matched the record then held by Isaac Murphy.

The following year Twenty Grand knocked a whopping one and three-fifths seconds off Old Rosebud's record time in winning the fifty-seventh Run for the Roses for Greentree Stable. Helen Hay Whitney, the daughter of former secretary of state John Milton Hay and widow of multimillionaire W. Payne Whitney, had taken over Greentree upon her husband's death in 1927. With Twenty Grand's win she joined her brother-in-law Harry P. Whitney, who won in 1915 with Regret and again in 1927 with Whiskery, in the ranks of Derby-winning owners. Interestingly, Twenty Grand's trainer was James Rowe Jr., the son of Regret's trainer.

The presence of both aristocrats and regular folk at the Derby continued to fascinate journalists in the 1930s. In covering Twenty Grand's victory, one reporter explained, "The Kentucky

Helen Hay Whitney, owner of 1931 Derby winner Twenty Grand. (Keeneland Library, Lexington, Kentucky.)

Derby is America's unique annual sporting event. It cannot be considered merely in light of a race. It is a great hegira of multitudes to Churchill Downs, a coming together of many thousands, a gathering where all meet upon the same plane, made equal and joined together by admiration for the Thoroughbred horse."[4] The interaction that year was an unusually peaceful one—for the first time in forty-three years, the police failed to receive a single complaint of unruly behavior—but it would prove to be a calm before a storm of unrest that would be unleashed at the Derby in the years to come.[5] Thirty-three detectives had been placed throughout the grounds to keep watch over a crowd that included U.S. vice president Charles Curtis. Curtis, seated in a special stand built the previous year for Lord Derby, reinforced the Derby's status as one of America's top sporting spectacles, and further added to the air of respectability that Lord Derby's presence had brought the year before. Curtis claimed to have had a "positively wonderful time" at the Derby, remarking, "The real Kentucky spirit has been manifested throughout."[6]

The Derby had long been a place to show off fashion and wealth, but these displays took on a greater significance during the Depression. The fact that the Derby was a favorite destination of the nation's elite was demonstrated by a 1932 petition circulated by a sophomore at Columbia University in Manhattan requesting that final exams be shifted to avoid a conflict with students' Derby travel plans. "Appreciating that many of our body will want to attend the Kentucky Derby," the petition stated, "we look with sadness at the triumph of bureaucracy which will prevent them from doing so without impairment to [their] scholastic standing."[7]

Those who made the journey that year witnessed the easy five-length victory of Colonel E. R. Bradley's Burgoo King over Economic and Stepenfetchit.[8] The *New York Times* reported that despite the tough economic times, "the Derby is still the Derby with all its old glamour and gayety."[9] News from the racetrack the following day told a different story, however; a large group of young men had defied mounted police by rushing a gate on the backstretch in an attempt to avoid admission charges, leading to as many as two thousand unpaid entries.[10] This embarrassment for Churchill Downs would lead to an increased security presence in the future.

The following year the action on the racetrack mirrored the clashes between patrons and officials. Rounding the final turn in the 1933 Derby, jockey Herb Fisher was in the lead aboard Head Play. Fisher brought the colt wide, forcing challengers to

Broker's Tip (pictured with jockey Don Meade) won the 1933 Kentucky Derby, which is better remembered for the "fighting finish" exchange between Meade and rival jockey Herb Fisher. (Morgan Collection, Keeneland Library, Lexington, Kentucky.)

the outside and opening a clear path along the inside rail for Don Meade, wearing E. R. Bradley's green and white silks aboard Broker's Tip. The stretch drive between Head Play and Broker's Tip would be one of the most dramatic and infamous in Derby history. Attempting to intimidate his rival, Fisher guided his horse left and to the inside, moving to within inches of Meade and Broker's Tip. While charging down the homestretch, the pair of jockeys exchanged a series of tugs and blows as the finish line neared.

From a trackside position lying on the ground near the wire, photographer Wallace Lowry captured one of the most famous images in American racing history. The photo, now popularly referred to as "The Fighting Finish," shows Meade grabbing Fisher's shoulder, and Fisher holding Meade's saddlecloth. After the horses crossed the wire, Fisher knocked Meade across the face with his whip and lodged a claim of foul against his rival, which was disallowed by the stewards. Following the announcement of Broker's Tip as the winner, a despondent Fisher broke into tears. Later, in the jockey's quarters, he again attacked Meade, this time with a bootjack (a solid U-shaped device used to aid the removal of footwear). Newspapers and newsreels across the country carried images of the on-track fracas, and "The Fighting Finish" would become an iconic piece of Depression-era American sports photojournalism, capturing the desperation of a society in flux. Purchased the day before the Derby for $30,000, Head Play would go on to a successful racing career, including a win in the Preakness Stakes and over $100,000 in lifetime earnings, while the Derby would prove to be the only race Broker's Tip would win in his entire racing career. But what a win it was. It was the second consecutive Derby win, and a then-record fourth overall, for owner E. R. Bradley.

As Derby Day approached in 1934, the first since the end of Prohibition, organizers prepared for what was expected to be Churchill Downs's largest-ever crowd. Falling profits had forced the track to lower admission prices and reduce the race's prize money. Organizers also hired detectives from cities around the country and installed units of mounted police in the infield to combat the growing problems of gatecrashers trying to enter the grounds without paying and attempting to access restricted areas. However, efforts to increase security, including a nine-foot wire fence to keep the masses out of the clubhouse area, were not enough to prevent thousands from gaining illegal entry.

On the racetrack that day, automobile heiress Isabel Dodge Sloane's top colt Cavalcade caught A. G. Vanderbilt's Discovery in deep stretch to win the Derby by a widening two-and-a-half-length margin. As the horses thundered toward the finish line,

Boy caught red-handed with tools to help Derby-goers enter Churchill Downs illegally in 1935. (Photographic Archives, 1994.18.0923, Special Collections, University of Louisville, Louisville, Kentucky.)

they were left with scarcely enough space to run by the horde of spectators that had jumped the outside rail separating the grandstand seats from the racetrack and recklessly swarmed toward the approaching field of Derby runners.

Enthusiastic reports of the return of alcohol to the Derby that year were tempered by widespread concern over the behavior of the infield crowd. People climbed ladders, dug holes, scaled roofs, trampled bushes and flower beds, and overran police to

Winning horse Cavalcade in the 1934 Derby winner's circle, surrounded by the crowd that had swarmed onto the racetrack during the race. (Photographic Archives, 1994.18.180901, Special Collections, University of Louisville, Louisville, Kentucky.)

gain admission to Churchill Downs. The security forces used nightsticks and engaged in fisticuffs to keep the infielders in line. Disturbances were not limited to the infield, however, as "swank in the boxes clashed with shoddy on the rail," according to one Louisville newspaper.[11] Nor was the rambunctiousness limited to the racetrack. *Time* reported that the previous night "Derby guests continued their yearly romp, the less restrained firing the annual barrage of empty bottles into the court of the Brown Hotel despite the fact that Kentucky is now wet and liquor is sold by the glass."[12]

Newspapers published the names of the notable members of the crowd as usual, but the descriptions of the people populating the infield carried a tone of disapproval. Rather than cel-

Guards try to keep order at the 1935 Derby. (Photographic Archives, 1994.18.0907, Special Collections, University of Louisville, Louisville, Kentucky.)

ebrating the variety of sights and sounds in the infield as had previously been the norm, the *Courier-Journal* expressed disgust at the scene: "Spread newspapers—California blankets—littered the clean greensward, some relics of a night's stay on the grounds," the paper complained. "Men lay about, dozing: some drunk, some just tired. Many failed to see any race. Dice games and cards flourished in the oval during the interludes between races. . . . And the people!"[13]

As violent disruptions continued at the Derby, track officials responded with increased policing presence, including state troopers, militia, city police, and National Guardsmen. Readers across the country saw a particularly violent newspaper image in 1935 that depicted a group of National Guardsmen trying to contain a small mob of infielders that was using a wooden post as a battering ram in an attempt to break out of the confines of the infield.[14] The guards were armed with clubs as they tried to keep the infielders, some of whom were wielding chairs as weapons, in their space. At least some of the infielders were attempting to access the covered grandstand to escape the rain. The battle between police forces and spectators continued all afternoon. Ultimately law enforcement prevailed, but not before "a few heads were cracked."[15]

Security forces were not limited to the infield, as Downs officials also employed thirty-two sharpshooters to protect the pari-mutuel handle. The "grim group of men" charged with guarding the till were led by special Churchill Downs policeman George T. Kinnarney, whose orders to the marksmen were, "If anybody tries to get through those doors, don't ask questions. Let them have it."[16] That armed guards would be hired to protect large amounts of cash at a major sporting event cannot be considered noteworthy. But the fact that journalists considered it a significant part of the Derby "story" underscores the heightened levels of tension present at the race during the 1930s.

In 1935 William Woodward Sr.'s Omaha joined his sire Gallant Fox as a Derby champion, taking the lead a half mile before the finish under jockey William "Smokey" Saunders and cruising to a one-and-a-half-length victory. During the trophy presentation, winning owner Woodward, a wealthy New York Republican, took the opportunity to declare his political sentiments in front of a national radio audience. Woodward caused the broadcast of the ceremony to be repeatedly shut down and restarted because of his verbal jabs at a member of the ceremony, Postmaster General James A. Farley, a prominent member of the Democratic Party. Referring to his horse's pedigree, Woodward told Farley, "This is not a New Deal. It is an old deal, and it is a good solid deal—because thoroughbred bloodlines bring out champions when properly crossed."[17] In addition to his political views, Woodward's comments suggested a distinction between

(*Above*) Omaha, winner of the 1935 Triple Crown, with jockey William "Smokey" Saunders wearing the famous polka dot silks of William Woodward's Belair Stud. (Cook Collection, Keeneland Library, Lexington, Kentucky.)

(*Left*) William Woodward Sr., master of Belair Stud and owner of Derby champions Gallant Fox and Omaha. (Cook Collection, Keeneland Library, Lexington, Kentucky.)

Ladies' clothing storefront window showcasing Derby fashion, ca. 1930s. (Caulfield and Shook Collection, CS.216434, Photographic Archives, Special Collections, University of Louisville, Louisville, Kentucky.)

those at the Derby who would appreciate a champion bloodline and those who would not. By implication this was a distinction between the well-to-do seated in dining rooms and boxes in the clubhouse and the masses in the infield.

Louisville clothiers were ready for those who wished to conspicuously display their status through fashion on Derby Day. An advertisement for Stewart's Department Store claimed that the store had the "correct fashion" for the Derby.[18] There had been fashion ads in Louisville newspapers aimed at Derby-goers before, but the notion that there existed such a thing as the "correct" fashion was new. Ads for ladies' dresses, including one called the "Dixie Belle," and men's hats and suits for the Derby continued to appear through the 1930s in Kentucky papers and in periodicals published as far away as Chicago. The advertisements for women's Derby outfits in Louisville newspapers suggested that at the Derby it was necessary to look like "a lady."

In the interwar period, when Victorian notions of "proper" appearance and decorum for women were being challenged, the Derby existed on the margin of the old and the new. Though the sight of females venturing over to the infield was still rare, women freely wandered the spacious grounds on the grandstand side unescorted and were surrounded by the vices associated with the Derby, including drinking, smoking, and gambling, while remaining safely within view of the clubhouse and boxes, where traditional gender roles were still very much the norm. Men and women alike found themselves in an environment that encouraged a paradoxical mix of liberation and restraint.

An editorial in the *Blood-Horse* voiced the concern of racing "purists" that the Derby had become too commodified, warning, "No tradition ever survived being converted into a marketable commodity." But for those racing fans who only wanted to "see the race and 'avoid the Derby,'" the environment at Churchill Downs would only get worse.[19]

In that environment Louisville hotel managers were forced to combat a growing trend among the tourists of minor vandalism and "souvenir taking." Although the Derby had become for some a forum to display status, there remained among many Derby fans a sense that they needed to access and participate in some of the elements of the Kentucky "experience" that ran in opposition to codes of gentility and sophistication. Broken glasses, bottles, and lamps, and guests masquerading as jockeys in sheets and towels were some of the scenes that hotel managers attempted to avoid with preventative measures. One hotel decided to issue complimentary cigarette cases to its guests, attempting to curb some of the unsanctioned requisitioning of hotel property in an early example of the commodification of the Derby experience.[20]

Garden area on the grounds of Churchill Downs on Derby Day, ca. 1930. (Photographic Archives, 1994.18.0874, Special Collections, University of Louisville, Louisville, Kentucky.)

Souvenir Kentucky Derby mint julep glasses were first made available at Churchill Downs in the late 1930s under similar circumstances. The glasses were introduced in an attempt to stem the rash of thefts of water glasses in the track's dining rooms on Derby Day. In 1938 prices for lunch were raised by $.25 and guests were allowed to take their glasses home with them. The following year, Churchill Downs began producing what would evolve into the souvenir glasses that are still collected by thousands today. Though persons traveling to the Derby imagined themselves to be like ladies and gentlemen from the Old South, they were witnesses to scenes reminiscent of the lawless, violent characters in the stories about the mountainous region of eastern Kentucky and the frontier era. They would return home to find their names and descriptions of their Derby outfits in the local society pages, but they might impress their friends even more with their tales of wild experiences in "Old Kentucky," or, perhaps, with a pilfered souvenir.

By the late 1930s the violence and disruptions at the Derby had largely dissipated. There were no more mounted police in the infield and National Guardsmen's nightsticks had been replaced by relatively benign devices made of rubber hose. Physical changes to the infield also had a pacifying effect on the crowd. A tunnel running beneath the track to the infield from the grandstand side allowed spectators to go to and from the infield more easily, and heavier wire mesh fencing, securely fastened to thick posts set in concrete, was installed to help ensure that people remained where they were supposed to be. Infield entertainment regularly included a "Confederate" marching band that the *New York Times* claimed "did much to assuage insurgents with wire clippers."[21] After the tension and violence at the Derby during the Great Depression subsided, Churchill Downs would not again become a site of major conflict until the 1960s.

As Derby Day approached in 1937, Louisville was still drying out from a historically catastrophic January flood. Scores of human lives had been lost, and the monetary damage caused in the city was estimated to be in excess of $50 million in Depression-era dollars.[22] But as spring returned, popular attention was once again focused on the big race. Samuel D. Riddle had the most celebrated three-year-old in the United States, just as he had with Man o' War in 1920. Riddle's prize colt in 1937 was a smallish son of Man o' War named War Admiral. Riddle had chosen to bypass the Derby in 1920, but seventeen years later War Admiral became Riddle's first Derby starter. Seventy thousand spectators watched the colt break from the rail and annihilate all but second-place finisher Pompoon in a field of twenty, collecting the winner's share of more than $50,000. War Admiral would go on to capture the Preakness and Belmont Stakes that year, earn-

1937 Triple Crown winner War Admiral with Mrs. Samuel D. Riddle. (Cook Collection, Keeneland Library, Lexington, Kentucky.)

ing recognition as a Triple Crown winner and one of the top American racehorses of the twentieth century. Since 1920, when Riddle chose not to send Man o' War to Louisville to compete in the Kentucky Derby, the Triple Crown had become the yardstick by which outstanding three-year-old Thoroughbreds were measured.

In the realm of sport, the term Triple Crown had first been used to describe three English horse races: the 2,000 Guineas, the Epsom Derby, and the St. Leger Stakes. American racetracks had attempted to establish racing series along the English model, but none achieved lasting national recognition. By 1930 the Preakness Stakes in Baltimore, the Kentucky Derby, and the Belmont Stakes in New York had clearly risen above all other American races for three-year-olds. That year Gallant Fox captured all three events and was referred to by the *New York Times* as a "Triple Crown Hero."[23] Five years later, Gallant Fox's son Omaha matched his father's feat (and the pair remains the only father-son combo to win the American Triple Crown). Once the term entered the popular vocabulary of sports fans and journalists in the 1930s, Sir Barton was recognized after the fact as the first to accomplish the feat in 1919.

Churchill Downs had moved the Derby from its traditional place on the opening day card to the second Saturday of the meet in 1923 in order to avoid a conflict with the Preakness, which was held the week prior. This arrangement continued until 1932, when the Derby was moved to the first Saturday in May, where it has remained, with two exceptions, ever since. The Derby was popular before the Triple Crown was even recognized. It could have survived with or without the Triple Crown. However, the association with the most important series of races in the country certainly raised the prestige of each of the races, including the Derby.

Matt Winn recognized the potential for a national Triple Crown series consisting of the Derby, Preakness, and Belmont and was an early proponent of a bonus to be presented to the winner of all three races, but the racetracks that hosted the events failed to cooperate. In fact, at least as early as 1919 Winn had proposed a Triple Crown modeled after the English version but consisting of three races run exclusively in Kentucky: the Kentucky Derby in Louisville, the Latonia Derby near Cincinnati, and a third race to be created at the Kentucky Association track in Lexington.[24] The Kentucky Triple Crown never came to fruition, but the Kentucky Derby was certainly a beneficiary of the increase in media attention paid to the American Triple Crown series beginning in the 1930s. That acknowledgment of the American Triple Crown gave the three races, including the Derby, a small connection to the history and prestige of the English version on which the American Triple Crown was based.

In 1935 the City of Louisville attempted to capitalize upon its connection to the Derby and assert some control over its public image by organizing the first Derby Week Festival. The festival included a pageant celebrating Kentucky's rich history as well as a series of parades, balls, and sporting events capped off by a dinner hosted by the Honorable Order of Kentucky Colonels.

The inaugural festival was a success: local hotels were booked the entire week and "traditional" Kentucky hospitality was extended to visitors from across the country. The main ball crowned a king and queen of the festival, and their royal court consisted of "knights and ladies." Over 150,000 people witnessed the parade, which included five thousand marchers and thirty-five floats. The overall tone of the festival projected an image of romance, gentility, and hospitality that matched visitors' expectations of Kentucky. More than anything else, the festival strengthened links between the Derby and the past, and emphasized that the Derby had itself become an American tradition, a fact not lost on 1930s journalists.

"The Kentucky Derby has long since ceased to be merely a horse race," one Florida newspaper explained during the festival. "In the 60 years since Aristides won the first Derby, it has accumulated a tradition which makes it a fixture in the national life, an event to stir the imagination even of those who have no interest in racing otherwise. There has been in recent years in America a revaluing of our traditions, a new feeling for those things in our lives which are linked to the romantic past."[25] This first attempt at the creation of a Derby Festival would last only three years, but it would be revived in 1956. In the interim the Kentucky Colonels' Dinner would survive and prosper, attracting celebrities and garnering attention for the organization and the Derby, as well as perpetuating an element of Kentucky iconography.

Besides Colonel Harland Sanders, the founder of the Kentucky Fried Chicken chain, no Kentucky colonel made better use of the title than Colonel Matt Winn. His name alone was fantastic publicity for the Derby, as it connected the event to all the imagery and romance of Old Kentucky that was so attractive to Americans in the early twentieth century. Winn always had a quote for journalists, and his name appeared in newspapers across the country each year. Having a "Kentucky colonel" as the face of the Kentucky Derby would be akin to a major event in Texas having a spokesman named "Tex" who wore a cowboy hat and a bolo tie and drove a large white sedan with longhorns as a hood ornament. For those reading about the Derby, or experiencing it through newsreels or radio, it did not require too much creativity to imagine the Kentucky Derby as a unique event.

The colonel icon evoked much of the romance of Old Kentucky, specifically that part of Kentucky's identity that had become associated with the genteel elements of the Old South and the Confederacy. The Kentucky colonel is an emblem of a time and place that never really existed, but that could nonetheless be celebrated in Louisville at Derby time. Historian Gerald Carson summed up the attractiveness of the Kentucky colonel image quite articulately: "We cannot do without Kentucky Colonels. They provide us with humor and a touch of poetry. They liberate us from things as they are, make it plausible that there is yet a crossing into a Kentucky of the imagination, where the dogwood blossoms all year around, taxes are low, the whiskey always prime and all men are as they'd like to be."[26] The harsh realities of life in the Great Depression made the fantasy land that was Louisville at Derby time all the more attractive to Americans in the 1930s.

The fictional Old South from which the Kentucky colonel emerged was best depicted in the 1930s in the immensely popular novel *Gone with the Wind* and the even more popular film by the same title. According to the film's prologue, this Old South was "a land of Cavaliers and Cotton Fields. Here in this pretty world, Gallantry took its last bow. Here was the last ever to be seen of Knights and their Ladies Fair, of Master and of Slave. Look for it only in books, for it is no more than a dream remembered, a Civilization gone with the wind." *Gone with the Wind* was set in Georgia, but Kentucky was the setting of another popular Depression-era cinematic portrayal of the romantic Old South: *The Little Colonel,* starring Shirley Temple, Bill "Bojangles" Robinson, Lionel Barrymore, and Hattie McDaniel. Though the film's depiction of Kentucky does not begin to approach any semblance of reality, it demonstrates that Depression-era audiences were willing to accept the notion that Kentucky was a place in which memories of the Old South remained alive. This moonlight-and-magnolia imagery associated with the romanticized South that contributed to the popularity of Depression-era films like *Gone with the Wind* and *The Little Colonel* was a part of the experience of the Kentucky Derby for many.

Based on a series of immensely popular novels written by Anne Fellows Johnson in the late 1800s and early 1900s, *The Little Colonel* is set in Kentucky in the 1870s and tells the story of a gruff, unreconstructed Confederate colonel (played by Lionel Barrymore) whose heart melts when his six-year-old granddaughter (Shirley Temple) returns to Kentucky with her mother, who had broken the heart of her father the colonel when she eloped with a Yankee veteran six years earlier. The colonel's Kentucky plantation and mansion look like they belong somewhere much farther south than Kentucky and are populated by a group of singing, dancing black servants and a pair of black children the colonel calls "pickaninnies," one of whom is named Henry Clay after the famous nineteenth-century Kentucky statesman. The film is set in the years after emancipation, yet the white characters treat the blacks very much like slaves. When the servants are not providing loyal service with a smile, they busy themselves with tap dancing to the melodies of Stephen Foster. The treatment of black servants by the white characters in the film helped to reinforce the connection between Kentucky and the Old South still very much alive in the 1930s and embodied in the Kentucky colonel caricature.

Any portrayal of a Kentucky colonel would be incomplete

without a glass of Kentucky bourbon in his hand. The connection between the Derby and Kentucky bourbon dates to the event's early years, including a famous story of Lutie Clark delighting world-famous Polish actress Helena Modjeska, in Louisville to perform Henrik Ibsen's *A Doll's House,* with her first mint julep at a pre-Derby breakfast. Whiskey making in Kentucky began with the first European settlement, and the name *bourbon* probably comes from the name of the Kentucky county that was home to many early distilleries and Kentucky's leading Ohio River port, Limestone (later called Maysville) in the late 1700s. Bourbon is a type of whiskey that is distilled from mash consisting of at least 51 percent corn and lesser parts of rye, wheat, and barley, but much of its unique flavor comes from being aged in charred barrels. In 1964 Congress recognized bourbon as a distinctively American product, but more than 90 percent of all bourbon is produced in Kentucky.[27] The first advertisement for Kentucky bourbon appeared in newspapers at least as early as 1820, and by the beginning of the Civil War Kentucky was nationally recognized for its distinctive intoxicant. Bourbon figures *heavily* in the Derby experience; the mint julep has become the traditional drink of the Kentucky Derby and the most celebrated bourbon-based cocktail in the world.[28] Mint juleps had been served at Churchill Downs from the beginning, but were not available in the now-famous souvenir glasses until the late 1930s.

The following poetic description of the mint julep was written by Lexington lawyer J. Soule Smith in the late nineteenth century and published as a small book in 1949, almost half a century after his death. This tribute to Derby-goers' favorite drink demonstrates the evocative capabilities of the mint julep and the significance of its attachment to the Kentucky Derby. The poem begins, "It is the very dream of drinks, the vision of sweet quaffings. The Bourbon and the mint are lovers. In the same land they live, on the same food are fostered." This ode to bourbon rambles on for pages in a similar fashion, ending with an invitation

This advertisement for Crab Orchard bourbon appeared in the November 17, 1937, issue of *Collier's*. It exemplifies the link between Kentucky and the Old South in the minds of consumers that advertisers tried to exploit.

to the reader: "Sip it and dream—you cannot dream amiss. No other land can give so sweet a solace for your cares; no other liquor soothes you so in melancholy days. Sip it and say there is no solace for the soul, no tonic for the body like Old Bourbon whiskey."[29]

Kentucky had long been known as a center of whiskey production, and Kentucky bourbon whiskey had been tied to the

Derby experience for years, but in 1919 the imminent arrival of Prohibition was for many in Louisville (a city once called the "whiskey capital" of the United States) a cause for concern. One journalist lamented, "While the forty-fifth Kentucky Derby will long be remembered for many reasons, it will always be remembered as the last Derby when that most delectable of drinks, Kentucky's own concoction, the famous Mint Julep, was available to take the sting from defeat and give edge to victory. No longer can our native poet sing of us 'The corn is full of kernels and the colonel's full of corn.' *Morturi te salutamus* ["In death we salute you"]."[30] Another expressed similar sadness when he described the first Prohibition-era Derby in 1920: "Well-bred nostrils sniffed disdainfully as 'Kentucky's finest' thrust them deep into goblets of foaming soda water and other denatured drinks in toasting the winner of the Kentucky Derby Saturday night. The aristocracy of the Bluegrass state mourned most the loss of the third of Kentucky's famous pre-prohibition trinity of attractions. Its beautiful women and incomparable horses were there but. . . . —tis sad but true!"[31]

Despite the concerns, Kentucky's reputation as a producer of booze was, surprisingly, enhanced by Prohibition. Kentucky moonshine temporarily replaced bourbon in the 1920s as the state's most famous distilled spirit, spread across the country by bootleggers, including Al Capone. A 1923 article in the *Louisville Times* revealed that the association between the Derby and liquor had not ceased: "The annual whiskey robbery preceding the running of the Kentucky Derby in Louisville was committed Friday night at the distillery warehouse of the old H. Southerland Co . . . and the stolen liquor, it is believed, eventually will be peddled by bootleggers among the crowd attending the race meeting."[32] The perception of Kentucky as a place where booze could be readily obtained during Prohibition had only increased the Derby's allure in the Roaring Twenties.

After the end of Prohibition in 1933, the return of newspaper ads for Kentucky bourbon often included imagery evocative of the Old South. By the mid-1930s, ads that cast Kentucky in a "southern" light often contained the image of a genteel, white-haired Kentucky colonel or a servile "Negro." Beginning in 1935 newspapers across the country carried a particularly interesting ad for Crab Orchard whiskey in which an elderly black waiter, dressed in a tuxedo and wearing a white-lipped smile, offered the reader a bottle of Crab Orchard placed on a serving platter in the shape of the state of Kentucky.[33] This ad explicitly tied Kentucky to an Old South image that included happy, servile blacks. One distillery skipped the process of attempting to subtly or abstractly attach its product to Kentucky or the Derby by simply naming its product Kentucky Derby Whiskey. In addition to national ad campaigns promoting their products, Kentucky distilleries advertised tours of their facilities during Derby Week, some even offering free bus rides to the plants.

Though Depression-era print ads for Kentucky whiskey most often used images of Kentucky colonels and their happy servants or horse racing scenes to market their product, a few brands chose instead to focus on the flip side of Kentucky identity: the rural Kentucky mountaineer. At least one, Mattingly & Moore Distilleries, used both sets of imagery, and indeed both remained quite salient with the American public in the 1930s.

Other distillers tied their product to Old Kentucky with advertisements that included coonskin cap–wearing frontiersmen reminiscent of Daniel Boone. During the Great Depression Boone's status in American popular culture rose appreciably. His portrait graced a U.S. half dollar minted from 1934 to 1938 in commemoration of the bicentennial of his birth, and Boone was also the subject of a major motion picture in 1936 and a major biography published in 1939. The Boone image of the 1930s was a celebration of American spirit, the spirit that had led Boone to overcome all obstacles in bringing civilization and "American-ness" to the untamed wilderness. To Americans dealing with their own obstacles during the Depression he was a role model, an American hero who served as a reminder of the possibility of emerging from the dark woods of hard times to triumph over adversity.

Kentucky governor Ruby Laffoon evoked Boone during the 1934 Derby trophy presentation to the winning connections, which included owner Isabel Dodge Sloane. The stuttering governor said that it gave him "inexpress—, inexp—unexplainable pleasure to present the cup." He then addressed the crowd, urging everyone to return to Kentucky that Labor Day to celebrate the bicentennial of the birth of "that great friend of horses," Daniel Boone.[34] Though Boone had died decades before the first Derby and had no particular connection to organized horse racing, Laffoon's reference to Boone underscores the significance of Boone-related mythology to Kentucky's identity and, indirectly, to the appeal of the Derby.

The often contradictory attributes of the mythical Boone allowed for broad appeal of the Boone character (much like that of Kentucky and its Derby). Successful capitalists and the downtrodden unemployed alike could hold Boone as a hero, because he simultaneously represented the march of American progress and its antithesis, a relationship with nature and a suspicion of modernity. Boone as an icon combined elements of the Old South and of the mountains to form an ideal composite stereotypical Kentuckian. He was violent and he was civilized. He comfortably interacted with Indians, yet he was completely "white." He was a "man of nature," but he came from the settled East. In the 1930s, when both the Kentucky hillbilly and the Kentucky colonel icons were ubiquitous, the mythical Boone existed somewhere in the middle, and the image helped to raise the stature and mystique of Kentucky.

The tenor of a 1934 *New York Times* article suggests that the dualistic imagery the United States associated with Kentucky had spilled over into the popular memory and understanding of the historical Daniel Boone. The article described a scene in Lexington as the Commonwealth of Kentucky celebrated the two

hundredth anniversary of Boone's birth: "Even the eternal pioneer [Boone], who could not breathe freely when he had an or-
dinary neighbor nearer than ten miles, or a Yankee neighbor
within a hundred, would thrill at this tribute to the man who
conquered the once 'Dark and Bloody Ground' for white settlement."[35] There is no reason to assume that Boone would have felt
any more resentment toward a "Yankee" neighbor than any other one, but the journalist's belief underscores how Kentucky had
become inextricably associated with the Old South in American
popular memory.

During the 1920s the backward mountaineer element of
Kentucky's identity had been overshadowed by depictions and
images that connected the state and its inhabitants to the Old
South. But by the 1930s and the onset of the Great Depression,
this dormant element of the state's identity reemerged as Americans tried to laugh at their collective unemployment and idle-
ness.[36] At the same time, some people sought to blame those who
were adversely affected by the Depression, suggesting that there
were some Americans—"hillbillies," for example—who were
just naturally lazy or inept and deserved their misfortune.

The use of the hillbilly icon in cartoons like Al Capp's *Li'l
Abner* and Paul Webb's *The Mountain Boys* during the 1930s reflected the changing viewpoints and attitudes of American audiences, including the fear of economic and societal collapse and a
need to explain the widespread poverty in the rural South. The
hillbilly cartoons of the 1930s told audiences that conditions really were not as bad as they seemed, while at the same time suggesting that these rural white southerners deserved their plight
because of their own laziness and ineptitude. In Depression-era
popular culture Kentucky was associated with both the positive and negative aspects of the hillbilly icon.[37] These cartoons
fostered the idea of backwardness associated with the marginal
rural South, but they also celebrated the hillbilly's rejection of
modern society, a society that seemed to be crumbling at its foun-

dation. These popular cartoons suggested that the hillbillies were somehow different from "regular" Americans in their backwardness, a distinction that allowed audiences to laugh at "those" people while they simultaneously celebrated them.[38]

Though the hillbilly image was not directly associated with Louisville, it had been for many years associated with Kentucky, and Louisville had come to represent Kentucky as the home of the Kentucky Derby. As representatives of Kentucky, then, Louisville and the Derby inherited some of the latent popular perceptions of the state that had emerged in the nineteenth century. Depending on the particular needs of a given era or set of social conditions, the genteel southern imagery (as represented by the Kentucky colonel) and the violent, backward, and simple imagery (as represented by the Kentucky hillbilly) have been alternatively, and sometimes simultaneously, used in popular culture in connection with Kentucky. To illustrate, practically any merchant selling Kentucky souvenirs and paraphernalia today is likely to have plenty of items depicting the familiar hillbilly image alongside products imbued with images of idyllic horse farms, bourbon whiskey, and Colonel Sandersesque Kentucky gentlemen.

This dualistic identity, which helped to sell Kentucky bourbon in the years after the end of Prohibition, also helped to keep Kentucky—and, in turn, the Derby—in the American popular consciousness.[39] During the 1930s, both the hillbilly and the colonel icons were attractive to Americans, allowing the state and its signature event to become further entrenched in American culture.

At times, Kentuckians themselves had difficulties choosing which elements of their state's identity to market to the public. In the 1930s, Louisville newspapers regularly suggested destinations for Derby Week tourists. Confederate monuments, Civil War battlefields, and plantation-style mansions were especially popular, but advertisements also regularly encouraged trips to Daniel Boone's grave, the site of Abraham Lincoln's humble log cabin birthplace, and places of natural beauty like Mammoth

Cave, furthering the notion of Kentucky as a place of intrigue and contradiction.

The return of the appeal of the hillbilly element of Kentucky's identity in the 1930s recomplicated Kentucky's place within American popular culture, but Kentucky's status as a neo-Confederate state endured as the decade came to a close. In 1939 a Louisville journalist described the prerace scene at Churchill Downs as post-time favorite (and eventual winner) Johnstown made his way from the saddling paddock toward the track: "A Negro stable boy pulled his harmonica from his pocket to play a few bars of 'My Old Kentucky Home' before an official waved him into silence. But the silence couldn't kill the memory of the melody. The memory seemed to linger in an unvoiced rhythm about sunny skies and fields of bluegrass. . . . It was about the shuffling of Negro feet on rough plank floors and in the soft earth of tobacco fields. ''Tis summer, the darkies are gay.'"[40]

During the early years of the Derby's national popularity and significance, Old South imagery had been salient with national elites, who made room for the Derby on their collective social calendar. In the 1930s the cultural cachet of the Kentucky hillbilly reemerged, reemphasizing the dualistic nature of Kentucky's identity within American culture. Like all enduring stereotypes, it was this dualism that helped to allow Kentucky—and, as a result, the Derby—to retain its special place of significance within American popular consciousness and culture, and to survive changes in the American political, social, and cultural landscape. Conflict was the recurring theme in and around the Derby in the 1930s, as discord was manifest on the racetrack, in the stands, and even in the ways in which Kentucky was portrayed within pop culture. But with America's full entry into World War II in 1941, conflict would turn to consensus as Americans rallied around their flag and around American institutions like the Kentucky Derby.

4

An American Institution

1940–1960

On an unseasonably cool May 4, 1940, Gallahadion caught previously unbeaten and odds-on favorite Bimelech in the homestretch to win the Derby at odds of more than 35-1 in one of the great upsets of Derby history. Gallahadion was owned by Ethel Mars, the widow of the founder of Mars Candies who raced under the name Milky Way Stables. The bedridden Mars, who netted the winner's share of the largest purse in Derby history, called it "the happiest day of her life."[1] The stable had entered at least one horse in every Derby since 1935 with lackluster results.[2] Among Milky Way's previous Derby finishes were a fifteenth, a thirteenth, an eleventh, and two last-place finishes. In contrast, Bimelech was owned by four-time Derby winner E. R. Bradley, and was by Black Toney (sire of 1924 Derby winner Black Gold), out of one of the most influential American broodmares of the twentieth century, La Troienne. Bimelech, arguably the best horse Bradley had ever owned, would be his final Derby starter.

The 1940 Derby crowd of around ninety-five thousand is believed to have been an American record at the time. Though few actually won money on the bay colt, the spectators greeted Gallahadion with loud cheers as he entered the winner's cir-

1940 trophy presentation. Left to right: president of Standard Oil Co. William E. Smith, Postmaster General James A. Farley, Colonel Matt Winn, trainer Roy Waldron, jockey Carroll Bierman, Kentucky governor Keen Johnson. (Morgan Collection, Keeneland Library, Lexington, Kentucky.)

cle, a giant killer and a popular champion. The celebration of Gallahadion's unlikely victory mirrored the popularity of other Depression-era underdog triumphs, including Seabiscuit's over War Admiral, and boxer Jim "Cinderella Man" Braddock's over world heavyweight champion Max Baer. But the resonance of victory by "the little guy" in the Great Depression would give way to celebrations of powerful racing stables and dominant equine champions at the Derby in the two decades that followed as Americans looked for examples and demonstrations of American strength and prosperity. The cultural climate of the Derby and the nation would be permanently altered in 1941 by the American entry into World War II, marking Gallahadion's victory as the end of an era. The Derby would survive the war, as it had the Great Depression, becoming even further enmeshed in the American cultural fabric in the process.

On the morning of the 1941 Derby, the last before the United States entered World War II, an advertisement appeared in the *Louisville Courier-Journal* promoting the newspaper's special Derby issue that would be on newsstands the following day. The ad included a cartoon Kentucky colonel saying, "Yes suh! It'll be a great hoss race!"[3] In the infield that year, the Indiana University marching band and drill team delighted fans as they had for years by spelling out "Dixie" while playing the tune. The *Courier-Journal* reported that the new entrance to the Churchill Downs clubhouse at the streetcar gate "represents a dignified beauty reminiscent of an old Southern mansion."[4]

Since the end of World War I, journalists had publicized and perpetuated a perceived connection between the Kentucky Derby and the Old South. But with the onset of American involvement in World War II, references to "Dixie," "darkies," "colonels," and "belles" in conjunction with the Derby would temporarily disappear. These connections would return by the 1950s, demonstrating that the Derby and its related imagery could be either "American" or "southern," as the tastes of national culture required, in much the same way that Kentucky was simultaneously (and alternatively) "backward" and "refined." The return of the "American" element of the Derby's identity in the early 1940s reflected changes in the American cultural landscape that included a reduction in the divisive celebration of sectional identity and a desire to downplay America's own racist past in order to distinguish itself from the racist Nazi enemy. This change also underscored the resiliency of the Derby, which could remain culturally relevant as an American event in a moment when the Old South was not an attractive element of popular historical memory or national identity.

When the United States became fully involved in World War II late in 1941, the immediate future of much frivolous activity like major sporting events was in serious jeopardy. But Colonel Winn, aware of the importance of continuity to the Derby's image and popularity, eagerly reminded people that the Kentucky Derby was the oldest continuously contested sporting event in the United States and deserving of special consideration. Signs around Churchill Downs, then as now, informed Derby-goers that the Derby has been held every year on the same racetrack since 1875. Winn had seen other racing events, like the Preakness Stakes and the American Derby, decline in significance and popularity when they were moved to different racetracks or put on hiatus; thus he felt it was very important that the Derby's continuity not be interrupted. In Winn's words, "part of its glory was centered in the fact that it had never lapsed."[5]

Because of restrictions on travel and consumption during World War II, Winn faced one of the toughest tests of his career in ensuring that the Derby was run in 1943. On February 6 of that year, American transportation administrator Joseph B. Eastman suggested that the Kentucky Derby might be cancelled. He admitted that his office had no direct control over sports, but threatened that his authority over transportation systems could be used to regulate or suspend some events. In the 1920s and 1930s the Derby had been the annual destination of dozens of special trains and private cars from across the country. This heavy Derby traffic fell in the category of unnecessary travel in the wartime environment, the kind of travel that Eastman was attempting to curb.

Colonel Winn responded to Eastman's threat a week later, promising to comply with the letter and intent of the Office of Defense Transportation's regulations. Winn told Eastman that "the track would not honor the requests for reservations from persons outside the Louisville area, would not ask for any sort of special transportation, and would run the Kentucky Derby on Saturday, May 1."[6] He pointed out that special Derby trains had not run to Louisville since 1941 anyway, because of the wartime restrictions. Administrator Eastman approved Winn's plans the same day.

In his memoirs, Winn recalled telling doubters that "the Kentucky Derby will be run in 1943, even if there are only two horses in the race, and only a half dozen people in the stands."[7] Approximately fifty thousand spectators attended and watched Johnny Longden ride heavily favored Count Fleet to an easy wire-to-wire victory for his owners, taxicab and rental car magnate John D. Hertz and his wife, who had previously entered the Derby winner's circle in 1928 with Count Fleet's sire, Reigh Count.[8] Count Fleet would capture the Triple Crown that year, with a victory in the Withers Stakes sandwiched in for good measure. His twenty-five-length margin of victory in the Belmont Stakes would not be bettered until Secretariat's famous 1973 performance. Count Fleet would eventually earn a spot in racing's Hall of Fame and a place on the lists of greatest American racehorses of the twentieth century. Despite his relative star power, attendance at Count Fleet's Derby was not as large as in previous years—but still a successful showing under the circumstances of wartime travel restrictions. Churchill Downs provided American servicemen with many of the out-of-town box owners' tickets for the Derby, and other soldiers were admitted at reduced rates, giving Churchill Downs a patriotic feel on Derby Day and garnering positive publicity.[9]

The 1943 Derby would be remembered as the "Streetcar Derby" because of the mode of transportation a great number of spectators used to arrive at the track that day. Even descriptions of the race itself included references to the war, which influenced nearly every aspect of American life by 1943. "It was as if the horses in the Derby captured the military spirit of the times. They marched around the track almost exactly according to their rank, as indicated on the mutual boards on the infield," the *Blood-Horse* reported.[10] Winn's ability to keep the Derby afloat during the war years is among his greatest accomplishments at

Churchill Downs, and Winn himself called the Streetcar Derby the "greatest Derby of them all."[11]

In 1944, travel restrictions again affected Derby attendance —but not enthusiasm—as the downtown hotels were jammed and the city possessed a "festival air."[12] Streetcars began arriving at Churchill Downs at 4:00 on a chilly morning with the first load of Derby patrons. A group of navy students from the University of Louisville performed their daily drills on the grounds of Churchill Downs at dawn so that they would be free to watch the races in the afternoon. Their military brethren stationed overseas were also able to follow the action. An Associated Press report from Naples, Italy, explained that American "G.I.'s had no mint juleps and no blue grass here in Italy today, but they were distinctly Derby conscious on this Kentucky Derby Day—so Derby conscious, in fact, that they had their own bookmaker handle wagers of a quarter or two on their choices."[13] A Derby Day cartoon in the *Courier-Journal* depicted a frustrated Adolf Hitler trying to spy on American radio transmissions, but unable to find anything but a broadcast of the Kentucky Derby.[14] The crowd of sixty-five thousand bet more on that year's race than any since 1929, and a $2 win ticket on Pensive returned $16.20 to his backers.

The Derby had been called an American institution before the war, and its survival in the face of wartime restrictions only helped to further its national reputation.[15] But at the end of 1944 James F. Byrnes, director of War Mobilization, shut down all American racing effective January 3, 1945, justifying his action thus: "The operation of race tracks not only requires the employment of more essential operations, but also manpower, railroad transportation, as well as tires and gasoline in the movement of patrons to and from the track, and in the movement of the horses. . . . The existing war situation demands the utmost effort that the people of the United States can give. . . . The Operation of race tracks is not conducive to this all-out effort."[16] The racing press criticized the decision, citing the fact that racing was allowed to continue in England and France in spite of the war. Some claimed that the ban was the result of Washington's anger over the $1 billion wagered on horses annually—money that was not being invested in war bonds. Others suggested that the ban was retaliation for a $75,000 contribution made to Thomas Dewey's 1944 presidential campaign by Santa Anita, a Los Angeles area racetrack. Regardless of what had motivated the ban, it was not in effect for long. Racing returned to the United States in May of 1945, following the German surrender in Europe, and proceeded to break national records for attendance and wagering handle: in less than eight months more than 19 million people visited American tracks, plunking down more than $1.4 billion in bets.[17]

With restrictions lifted, Churchill Downs readied itself for another running of its signature event. The 1945 Derby was run on June 9, the last time the Derby was not contested on the first Saturday in May. Though the date was different, national newspapers were happy to report that things were largely back to normal at Churchill Downs: "This wasn't the first Saturday in May, but it was the same old Derby Day. It had all the color, all the pretty women, all the second guessers and all the crowd with its hustle and bustle of past Derby Days," the *New York Times* reported.[18] The Derby's survival during World War II confirmed its status as one of the premiere events in the nation and reinforced its ties to a distant American past. To an American population that had learned patriotic consumption practices during the war, the Derby came to represent the nation (not just Kentucky and the South) in the "Consumers' Republic" that emerged in postwar America.[19]

If Kentucky had been located in the Deep South, it might not have been possible for the Derby to become an "American" institution as early as it did. However, the geographic, cultural, and political location of Kentucky had allowed the identity of the state and the Derby to evolve over the years to suit the cultural needs and tastes of different eras. By celebrating American patriotism, especially during times of war, Churchill Downs leaders had helped to foster an American identity for the event. In 1902, when American forces were fighting in the Philippines, coverage of the Derby had included journalists' description of the American flags around the track.[20] During World War I, Matt Winn and other Churchill Downs officials had trumpeted their charitable efforts and support of the U.S. military, even planting crops in the infield to support the war effort. Thus, by the time the United States had become involved in World War II, the Kentucky Derby no longer needed to be metaphorically draped in the American flag to be perceived as patriotically acceptable in a time of war; it was already an American institution, and was celebrated as such. Whereas other high-profile American sporting events, like the Masters golf tournament and the Indianapolis 500, were suspended during World War II, the Kentucky Derby was a rallying point for Americans at home and abroad.

It was the Kentucky Derby's considerable cultural clout that enabled Churchill Downs officials to negotiate with the U.S. government to allow the Derby to continue when other events were cancelled. The Derby had reached such a stature, and continuity was perceived to be such a significant piece of the popular appeal of the event, that there had again been serious talk of staging the race without spectators if the ban on horse racing and wartime travel had not been lifted after V-E Day.[21]

The Derby's association with the Old South had not been emphasized during the war, but the connection remained potent, and it didn't take long for the Old South imagery to return. In 1946 a journalist for the *Blood-Horse* wrote, "If the visitors go away with the impression that central Kentuckians live exclusively on fried chicken and country ham biscuits, and that you are met at every doorway by a dark servitor carrying a tray of mint juleps it will not surprise anyone."[22] In 1950 a photograph appeared in the *Courier-Journal* that depicted a Wake Forest student waving a Confederate battle flag in the Churchill Downs infield, and in 1952 a U.S. Army band from the "Dixie Division," dressed in Confederate gray and "rebel hats," marched into the Derby infield playing "Dixie," led by their cocker spaniel mascot bearing a Confederate flag.[23]

The following year a popular Warner Bros. cartoon reaffirmed the connection between Kentucky and the Old South in American culture. In *Southern Fried Rabbit,* Bugs Bunny travels south in search of carrots during a famine in the North.[24] Bugs encounters Yosemite Sam, unaware that the Civil War has ended, dressed in a Confederate uniform and guarding the Mason-Dixon Line. In an attempt to get by Sam, Bugs dons a blackface disguise and strums a banjo, singing "My Old Kentucky Home."

In 1956 four Louisville business leaders reestablished the Kentucky Derby Festival that had been first attempted briefly in the 1930s, giving the City of Louisville and festival sponsors an opportunity to shape the image and identity of the Derby and its host city during Derby Week, when Louisville had the attention of the nation. The festival's events helped city leaders to reemphasize Louisville's reputation as a southern city. Although the festival has grown to the extent that it now lasts for two weeks, consists of dozens of events, and attracts hundreds of thousands of visitors to Louisville each year, the first modern Derby Festival in 1956 consisted only of a parade.

In the festival's early years designers competed for awards given to top parade floats sponsored by local companies. Themes of the floats reflected both Cold War patriotic spirit and a fondness for evocations of the Old South. Winning floats had titles like "The Great U.S.," "Heritage of the Old South," and "Medleys of Stephen Foster."[25] A float called "Dixie" won the "Bluegrass Trophy for the float most representative of the romance of Kentucky."[26] Another, sponsored by the Louisville and Nashville Railroad, won "most beautiful commercial entry" with a float depicting a "smoke-belching 'iron horse' surrounded by a Southern plantation and ladies in hoop skirts."[27] In 1957 the first Derby Festival queen was crowned at the Coronation Ball, which has been held under the name the Fillies Derby Ball since 1959. Today, organizers describe the event as "a grand affair representing Louisville's tradition of southern hospitality," demonstrating the continued connection between the Derby and the South that festival organizers have worked to maintain.[28]

Another way in which the prewar links between the Derby and the Old South reemerged in the 1950s was in newspaper coverage of the Kentucky Colonels' annual pre-Derby dinner. Reports often included photos of all-black servant staffs carrying trays of mint juleps and singing Stephen Foster tunes, reminiscent of scenes from films like *The Little Colonel*. The following description is typical in the writer's knowing nod to his readers regarding Kentucky's lingering pseudo-Confederate status: "The night's festivities really got underway when a procession of [black] waiters marched into the Flag Room singing and bearing trays of mint juleps. A toast to the President of the United States was proposed. Everyone arose, waited expectantly, but nothing happened. Then everyone drank to the health of Governor Chandler."[29]

Though the winking recognition of an imagined Confederate identity being celebrated at the Derby continued after the war, the days of cartoon depictions of black-faced clowns in newspaper coverage of the Derby were gone for good. The cultural and political climate had changed since the start of American involvement in World War II, and while there was still a place for commemoration of the Old South in 1950s America, the Derby had become more than just a celebration of the regional past. The Derby had also become a site that celebrated the *American* present, where equine champions and their human connections were praised for possessing the power, strength, and virtue of a nation recently victorious in the largest war in the history of humankind.

After the end of World War II, American horse racing entered a "golden age." Seven hundred thousand Americans would visit one of the nation's 130 racetracks each week; racing surpassed baseball as the number-one spectator sport in America by 1952.[30] Racing had a virtual monopoly on legal gambling in the United States and provided spectators an opportunity for excitement and escape while participating in a sport with deep American roots. Horse racing, boxing, and baseball, the most popular sports of the 1950s, could all trace their lineage back for generations, which appealed to a society trying to establish itself as a model for the world. In the immediate aftermath of World War II, some of the most successful and celebrated teams and athletes were held up as examples of American strength, success, and prosperity.

The most dominant horse racing operation in the 1940s and 1950s, Calumet Farm, was on a plane of national celebrity similar to that of heavyweight boxing champion Rocky Marciano or Mickey Mantle and the New York Yankees. From 1941 to 1961, Calumet Farm dominated all American racing, including the Kentucky Derby. In that period Calumet was the leading owner in terms of annual purse money won in America twelve times, and was never out of the top three.[31] Overall, Calumet Farm owned eight Derby winners and bred nine.[32] Those eight Derby wins came in just twenty starts. In addition, Calumet Farm had four seconds and a third-place finish from those twenty starts, a remarkable record that is unlikely ever to be matched. Calumet's dominance of the sport came at a time when Americans were happy to celebrate signs of national strength and dominance. The Kentucky Derby was horse racing's brightest stage, and horses carrying Calumet's famous "devil red and blue" silks shone brightly upon it. Calumet's eight Derby wins doubled the total of its nearest competitor, Colonel E. R. Bradley, and its success helped to increase not only its own popularity but also that of the Derby.

Whirlaway (in front) capturing the Belmont Stakes en route to the 1941 Triple Crown. (Keeneland Library, Lexington, Kentucky.)

The name Calumet Farm first became commonplace in the headlines of the nation's sports pages in 1941, when Whirlaway won the Kentucky Derby in record time on his way to the Triple Crown and two consecutive Horse of the Year honors, beginning a run of two decades of dominance for Calumet Farm in American racing. Whirlaway, known for his freakishly long tail, which reached almost to the ground, and his unpredictable running style, is still regarded as one of the greatest American horses of the twentieth century. He would go on to break the American career earnings record set by Seabiscuit and eventually joined his jockey Eddie Arcaro and his trainer Ben Jones in racing's Hall of Fame. He helped make Calumet Farm a household name in the American sports vernacular, but he would not even be the greatest horse to carry the Calumet colors in the 1940s.

In 1948 Calumet's Citation completed the most impressive three-year-old campaign of any American racehorse in history af-

Citation, ridden by Eddie Arcaro, Kentucky Derby, 1948. (Keeneland Library, Lexington, Kentucky.)

ter crushing his competition the previous year to earn two-year-old champion honors. As a three-year-old the mahogany-colored colt captured the Derby as an odds-on favorite, becoming Calumet's third Kentucky Derby winner of the decade.[33] He would go on to win the Triple Crown that year, the last horse to do so until Secretariat a quarter century later. In his 1948 three-year-old season Citation won nineteen of twenty races, including fifteen in a row and eight against older horses, a record that is most unlikely ever to be matched.

Citation earned comparisons to the theretofore incomparable Man o' War but, unlike Man o' War, Citation competed in and won the Kentucky Derby. This fact does not diminish Man o' War's legacy, but it does reinforce the fact that the Kentucky Derby had unquestionably become the most important race on the American three-year-olds' calendar, a status that had not been so certain in 1920, when Man o' War's owner Samuel Riddle had decided that his horse would bypass the Derby.

Mr. and Mrs. Warren Wright, at Hialeah, 1948. (Morgan Collection, Keeneland Library, Lexington, Kentucky.)

Calumet owner Warren Wright was in the midst of an unprecedented run as an owner and breeder of champion racehorses. He had endeavored to make Calumet Farm the finest Thoroughbred racehorse factory in the nation when he inherited what had been a top-notch Standardbred farm from his father in 1931, and he was succeeding in that endeavor.[34]

At the beginning of the Depression, the Wrights were among the wealthiest families in America. As president of the Calumet Baking Powder Company in the 1920s, Warren Wright negotiated its sale for $32 million to an operation that would soon be called General Foods. Warren Wright's father, William Wright, had founded the baking powder company at age thirty-seven in 1888 with $3,500, his life savings accumulated over his years as a salesman. His product was marketed as containing a special ingredient (egg whites), which gave the baking powder "double leavening action," according to advertisements.[35]

In 1931 William Wright died, leaving the vast majority of his estate, including his Calumet Farm in Lexington, Kentucky, to his son Warren. By the 1940s, Warren had established Calumet Farm as America's greatest Thoroughbred racing and breeding dynasty. After Calumet's victory in the 1941 Derby with Whirlaway, the farm became one of Kentucky's most popular tourist attractions, drawing hundreds of visitors per day. *Time* magazine ran a cover story on Calumet's trainer "Plain" Ben Jones in 1949, and by 1950, the farm was forced to limit public access to the farm because of the swell in visitors due to Citation's success.[36]

In 1952, when Hill Gail became the fifth horse to carry Calumet's colors to a Derby victory, a writer for the *Blood-Horse* asserted, "The folklore of sports is filled with exploits of underdogs who sandbagged a champion, but the world loves a consistent winner, and the Man in the White Hat always gives the citizenry something to anchor to."[37] This argument is not a universal truth; the history of American sport is full of "consistent winners" who were not embraced by the public, and of "underdogs" who were. But the quotation does shed some important light on an element of the collective mindset of Americans in the 1950s, and offers some insight into how Americans may have been experiencing and perceiving the Kentucky Derby in the aftermath of World War II.

Like Calumet, the Derby was itself a "consistent winner" and an example of American perseverance and strength. It was an event that Americans could legitimately call "American" at a time when the nation was ready to celebrate its own past, present, and future. In other eras in American culture, underdogs and unlikely victors would be more enthusiastically celebrated, and later in the twentieth century journalists and spectators at the Derby would do just that. But in the early Cold War era journalists and race fans tended to pay more attention to institutions with records of longevity and success; Calumet Farm and the Derby were two such institutions.

An exception to the rule was the mixed reaction to Calumet's sixth Derby victory with Iron Liege in 1957 over a field that many hold as the greatest in the history of the race. Jockey Bill Shoemaker misjudged the finish line aboard Gallant Man, standing up in the stirrups a sixteenth of a mile too early and allowing Iron Liege to prevail by what the *New York Times* called a "lucky nose."[38] Bold Ruler's jockey Eddie Arcaro was embarrassed by his fourth-place finish aboard the favorite and blamed himself for the horse's loss.[39] Iron Liege, called the "junior varsity colt" by one writer, rather than being celebrated as an unlikely victor, almost seemed to be blamed by writers for circumventing the "correct" outcome at the Derby, which should have been a victory by the superior talent.[40] Despite some spectators' disappointment, all could take some solace in knowing that they had indeed witnessed greatness that day, including the talents of jockeys Eddie Arcaro, Bill Hartack, and Bill Shoemaker, who would finish their careers with a combined fourteen Derby wins. In addition to the riders who would eventually be enshrined, the crowd also saw three future Hall of Fame horses that day, though the winner, Iron Liege, was not one of them.[41]

The only equine outfit to even approach Calumet's success in the Derby in the 1940s and 1950s was Robert Kleberg's King Ranch, an enormous cattle operation founded by Kleberg's grandfather in the 1850s that encompassed hundreds of thousands of acres of south Texas brush country. Under the guidance of Hall of Fame trainer Max Hirsch, King Ranch won the Derby in 1946 and 1950 with Assault and Middleground, respectively, the former going on to capture that year's Triple Crown. As a young horse Assault barely survived an injury to his right front foot sustained when he stepped on a surveyor's stake. The injury left the colt with a deformity that made walking and trotting difficult. Fortunately for Assault, galloping was another story. Popularly known as the "Club Footed Comet" (despite the fact that he did not actually have a club foot), Assault equaled a Derby record when he won in 1946 by eight lengths with Jockey Warren

Bill Shoemaker, four-time Derby-winning jockey, weighing in.
(Keeneland Library, Lexington, Kentucky.)

Mehrtens. A crowd estimated to be as large as 105,000 showed up to witness the first peacetime Derby in five years, and the winner's share of the record Derby purse amounted to $96,400.[42] "The Lone Star yesterday from the Lone Star State won by the width of Texas," one newspaper reported. "As he flew away from them in the stretch, the only hope the other horses seemed to have of ever catching Assault was to hang around when the race

Assault with jockey Warren Mehrtens and groom after his record-setting win in the 1946 Kentucky Derby. (Morgan Collection, Keeneland Library, Lexington, Kentucky.)

was over and wait for him to revisit the scene of his crime."[43] Only a week later, Assault won the Preakness Stakes by a head before a record crowd for that event.[44] He went on to capture the Belmont Stakes to become the seventh Triple Crown champion in American racing history.

The following year a colt named Jet Pilot won the Derby for trainer "Silent" Tom Smith, who had first made a name for himself by developing Seabiscuit into a champion racehorse. In the 1940s Smith was nationally known as the trainer for Main Chance Farm, one of the leading racing stables of the 1940s and 1950s, owned by cosmetics giant Elizabeth Arden. Born Florence Nightingale Graham, Arden began her cosmetics empire in the 1910s, at a time when women who "painted" (wore make-up) were presumed to be whores or actresses. Graham marketed her "Concept of Total Beauty" brilliantly, becoming one of the world's wealthiest women by selling the idea that youth and beauty could be bought in the form of lotions, cosmetics, and perfumes. A contemporary of Graham's, Matt Winn must have been impressed by her ability to sell a vision and a lifestyle, something Winn had also done in his promotion of the Derby as a consumable experience.

In 1950 the formidable tandem of King Ranch and Max Hirsch again found the Derby winner's circle with Middleground, who missed Whirlaway's record time by one-fifth of a second beneath apprentice rider Bill Boland. In capturing its second Derby the King Ranch became, to that time, only the seventh owner in history to have won at least two Derbies, a list headed by Calumet Farm, which would break a tie with Colonel E. R. Bradley two years later with its fifth Derby victory by Hill Gail in 1952. At the dawn of the golden age of the television cowboys, including Gene Autry, Hopalong Cassidy, and Roy Rogers, King Ranch's Texas-bred horses and trainer proved to be popular Derby champions in the postwar culture of mass consumption in America.[45]

In 1956 Needles became the first Florida-bred horse to win the Kentucky Derby. His father and paternal grandfather, Pensive and Ponder, were both Derby winners who had been bred and owned by Calumet Farm.[46] One of those on hand to witness Needles's Derby win was the great American writer John Steinbeck, who had been invited by the *Courier-Journal* to write a guest piece on that year's event. In what has become one of the more famous descriptions of the Derby, Steinbeck wrote:

At this sacred moment, in this place of pilgrimage, I have several towering but gossamer convictions. During Derby Week, Louisville is the capital of the world. This lively, lovely city has a temporary population of foster-citizens second only to China. I am also sure that if the national elections took place today, our next president would be a horse. . . . I am fulfilled and weary.

This Kentucky Derby, whatever it is—a race, an emotion, a turbulence, an explosion—is one of the most beautiful and violent and satisfying things I have ever experienced. And I suspect that, as with other wonders, the people one by one have taken from it exactly as much good or evil as they brought to it. What an experience. I am glad I have seen it and felt it at last.[47]

The year before Steinbeck's Derby coverage appeared in the *Courier-Journal,* William Faulkner was given a similar assignment to produce a piece on the Derby for the then-fledgling *Sports Illustrated.* Faulkner, like countless writers who had covered the Kentucky Derby before him, referred to Stephen Foster and called Kentucky "my old Kentucky home," but he was somewhat atypical in his inclusion of Daniel Boone and Abraham Lincoln in his unusual and evocative description of the Derby experience: "This saw Boone: the bluegrass, the virgin land rolling westward wave by dense wave from the Allegheny gaps, unmarked then, teeming with deer and buffalo about the salt licks and the limestone springs whose water in time would make the fine bourbon whiskey; and the wild men too—the red men and the white ones too who had to be a little wild also to endure and survive and so mark the wilderness with the proofs of their tough survival—. . . the dark and bloody ground."[48]

This excerpt would seem to have nothing to do with the horse race that Faulkner was nominally covering. But the writer was trying to capture the essence of the event, and he understood very well that the Derby was more than just a horse race. The Derby was an embodiment of Kentucky and all that the state represented, but it had also become a slice of Americana. In the environment of the Cold War, the Derby was in many ways an American celebration, and Kentucky's rich history and malleable identity allowed Faulkner to evoke images of Abraham Lincoln, born in a Kentucky log cabin, in the same report with Boone and the 1955 Derby, making Kentucky a cradle as well as a keeper of American national identity. Faulkner continued:

And knew Lincoln too, where the old weathered durable rail fences enclose the green and sacrosanct place of rounded hills long healed now from the plow, and big old trees to shade the site of the ancient one-room cabin in which the babe first saw light; no sound there now but such wind and birds as when the child first faced the road which would lead to fame and martyrdom—unless perhaps you like to think that the man's voice is somewhere there too, speaking into the scene of his nativity the simple and matchless prose with which he reminded us of our duties and responsibilities if we wished to continue as a nation.[49]

In celebrating the Kentucky Derby with Faulkner, Cold War Americans could embrace the popular memory of Daniel Boone, the man who brought American values to the untamed wilderness, and Lincoln, the man who preserved them by saving the Union.

Faulkner and Steinbeck published their evocative Derby descriptions at a time when national sports telecasts were still in their infancy. But it would not be long before sportscasters would come to overshadow sportswriters as national celebrities and as popular sources for description, analysis, and interpretation of sport. With the growth of national television broadcasting in the 1950s came a homogenization of Derby coverage in some respects. Television networks needed to appeal to as broad an audience as possible in national broadcasts, which ironically led to a reduction in media focus on the aspect of the Derby that had helped it to become so culturally significant in the first place—its evocation of the Old South. Although elements of southern-ness like singing "My Old Kentucky Home" and tossing back mint juleps remained part of the story in the age of television, the advent of network broadcasting helped to further reshape the Derby as an *American* event, not just a "southern" one.

In 1928 radio broadcaster Credo Harris had lamented to his Derby audience, "In such a condition of color and motion the task of describing it to you seems almost hopeless. I wish that television were in general use—as it will be shortly—for then I could turn it on and let you thrill with the actual picture, instead of asking you to follow a most inadequate word printer."[50] Two decades later, in 1949, Louisville's WAVE television station carried the first live telecast of the Kentucky Derby. The telecast, which could be seen only in the homes of the few owners of television sets in Louisville and the surrounding area, included an interview with an aging Colonel Matt Winn.

Only months after appearing on the first limited television broadcast of the Derby, Matt Winn died at the age of eighty-eight. He had seen each of the first seventy-five Kentucky Derbies in person, and was widely acknowledged as the man most responsible for the event's survival and prosperity. Legendary sports columnist Arthur Daley described the considerable role Winn played in shaping the Kentucky Derby: "A fabulous character in every respect was the man who was christened Martin Joseph Winn but became Matt Winn. He could give cards and spades to Barnum and beat him. [The Kentucky Derby] is his baby and his alone. He will always be a part of it, even more a part of it than the spired towers at Churchill Downs. He alone made it what it is today."[51]

From the beginning of his association with Churchill Downs, Winn had a friendly relationship with members of the press. Winn spent much of his winter "off season" in New York at the Waldorf-Astoria, where he often entertained sportswriters and picked up their tabs.[52] He encouraged top sports journalists to come to the Derby, and made sure they were well treated while in Louisville. His list of friends within the industry included some of the most famous names of that generation: Grantland Rice, Damon Runyon, and Jimmy Cannon. Bill Corum was another of Winn's favorite writers. Corum coined the phrase "Run for the Roses" in 1925, and later succeeded Winn as president of Churchill Downs, Inc.

The respect that Winn had for writers was reciprocated, and the writers knew that he was always good for a useful quote

Matt Winn, always dapper, always promoting the Derby. (Photographic Archives, 1994.18.4644, Special Collections, University of Louisville, Louisville, Kentucky.)

and a free drink. Writers returned Winn's kindness by regularly heaping praise and attention upon him in their columns. Arthur Daley wrote of Winn, "The colonel took a hinky-dink country race and converted it into the most glamorous and widely publicized hoss event in the world, the Kentucky Derby."[53] *Time* magazine claimed that the popularity of the Kentucky Derby could be attributed "to the industry and wily determination of a fat, white-haired Louisville Irishman who, as General Manager of Churchill Downs since 1902, has transformed the event from a pipsqueak Dixie picnic to a major U.S. sport fiesta."[54] Such explanations of the Derby's rise to prominence were gross simplifications, but articles like these nevertheless helped to promote both Winn and his beloved Kentucky Derby.

Much of the longevity and success of the Derby can be attributed to the many contributions made by Matt Winn, who worked tirelessly to make the Derby the annual spectacle that it has become. Winn continued the efforts of M. L. Clark to make Churchill Downs and the Derby appealing to high society, and to establish a reputation of legitimacy and integrity for the Downs. Under Winn's watch the Derby's attendance grew along with its national stature. Thanks in large part to Winn's leadership, Churchill Downs and the Derby survived antigambling and antiracing reform movements, two world wars, the Great Depression, and a major flood.

In promoting the Derby, Winn sold a vision, a dream, and a lifestyle. He was selling romantic notions of Old Kentucky and the Old South. The Kentucky Derby was an opportunity for the swells to indulge in vice and a chance for the masses to experience a bit of luxury. Eventually the Derby would become a celebration of the American Dream, a place where patrons had an opportunity to shoot for success on the highest stage with a $2 ticket to win on a Derby champion, or for dreamers to imagine themselves in the winner's circle. The Derby was always more than just a horse race. From its inception it was a romantic celebration of past and present. Winn, more than anyone else, recognized and effectively exploited the Derby's potential for mass appeal.

Above all, Winn was a walking, talking, living embodiment of the myth and romance that the American public had come to associate with Kentucky. He called himself "colonel"; he drank bourbon, smoked cigars, wore light-colored suits, and employed a black valet. Those who have called Winn indispensable to the success of the Kentucky Derby are correct in their assessments, but they have generally missed the nature of his significance. Winn was not merely a "tireless promoter," a term that calls to mind a mustachioed, cane-twirling carnival barker with an uncanny ability to attract rubes with fast talk. He was not an example of someone whose touch turned everything to gold. He had

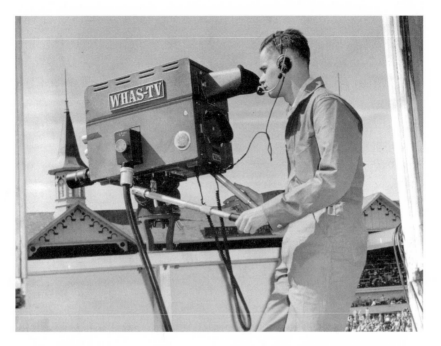

WHAS TV camera, 1953. Worries that televising the Derby would lead to decreased attendance proved to be unfounded. (Radio Photographic Collection, 79PA104-0437, University of Kentucky, Lexington.)

a hand in dozens of other racetracks with signature races in the United States and Mexico over a long career, but no event that he promoted or managed ever began to approach the popularity or cultural significance of the Kentucky Derby.

Winn attracted attention to the Kentucky Derby because he was able to provide an image of what people wanted or needed Kentucky to be. He invited Americans to experience the image that he embodied by coming to Louisville each May or by following the event via newspapers, radio, newsreels, and television. No person was more important to the story of the growth of the Kentucky Derby than Colonel Martin J. Winn. Behind the scenes he was a capable manager, administrator, and businessman. He was an innovator in the world of horse racing. He had a warm and symbiotic relationship with many of the nation's greatest sportswriters. But for millions of Americans who attended, read about, listened to, or watched the Kentucky Derby every year, Winn was a real-life Kentucky colonel who served as both spokesman and pseudo-mascot for the event. This was his greatest contribution to the Derby.

In 1952 millions of people beyond Louisville had the opportunity to experience the Derby in their living rooms with the first live national television broadcast of the event. It was believed to have been the costliest half-hour show in television history at that time and was picked up by more than forty television stations on the Columbia Broadcasting System network. The television audience was roughly estimated at between 10 and 15 million viewers, and millions more heard Fred Capossella and Mel Allen call the race on a national radio broadcast that was carried by 208 radio stations across the United States, Alaska, Hawaii, and Canada, and was rebroadcast around the world to the American Armed Forces Network.[55] Churchill Downs officials had been concerned about the broadcast's potential effect on attendance, but track president Bill Corum happily reported after the 1952 Derby that attendance and betting figures were both up from previous years.

Other tracks did not learn from the Derby's successful relationship with media technology, and American racing in general suffered as a result of its failure to take advantage of the enormous growth of televised sports in the second half of the twentieth century. The general reluctance to use television among racing industry leaders had been due to their fear that because people could not bet on the races if watching from their homes, the racetracks would lose income with televised racing. This was a shortsighted fear that proved to be costly. But the Kentucky Derby would remain a fixture on American television, which helped keep the event relevant throughout the twentieth century.

An estimated 20 million people tuned into the CBS telecast of the 1953 Kentucky Derby.[56] Seventy-two percent of American televisions that were turned on at the time of the race were tuned to the Derby coverage when American racing's first television superstar, a gray colt named Native Dancer, was defeated by H. F. Guggenheim's Dark Star after being bumped badly on the first turn.[57] This shocking defeat before an estimated one hundred thousand fans was the only loss in the career of the immensely popular gray colt. His late-running style and his distinctive color were part of his appeal to audiences, but the reasons for his popularity were more complicated, as a biographer of the horse explained. "It was an epic time for mythmaking in America. In the aftermath of a depression and war, at the dawn of the television age, the country was moving to the suburbs and learning to commune over heroes hatched in living rooms on flickering black-and-white TV sets."[58] Native Dancer, affectionately known to his supporters as the Grey Ghost, was owned by the handsome and wealthy sportsman Alfred Gwynne Vanderbilt. The horse and owner seemed to Americans to embody what they wanted to believe about themselves and their nation—success, confidence, and power.[59] Although American sports history had been replete with unlikely victories by popular underdogs, Dark Star's upset of Native Dancer came in the 1950s, not the 1930s, and it was not popular. *Time* magazine reported, "Thousands turned from their TV screens in sorrow, a few in tears."[60] Arthur Daley admitted, "This reporter was never as emotionally affected by a horse race."[61]

Native Dancer's popularity had transcended the sport of Thoroughbred racing and the Kentucky Derby; he appeared on the cover of *Time* magazine in May of 1954. His popularity helped to demonstrate that the Derby was a marketable television event. The following year the Gillette Safety Razor Company agreed to pay $150,000 to sponsor the Derby's CBS telecast for the next three years. The national broadcasts allowed millions of fans across the country to experience the Derby from their living rooms and helped the Derby to secure a place in the changing American culture of the television age.

The next equine television superstar and popular hero of Thoroughbred racing to emerge was Silky Sullivan, named for boxer John L. Sullivan.[62] Silky had a habit of spotting his rivals dozens of lengths before catching them at the wire in a blazing finish. But in 1958 he became one of the first victims of the *Sports Illustrated* jinx (which, some believe, has caused an uncanny number of athletes appearing on the magazine's cover to subsequently underperform or suffer injuries) when he appeared on the cover the week before the Derby.[63] The Derby was America's most popular race, and Churchill Downs would have served as a fitting setting for Silky's coronation as king of American racing. The national television coverage of the Derby even had a camera dedicated to Silky so that his fans could keep him in view as he employed his usual tactic of dropping far behind the rest of the horses in the race, far out of the typical frame of televised racing.[64] But his triumph was not to be. Rain had caused the track conditions to deteriorate, and one trainer later recalled that it was "like racing in chewing gum."[65] Calumet Farm's Tim Tam prevailed, adding to the farm's already impressive Derby record.[66] Nevertheless, the Derby was the beneficiary of increased attention and publicity when a horse as popular as Silky Sullivan competed in the event.

The Derby achieved its lofty national reputation and stature in the early twentieth century in large part because of the event's perceived connection to romantic elements of Kentucky and the Old South. But even as the Derby gained popularity because of its southern ties, it had become, at least by the time of the American entrance into World War II, an *American* institution and a significant piece of Americana. This status helped the Derby to remain popular and culturally relevant in the second half of the twentieth century, when many of the aspects of the Old South were not as widely appealing as they had been in the first half of the century. By the end of the 1950s the Derby's increasingly *American* status, combined with the continued growth in media coverage of the event, which by then included a week's worth of prerace festivities, made Louisville a national stage during Derby Week. In the increasingly homogenized American culture in the 1950s, which included network television, Levittowns, the interstate highway system, and chain stores, the Derby remained a distinct piece of regional culture even as it became increasingly American.

5

A Stage for Social Protest and a Site of National Healing

1960–1980

By the 1960s the Derby's status as an important piece of Americana, combined with the glut of media attention focused on Louisville during the first week of May each year, had transformed the event into a national stage. As baby boomers came of age and challenged the conventional wisdom of their parents' generation, many of the American cultural and social battles of the 1960s and 1970s would be waged on that stage, including the clash between youth and the "establishment," and the struggle for black civil rights.

The first of these conflicts to appear at Churchill Downs accompanied the young people who made Louisville an important date on their social calendar beginning in the early 1960s, in hindsight a relatively simple and innocent time as compared to the social and political environment at the Derby and around the world that would emerge just a few years later. These teenagers and collegians invaded the infield at Churchill Downs in unprecedented numbers, creating a visible "generation gap," between the youth in the infield and the older folks across the track in the grandstand and clubhouse. In the 1950s the infield had been a place where adults could enjoy a "picnic" atmosphere, but by the mid-1960s the infield began to embody the "spring break" envi-

Group from Frankfort relaxes in the infield, 1950s. The picnic atmosphere in the Derby infield of the 1950s turned much more rambunctious in the 1960s. (Kentucky Historical Society, Frankfort.)

ronment that it retains today, populated by a young crowd and dominated by college-aged revelers.

A Louisville reporter stationed in the Derby infield in 1965 spoke with some of the spectators, questioning them about their Derby experience as if they were members of an exotic species. "I'm out of my gourd," shouted "a barefooted young blonde woman wearing the 'omnipresent' madras skirt." Another college-aged reveler bristled at the large presence of law enforcement in the infield. "What makes this place so great is all the authority around," the young man sarcastically explained. "I mean everywhere you look there's fuzz or National Guard, or even Army. You know we can't have fun unless there's authority around."[1] Those who were paying any attention to the nominal reason for the party saw Lucky Debonair and Bill Shoemaker just outlast a hard-charging Dapper Dan to win the big race, the third Derby score for the popular rider.

By the mid-1960s young people, especially college students, were doing their best to create an environment of contained debauchery in the infield that contrasted with the stuffier setting across the track in the clubhouse. They were engaged in a mild form of social protest that was part fraternity party and part carnival right in front of their parents' eyes. Not everyone understood what the teenagers and college students were doing at the Derby, but everyone knew that the party atmosphere helped attract people to Louisville for Derby Week. Even the Roman Catholic Church relaxed its rules and regulations; in recognition of the Derby's status as an important civic holiday, in 1965 the Church announced that Louisville Catholics—natives and visitors alike—would be granted a Derby Eve dispensation from the rule against eating meat on Fridays. But, as is the case with each new generation, the baby boomers were unaware of the fact that the ground they were treading upon was not entirely new territory.

The Derby had possessed a certain antiestablishment air since the 1910s and 1920s, when vestiges of Victorian morality codes still lingered and activities like drinking and gambling were frowned upon by conservative segments of society. But the Derby had since become an American institution; this institutional status, combined with the national attention focused on Churchill Downs at Derby time, made it an ideal location for displays of protest and antiauthoritarianism. In an environment of conflict over the direction of American society, politics, and culture, the Kentucky Derby became a stage upon which various groups attempted to define America in a period of political and social unrest. The fact that the Derby was also a site of celebration of vestiges of the Old South only increased its attractiveness to progressive protesters and activists.

A new nod to bygone days celebrated at the Derby was born in 1963: the annual steamboat race on the Ohio River, which remains a popular part of the annual Derby Festival. The *Chicago*

Tribune reported beneath the headline "Shades of Huck Finn!" that the scene surrounding the first Great Steamboat Race "was almost as it might have been in granddad's day. Calliopes blared off key with those old time tunes. Bunting and flags fluttered in the afternoon's raw wind."[2] The popular race between *The Belle of Louisville* and New Orleans's *Delta Queen* was run for fourteen miles up and down the Ohio River, with a prize of a golden set of elk's antlers awarded to the winner. The race evoked visions of Louisville in a time when the Ohio River played a more important role in the city's economy and culture than it does today. The race also evoked images of a Twainian Mississippi River past that did not exactly match the reality of Louisville's historical experience. The steamboat race may be responsible for the following description of the Kentucky Derby by racing historian and *Baltimore Sun* sportswriter John Eisenberg: "The event was an American Bacchanalia, the scent of big money and fast horses colliding with Kentucky bourbon and pretty women to create a weekend of Roman excess in a conservative Mississippi River town."[3]

It is not entirely surprising that Eisenberg would confuse Louisville's Ohio River with the Mississippi; the imagery associated with Louisville at Derby time had much more in common with Mississippi River cities like Memphis and New Orleans than it had with cities along the Ohio like Cincinnati or Pittsburgh. In reality, Louisville was probably somewhere in between, but the romantically "southern" Louisville that played host to the Kentucky Derby in the imaginations of Americans would fit much better on the banks of the Mississippi, the river that had been romanticized in works like *Huckleberry Finn* and *Show Boat*.

In the spring of 1966 American newspapers were dominated by coverage of civil rights demonstrations and the war in Vietnam. But on the first Saturday in May, national attention again turned to Louisville. A cartoon that appeared in the Derby Day edition of the *Louisville Times* acknowledged this shift in attention. Below a drawing of U.S. soldiers wading through muck in a Vietnamese rainstorm with a helicopter flying overhead, the caption read, "Well, I hope they have a dry track in good ol' Louisville today."[4]

Journalists covering the buildup to the 1966 Derby echoed racing fans' disappointment that the two most celebrated three-year-olds of the year, Graustark and Buckpasser, would not be able to run in the race because of injuries. Days before the big race, *New York Times* columnist Arthur Daley suggested that the 1966 Derby "bears an embarrassing similarity to 'Hamlet' without the Dane."[5] Despite the conspicuous absences, the race provided a compelling story line and was dubbed "Native Dancer's Revenge" by journalists. The 1966 Derby winner was Kauai King, a son of Native Dancer, whose only loss in a twenty-two-race career had been in the Derby twelve years before. The "Grey Ghost" had been the first superstar in horse racing's television age, and his son Kauai King would be the first Derby winner in the age of color television coverage of the event.

Derby spectators had been part of the "story" of the Derby for journalists from the very beginning, but by the mid-1960s there was a clear tone of curiosity and suspicion in the descriptions of an infield increasingly dominated by exuberant youths. One journalist reported, "The Derby is very 'in' these days because the [youth] which sets the fashions of our times has extended its stylish vandalism from the jazz festivals of Newport and the beach conventions of Ft. Lauderdale to the infield of the Downs. There is probably no place in America where ladies and gentlemen at their tea, a dowager reading a novel in a lounge chair, gaudily clad bandsmen, soldiers in combat clothes, kids perched on 12-foot ladders, the beatnik fringe of the college set and lanky young men in ten-gallon hats could merge and mingle so freely."[6] Though serious disturbances were rare, beginning in the 1960s the Derby infield became an increasingly rambunctious environment and gained a national reputation as a first-rate opportunity for youth to participate in unbridled revelry and to thumb their collective nose at the representatives of the old guard and the status quo situated across the racetrack in the grandstand.

As the Derby's status as an American institution became more entrenched, the infield crowd and culture were increasingly targeted in journalists' rants about the ills of society. Whereas some commentators were concerned about the hedonism on display in the Derby infield, just as many complained about the commercialization of the event. Though it was the commercialized status of the Derby in general that was ostensibly offensive to traditionalists, their complaints about excessive Derby-related souvenirs and paraphernalia possessed a tinge of elitist snobbery. The enormous crowds whose tastes were reflected in these items were part of the Derby spectacle, and part of what made the event interesting to a nation of television viewers. The infield scene was part of the show, as evidenced by the amount of journalistic attention paid to the goings-on there, yet many print journalists, particularly turf writers, seemed to find the masses and the products presumably marketed toward them to be distasteful.

There were "too damned many promotions," one commentator lamented. "In addition to the traditional Derby mint julep glasses, there were stamps on sale, three different books, two different silver medallions, julep cups, limited edition prints, bracelets, charms, necklaces, trays, Wedgwood bowls, silver plates, regular plates, whiskey bottles, several plaques, hats, T-shirts, banners, balloons, buttons, [and] shingles from the roof."[7] Calling the Derby "formalized, certified, organized Americana," columnist Frank Deford opined, "'Kentucky Derby' is a registered trademark and would surely be franchised if they could find a way to put ketchup on it."[8] Local businesses capitalized on the Derby each year in a ritual price and rate hike that the *New York Times* called an "annual orgy of greed and opportunism."[9] Another writer, using a nom de plume in the *Thoroughbred Record*, observed that the commercial emphasis at Churchill Downs on Derby Day detracted from the romance of the sport of horse racing. He called the grandstand "a monstrous people-processor," and noted that in the infield "the throngs are penned in by eight-foot high chain-link fencing. They peer through the railings behind the winner's circle like animals at the zoo. No wonder the newspapers come out with headlines like 'Derby Decadence Reigns in the Infield.'"[10]

By the 1970s the cultural divide between the infield and the grandstand area had become even more rigid, mirroring rifts between generations, social classes, and political persuasions in American society at large. An artist named W. B. Park, assigned to cover the 1972 Derby for *Sports Illustrated,* declared, "Status consciousness and elitism are rife at Churchill Downs, and the higher you climb in the stadium, the thicker this atmosphere becomes. The pecking order runs from the surging masses in the infield up through the bleachers, seats in the Grandstand, boxes in the Clubhouse, and finally to the lofty Penthouse, enclosed, air conditioned and incredibly exclusive."[11] There had been social stratification at the Derby since the beginning, though the journalists who praised the "democratic" crowds had largely ignored it. But the disparity between the infield and the grandstand was becoming too great for journalists to ignore by the late 1960s and early 1970s. Many journalists admitted that they could not understand the attraction of the infield, a place where one typically could not even see a horse.

Park described the 1972 infield as a vast melting pot of humanity: "Squeeze your way between the writhing, perspiring bodies in all stages of dishabille. . . . A thousand square yards of overlapping blankets, umbrellas, Kentucky Fried Chicken, discarded clothes, newspapers, clever hats, transistor radios, books, footballs, Frisbees, and fraternity banners. There are hippies, heads, straights, rednecks, coeds, jocks, teeny boppers, and weirdoes. It is a young crowd, a crowd only vaguely aware that horse racing is going on around them (when do they play 'My Old Kentucky Home?'), and packed in there, eyeball to elbow. It is just as well; they couldn't see anything if they wanted to."[12]

In 1975 an editorial in the *Blood-Horse* expressed similar incredulity about the charm of the infield. "This year the admission price doubled, from $5 to $10, and the infield crowd was halved, total attendance dropping some 50,000 to 113,324. We can understand the thinking of those who did not return to the infield this year—increased admission price and a forecast of rain. We cannot account for those who did, for none of the races can be seen from the infield, and as a social gathering, it has no pizzazz." The article went on to criticize the behavior of the infield patrons. "Overcast skies and knots of uniformed police reduced displays of nudity to some extent, but could not restrain some individuals who, through boredom and cultivated antagonism to barriers, broke through the chain-link fence to get to the backstretch rail. A thrown beer can struck [last-place finisher] Bombay Duck for no plausible reason."[13]

Journalistic reports of the consumption of copious amounts of alcohol in the infield had been published since at least 1911, when the *Courier-Journal* described a "German village" beneath a tent in the middle of the infield in which "a score or more of coatless men, perspiring from every pore, were kept busy dispensing beer and sandwiches."[14] Activities like drinking and gambling, although considered taboo by certain elements of society, had been a part of the attraction of the Derby, and its infield, since the event's inception, and part of the Derby's appeal was the presence of all different kinds of people in the infield: gamblers, minorities, women, drunks, and thieves helped to create an environment of excitement. But in the 1960s and 1970s, the drinking, drug use, and nudity in the Derby infield were objectionable to some conservative elements of society seated in the grandstand. The Derby had become a site for challenging and reshaping American cultural and social norms.

Famed writer and Louisville native Hunter S. Thompson described the contrast between patrons in the clubhouse and those in the infield in a 1970 article for the short-lived *Scanlan's Monthly*. The fame of Thompson's piece would outlive the publication and give rise to what was later called Thompson's "gonzo journalism." Thompson described his attempt to access the more exclusive sections of the clubhouse at the Kentucky Oaks (a race for three-year-old fillies run the day before the Derby): "The only thing we lacked was unlimited access to the clubhouse inner sanctum in sections 'F and G' . . . and I felt we needed that, to see the whiskey gentry in action," Thompson wrote. "The governor, a swinish neo-Nazi hack named Louis Nunn, would be in 'G' along with Barry Goldwater and Colonel Sanders. I felt we'd be legal in a box in 'G' where we could rest and sip juleps, and soak up a bit of atmosphere and the Derby's special vibrations."[15]

Thompson used his press credentials to acquire a "walkaround" press pass and soon found himself in a clubhouse bar, "a very special kind of scene. Along with the politicians, society belles and local captains of commerce, every half-mad dingbat who ever had any pretension to anything at all within five hundred miles of Louisville will show up there to get strutting drunk and slap a lot of backs and generally make himself obvious." From his vantage point in the press box, Thompson described to his companion, an artist named Ralph Steadman assigned to illustrate the article, what would happen in the infield the next day. "That whole thing . . . will be jammed with people; fifty thousand or so, and most of them staggering drunk. It's a fantastic scene—thousands of people fainting, crying, copulating, trampling each other and fighting with broken whiskey bottles. We'll have to spend some time out there, but it's hard to move around. Too many bodies."[16]

The Derby didn't remain attractive to the infield and clubhouse crowds in spite of the presence of the other but *because of* the presence of the other, at least in part. As it had been for decades, the Derby was a place where the rich could misbehave and experience something a bit exotic and risqué. It was also a place where regular folk could come into contact—or at least share the same time, place, and experience—with the rich, famous, and powerful. The presence of each group contributed to the experience of the other.

Both the rich and the regular folk could return home with wonderful and fantastic tales for their friends. One man who had been coming to the infield for decades claimed that it had "gotten better year by year" despite (or perhaps because of) the fact that the air had increasingly "become filled with Frisbees and the smell of marijuana."[17] In 1972 a female clubhouse patron at the Derby described to a reporter her view of the infield: "The only thing I have to say is that I've never seen as many naked men in my life."[18] To a certain degree the infield was simply a place where young people could gather by the thousands and have fun. But because it was a place where traditions were valued and ties to yesteryear were celebrated, the Derby infield also provided an opportunity for young people to extend a metaphorical middle finger toward "old ways" and "the establishment," some representatives of which were seated right across the track in the clubhouse and grandstand. Public displays of nudity and sexual activity in the infield challenged gender norms and declared sexual liberation on a stage made bright by the Derby's popularity and significance to national identity and culture.

For millions of American television viewers in the mid- to late 1960s, Kentucky became a destination of escape from the currents of change sweeping through American society. From 1964 to 1970 *Daniel Boone* was a staple of NBC's primetime lineup, entertaining audiences with tales from a simpler time in frontier-era Kentucky. Actor Fess Parker played the title character in something of a reprise of his portrayal of Davy Crockett in the 1955–1956 Disney miniseries that had sparked a merchandis-

Couple attending the Kentucky Derby. Louisville, Jefferson County, Kentucky. 1976. (© Ted Wathen, 1976.)

ing bonanza. Parker's Boone wore a coonskin cap like Crockett's, and he befriended people of all nationalities and skin colors, including Indians and runaway slaves, in the pursuit of righteousness and justice. This fictional depiction of Old Kentucky fit the long-held popular notion that Kentucky was more racially tolerant and harmonious than other southern states. In 1969 Parker

153

would serve as grand marshall of the Derby Festival Parade in a nod to his television-born connection to the Bluegrass State, but as the Derby approached in 1967, tensions over race-based housing discrimination in Louisville underscored the fact that depictions of eighteenth-century Boonesborough on TV were a far cry from the complex realities of the late 1960s in America.

Just as the Derby had been a stage upon which 1960s youth had challenged some of the tradition and culture of their parents' generation, protesters including Martin Luther King Jr. used the platform that was Louisville during Derby Week to speak out against racial discrimination in the city's housing market in 1967, as the city and nation were becoming more culturally fractured and polarized than they had been at the beginning of the decade. The glut of media attention focused on Louisville during Derby Week ensured that anyone promoting a cause would receive plenty of exposure. Just as significantly, the Derby symbolized a tradition and history that was both American and Southern, making a Derby Week protest against race-based discrimination all the more poignant and controversial.

On May 2, 1967 (the Tuesday of Derby Week), the feature race at Churchill Downs was the Derby Trial Stakes, but five black teenagers stole the spotlight by running onto the track during the first race in front of ten horses barreling down the homestretch. In demonstrating their support for the open-housing protesters, the young men employed a tactic previously attempted in 1913 by suffragette Emily Davidson at the Epsom Derby in England: in support of women's rights, she attempted to interfere with King George V's horse Anmer during the race. Whereas Davidson suffered a fatal fracture of the skull in the process, the teenaged protesters at Churchill Downs were uninjured, diving to safety in the track's infield as the horses approached. Jockey Bill Shoemaker responded lividly to the dangerous act, telling reporters, "If they get out there again, somebody's going to get run over."[19] Another jockey threatened, "If they get out there again, I'm going to nail them. If they want to play games, we'll play games."[20]

Later that week, a reburial ceremony at Lexington's Man o' War Park for jockey Isaac Murphy (who had been nationally famous in the nineteenth century and largely forgotten since) provided an opportunity for opponents to express disapproval of the protests. Andrew Hatcher, assistant press secretary to the late president John F. Kennedy, told the crowd gathered for the ceremony, "Isaac Murphy was not interested in black power or green power but was content to let his own talent and abilities as a rider carry him to success."[21] The *Thoroughbred Record* favorably compared Murphy with the "members of Murphy's race" who "marched and chanted and flaunted picket signs."[22]

Others, however, praised the activism. Southern Christian Leadership Conference (SCLC) leader Hosea Williams told reporters, "Those children did a great thing. They brought to light on a national arena the problems here in Louisville."[23] The problem Williams referred to was the failure of Louisville city leaders to pass a proposed open-housing ordinance for the city that would address Louisville's unofficial but habitual practice of denying blacks the opportunity to purchase or rent housing in traditionally white neighborhoods. The Louisville Board of Aldermen had voted down the proposed ordinance in April, sparking a series of protest demonstrations throughout the city. Threats of trouble from open-housing supporters, combined with the disruption at Churchill Downs, led to the announcement that the Derby Festival Parade scheduled for later that week would be cancelled to "protect the best interests of the participants and spectators."[24] City leaders acknowledged that the threat of disturbances came from both open-housing supporters and opponents, but the executive director of the Kentucky Derby Festival Committee, Addison F. McGhee, placed the blame squarely on the shoulders of black protesters when he explained that "a small city has completely capitulated to a dissident minority."[25]

Open-housing advocates clearly had the attention of Louisville leaders, and they were threatening more action if their demands were not met. "No open housing, no Derby" was a rallying cry heard around Louisville as Derby Day approached. But Mayor Kenneth Schmied assured the city that nothing would prevent the running of the ninety-third Kentucky Derby: "The Kentucky Derby is one of the world's greatest sporting events, and we will do everything possible to see that it is run in its richest tradition."[26] Governor Edward T. Breathitt used stronger language, assuring Derby-goers that he would do "whatever is necessary" to make certain that the event would be undisturbed.[27] "The Derby must be run. It is our state's showcase," Breathitt told the director of the Kentucky State Police, Ted Bassett. "We're on national television. We're going to have 100,000 people coming through the gates at Churchill. The race is a huge economic entity. Tell me what you need, and we'll get it for you."[28]

Because of the bright spotlight shining upon Louisville during Derby Week, the city's housing battle became a national issue. National groups including the SCLC and the Ku Klux Klan stormed into the city, fully aware that the nation's eyes were fixed upon Louisville during the first week in May. The day after the on-track incident, plain-clothed leaders of the KKK, along with a handful of robed members, visited the track to offer to help police "keep order" there. One leader told reporters that "thousands" of Klansmen would attend the Derby that Saturday. "The Kentucky Derby is an important national event," the Klansman explained, "and we don't see that it has anything to do with open housing. We suggest that they either bar Negroes from Churchill Downs Saturday or find some other way to control them."[29]

Later that day, the Reverend Martin Luther King arrived in Louisville to aid in the organization of protests planned for Derby Week. "The matter is now at a crucial stage and we must use all our resources to get open housing in Louisville," King explained at a news conference. He declined to comment on whether the open-housing supporters would attempt to interfere with the Derby on Saturday, adding, "I'll have to confer with the leaders here before I can say anything about that."[30]

Uncertainty loomed in Louisville throughout the week about what might take place at the Downs on Saturday. Law enforcement groups even took seriously the possibility (reported via a tip from a Mafia-related informant in Detroit) that protesters were planning to gather in the infield near the starting gate where they would disrupt the start of the Derby by blowing dog-training whistles to prevent the horses from being loaded.[31] Late on Derby Eve word leaked from the King camp that there would be no disruption of the Derby. King announced there would be a demonstration downtown, but there would be no such presence at the Derby. King admitted his fear that tension and hostility amid the expected Derby crowd of one hundred thousand could spark a race riot.

Despite these assurances, a major police and military presence was in place at Churchill Downs on Derby Day. Twenty-five hundred National Guardsmen, state troopers, and local law enforcement officers were at the track, which resembled an armed camp. As post time for the big race approached, National Guardsmen formed a ring around the inside of the one-mile track at intervals of twenty-five feet, armed with riot batons, creating a barrier between the infield and the race participants. "I want you men to look to the left, and I want you men to look to the right," one officer barked, "and if anybody comes over [the fence] I want you to hit 'em in the head."[32] The *Courier-Journal* noted, "Only a few Negroes were in the big infield, and they appeared to go unnoticed by the crowd. What tension there was appeared directed at badges and helmets."[33] A cartoon in the Derby Day edition of the *Louisville Times* was a telling comment on the state of affairs in Louisville and in the nation at large. The drawing depicted a military tank in motion, with the caption, "Are they sending us to Vietnam, Mac—or Churchill Downs?"[34] The infield truly looked like occupied territory.

Like the threats of disturbance and violence at Churchill Downs that day, the equine action on the track failed to meet expectations. The post-time favorite Damascus entered the Derby off an easy score in the Wood Memorial Stakes, New York's most important Derby prep. Though he would go on to be voted champion three-year-old and horse of the year for 1967 on his way to the Hall of Fame, Damascus could manage no better than third for jockey Bill Shoemaker after becoming unnerved by the large crowd before the race on what was a hot and humid afternoon. Darby Dan Farm's Proud Clarion was a surprise winner at odds of more than 30-1 under the urging of jockey Bobby Ussery.[35]

The fact that the eyes of the nation annually focused on Louisville in the first week of May placed the city's problems in a spotlight and made Louisville a stage with a national audience during Derby Week. Any disturbance in Louisville would have received more national attention the first week of May than at any other time of the year, but this was a conflict with clear racial overtones: the Derby's historical association with the Old South made this battle more contentious and more significant than those in other cities. The Derby's lofty place within American culture increased the stakes for both sides of the conflict. Neither the black protesters nor their opponents wanted to lose such a high-profile battle, and neither side wanted to allow the other to affect the tone or the identity of the Kentucky Derby—or the nation—in any way.

As trying a time as 1967 had been for Churchill Downs, things would get even worse the following year. History books and souvenir julep glasses show that Calumet Farm won the Kentucky Derby for a record eighth time in 1968, but the story is much more complicated than it might appear. Dancer's Image, a son of Native Dancer, finished first in the 1968 Derby, and Calumet's Forward Pass crossed the finish line in second place. Dancer's Image's jockey, Bobby Ussery, "with a hippie haircut and a hippie grin, waving two fingers at the crowd," crossed the finish line first for the second year in a row, becoming only the third jockey (and the first white one) to accomplish that feat.[36]

The colt was owned by Peter Fuller, a wealthy Massachusetts businessman and former amateur boxing champion who had invited controversy in the previous month when he donated the prize money he won in one of Dancer's Image's Derby preps in Maryland to the recently widowed Coretta Scott King, whose husband had angered city and track leaders the previous year with his Derby Week protests in Louisville. The *Thoroughbred Record* expressed disapproval of the gesture, claiming that Fuller had "made a mistake of injecting the racial situation into thoroughbred racing when he donated the Gold Cup purse to the widow of M. L. King."[37] Fuller later recalled that his gift to King led to the reaction from racing gentry of "Let's jump on this guy in no uncertain terms. It became something that it should not have become."[38] He ruffled more feathers once he arrived at Churchill Downs for Derby Week, brashly predicting victory for his colt, going so far as to rehearse the walk from his box seats to the winner's circle, and demanding that Churchill Downs president Wathen Knebelkamp increase his ticket allotment from four to fifty to accommodate his large group of friends and family, threatening that he would not run his colt if his needs were not met.

On the Tuesday following the Derby, Churchill Downs stewards released the following statement: "The chemist of the Kentucky State Racing Commission has reported that the analysis of the urine samples taken from Dancer's Image, winner of the 7th race on May 4 1968 contained phenylbutazone and/or a derivative thereof. Pursuant to Rule 14.06, when said sample indicates the presence of such medication, such horse shall not participate in the purse distribution, and, under the rules of racing, the wagering on said race is in no way affected."[39] The drug in question, a nonsteroidal anti-inflammatory drug prescribed to treat joint pain, commonly referred to as "bute" and sold under the brand name Butazolidin, was regularly prescribed for human and equine athletes at the time but was not allowed to be in a horse's system on race day in Kentucky.

The rule was clear regarding the distribution of purse money but left some ambiguity regarding which horse would be the official winner of the Kentucky Derby. News reports were calling the ruling a "disqualification" of Dancer's Image. But the stewards' ruling actually used no such language, only a prohibition against Dancer's Image receiving any prize money. The decision of the stewards to award the $122,600 first prize to the owners of Forward Pass began a four-year process of appeals and hearings filled with allegations, rumors, and confusion that would ultimately cost Fuller $250,000 in legal fees, and perhaps much more in lost stud fee revenue, as the title of Kentucky Derby champion would almost certainly have raised Dancer's Image's value for breeding purposes. In December 1968 the Kentucky Racing Commission declared Dancer's Image the record-book winner of the Derby but awarded the first-place purse to Forward Pass. In 1970 a Franklin County Circuit Court decision awarded the first-place money to Dancer's Image; then in 1972 the Kentucky Court of Appeals overturned the circuit court ruling and awarded the money to Forward Pass. Later that year the Kentucky State Racing Commission, appointed under a new Democratic gubernatorial administration, officially named Forward Pass the winner of the 1968 Kentucky Derby. The long course of action frustrated everyone involved, even the ultimate "winner," Lucille Markey, widow of Warren Wright and owner of Calumet Farm, whose experience with the process left a sour taste in her mouth and caused her to boycott all Kentucky racing for a time.

Knebelkamp tried to give the controversy a positive spin: "If there's anything good that comes out of this, it is that everyone will see how effectively racing polices itself. This will hurt Churchill Downs temporarily, but in the long run it will help."[40] Churchill Downs leaders believed that they were serving their event and society by applying strict interpretations of existing regulations. Racing historian William Robertson agreed: "So long as a rule is in the books, it ought to be respected—even if it's a rule against mare's milk. The rule should not be changed merely because it pinches at the moment. A rule which *never* pinches is worthless." Robertson then took the opportunity of the controversy to air his opinions on the state of American society in general: "There is ample opinion that the ban against [bute] is no good. I happen to feel that it is not as bad as the free use of the drug would be. On the other hand, it seems to be the fashion nowadays to literally wallow in self-criticism. When rioters riot and looters loot, it is not the fault of the rioters and looters but the fault of the 'system' controlled by non-rioters and non-looters, who thereupon are expected to engage in morbid introspection and go into fits of penitence. Nuts to that."[41]

Forty years after the fact, Fuller still believed that he had been treated unfairly in a racist environment that surrounded the Derby and the Kentucky horse industry. "I mean, baby doll," Fuller opined in 2008, "the Civil War was still pretty good down there. I've heard from people there who say we absolutely got screwed and from other people who say, 'please, Peter, shut up and go away.'"[42]

Perhaps leaders of less culturally significant events could have resolved controversies differently in 1968. But in the sociocultural environment of the late 1960s, Kentucky Derby officials would not have wanted to appear soft on drugs or tolerant of rule bending. The Derby was a part of American national culture and national identity. In an era when the definition and direction of the United States were being contested, leaders at the Derby took a stand for law and order. Leaders at two other high-profile sporting events took a similar stand in 1968. At the 1968 Masters, Argentine golfer Roberto De Vicenzo signed an incorrect scorecard after finishing the tournament tied for first place, resulting in his disqualification, despite the precedent of a more lenient interpretation of the rules.[43] Later that fall at the Mexico City Olympic Games, Americans John Carlos and Tommie Smith raised their black-glove-clad fists during the playing of the American national anthem on the medal stand after the two-hundred-meter sprint in order to raise awareness of racial injustice in the United States. Like leaders at the Derby and the Masters, Avery Brundage, the International Olympic Committee president and former United States Olympic Committee president, took a stand for "law and order" and banned Smith and Carlos from the Olympic Village and saw to it that they were removed from the U.S. Olympic team.

In a year chock-full of controversy in the sports world, *Sports Illustrated* put the Derby scandal on its cover, calling it "the story of the year."[44] The storm at the Derby made large waves in American popular culture. CBS News was prepared to run the story on Walter Cronkite's newscast under the headline "Derby Winner a Hop-Head" until a racing correspondent explained that the drug did not actually "hop" a horse—it was an anti-inflammatory medication.[45] The broad media coverage that accompanied the controversy until its conclusion in 1972 was a testament both to the significance of the Derby to Americans and to the pervading sociocultural environment.

It should not be surprising that in the most divisive of times in the late 1960s and early 1970s the Kentucky Derby found itself squarely in the middle of controversies so representative of a divided nation. The Derby was one of America's signature events, making it a fertile battleground for those who wanted to influence national culture. In the late 1960s, events like the Kentucky Derby were bastions against the tides of change that threatened the traditional order of American society. They were institutions at a time when institutions were being questioned and challenged. The Derby was representative of an established American tradition and culture. This institutional status the Derby had attained attracted groups that wanted to influence national opinion, direction, and identity.

The next major attempt to make use of the Derby spotlight to influence public policy and attitudes emerged out of the white backlash to desegregation, specifically the forced busing upheld as constitutional by the U.S. Supreme Court in its 1971 decision in *Swann v. Charlotte-Mecklenburg Board of Education*. Because of threats of disturbances made by groups opposed to court-ordered busing in Louisville and the surrounding suburbs, the police presence at the 1976 Derby was greater than ever before. The track had installed barbed wire atop the fence that surrounded the infield area after some of the infield crowd at the previous year's Derby broke through the fence in order to get closer to the backstretch railing. The threat of violence and the new prison-yard décor at the infield cast a pall over the atmosphere. Unlike 1967, when threats of disturbance ultimately proved to be empty, protesters made their presence felt in 1976.

Tension had been high in Louisville since the previous September, when the court orders to bus students to schools outside their neighborhoods in the interest of achieving racial diversity were first implemented. Manifestations of the tensions included major riots, bonfires, school boycotts, a KKK presence, and a cross burning at a white suburban Louisville high school.[46] At the 1976 Derby an antibusing group, the National Organization to Restore and Preserve Our Freedom, distributed handbills around the track calling for a chant after the singing of "My Old Kentucky Home." The flyer proposed that supporters shout the slogan "Stop forced busing and we'll stop fussing." A helicopter trailing a banner with an antibusing message was also spotted above the track periodically throughout the day. The real disturbance, however, came after the Derby horses passed the stands for the first time during the race. A grenade spewing green smoke hurled from the infield landed on the track, but crisis was averted when a National Guardsman used his helmet to remove the object before the horses appeared again.

A photo of the incident appeared on the front page of the *Chicago Tribune* with the accompanying caption "Violence Hits Derby."[47] The event was not given much attention in the major

Louisville papers, however. There was no specific evidence that the smoke bomb was related to the antibusing movement, but the environment at Churchill Downs in 1976 again demonstrated that the Derby was a national stage. The Derby was part of the national identity, and Derby-goers felt entitled and compelled to make known their visions for the proper direction for American society and culture.

The antibusing movement grabbed plenty of attention at the 1976 Derby, but another major theme that year was the American bicentennial. Ads and promotional material wrapped the event in red, white, and blue, as they had previously during the First and Second World Wars. A reporter described the unusual number of American flag bowties to be seen as well as the usual assortment of horse-related neckwear and "Kentucky colonel" black string ties. Even the lead ponies were decked out in patriotic colors at Churchill Downs in 1976.

When the starting gate opened, Bold Forbes and jockey Angel Cordero broke alertly and maintained their lead over heavily favored Honest Pleasure all the way around the track for a wire-to-wire victory. Called "the Puerto Rican Rolls-Royce" by Cordero, Bold Forbes had been born in Kentucky and sold at auction there as a yearling, but had raced extensively in his owner's native Puerto Rico. The press played up the horse's "Latino ethnicity," just as it had in 1971 with winning colt Canonero II, born and sold at auction as a yearling in Kentucky before being shipped to Venezuela. When Canonero II returned to his native state to take American horse racing's biggest prize, American sportswriters dubbed the colt "the Caracas Cannonball" and "the pride of Venezuela, a South American kid who came north to beat the yanqui at his own game."[48] The media's focus on the ethnicity of Derby horses and riders in the 1970s reflected a national interest in the subject of ethnicity, as illustrated by popular and award-winning 1970s films such as *Fiddler on the Roof, The Godfather, Rocky,* and *Saturday Night Fever.* Interest in "foreign" horses like "the Puerto Rican Rolls-Royce" and "the Caracas Cannonball" at the Derby would continue to grow in the decades to come as the Thoroughbred industry became increasingly global and as major international owners made the Kentucky Derby an important goal of their racing programs.

The United States was a nation looking for inspiration in the 1970s. The war in Vietnam, Watergate, a problematic economy, and the unfulfilled hope of the 1960s had damaged the national psyche. In this environment, Americans found heroes in unusual places, including on the racetrack. Though they were incapable of patriotic rhetoric, the three American Triple Crown champions of the 1970s, Secretariat, Seattle Slew, and Affirmed, were celebrated as examples of American strength and success in times that were not the country's brightest, and these equine stars would find no brighter stage than the Derby. As Secretariat made his way through the Triple Crown in 1973 he was featured on the covers of *Newsweek, Time,* and *Sports Illustrated. Newsweek* editor Osborne Elliott remarked, "We're going from Watergate to the starting gate."[49] California racing secretary Jimmy Kilroe said of the great horse, "I think he absolutely revitalized racing. We must believe in something."[50] After Secretariat annihilated the field at the 1973 Belmont Stakes, turf writer Arnold Kirkpatrick wrote, "There's absolutely no doubt in my mind that he is the finest athlete of any race, color, family, genus, or species ever to have lived. . . . His name is Secretariat and, with a crushing 31-length victory in the 105th Belmont Stakes June 9, he sent practically every sportswriter and racing fan in the country rushing for his thesaurus in search of the Ultimate Superlative. It has been found. The Ultimate Superlative is Secretariat himself."[51]

Though no horse would soon match the popularity of the great Secretariat, both Seattle Slew and Affirmed would join him on the list of Triple Crown winners in the 1970s. Owned by a pair of thirty-something couples, Mickey and Karen Taylor and

1973 Triple Crown champion Secretariat, in retirement at Claiborne Farm. (Photos by Z.)

Jim and Sally Hill, Seattle Slew had been purchased for $17,500 at the Fasig-Tipton July Yearling Sale in Lexington, Kentucky, in 1975, a relative bargain in hindsight. Slew showed early brilliance, and was named champion two-year-old of 1976. The following year he cruised through the Triple Crown undefeated for his career, the first horse to accomplish that feat, with the ownership keeping a high profile throughout his career, serving as living advertisements for the sport.

The following year Affirmed and teenage jockey sensation Steve Cauthen captured the attention of the nation in sweeping the 1978 Triple Crown. They had the help of a foil in Calumet Farm's Alydar, who finished second to Affirmed in each of the three Triple Crown races. In 1979 Spectacular Bid fell just short in his attempt to join the ranks of Triple Crown champions, but he earned a place alongside Secretariat, Seattle Slew, Affirmed, and Alydar among the elite horses of the 1970s and of the twentieth century.

Each of these horses not only contributed to the popularity of horse racing as a sport, but also helped to further the Kentucky Derby's status as a national event in the 1970s, a time when Americans were seeking American heroes but having difficulties finding them among the human set. As one reporter explained, "The Kentucky Derby is more than a horse race. It's an American institution, perhaps the only one left. The Derby has survived a hundred springs, despite wars and riots, despite panics, depressions, recessions. It flourishes because everyone believes it's a ritual handed down from a more elegant century. The Derby's anachronistic caress soothes the nation with visions of bluegrass farms and mint juleps and Kentucky colonels."[52] Another journalist placed the appeal in the context of 1970s turmoil. "In these days of Watergate . . . when the basic concepts of what is right, proper, [and] respectable are being slapped smartly about the head and shoulders, [the Derby] emerged in welcomed, sharp relief."[53]

The 1974 Centennial Derby shattered attendance records when 163,628 spectators passed through the turnstiles. (That record would eventually be broken, but not until 2011.) The success of Secretariat the previous year had enhanced the status of the Derby, but his exploits were not the focus of the media coverage and promotion of the 1974 Derby. The fact that it was the one hundredth running of the race was the major story that year. Kentucky was also celebrating the two hundredth anniversary of the founding of the state's first permanent settlement at what would later be called Harrodsburg. The two anniversaries combined to create unprecedented interest in and attendance at the Derby. Part of the appeal of the Derby for many spectators had long been the desire to be a "part of history." For those who wanted to participate in history making, the one hundredth Derby would be "one for the ages." Kentucky governor Wendell Ford boldly predicted, "The 100th Kentucky Derby will be the greatest thing that ever happened on the face of the United States."[54] He was not laughed out of the building. The advent of the centennial Derby turned everyone into nostalgic romantics.

In a preview of the 1974 Derby, *New York Times* columnist Joe Nichols included an excerpt from the *Courier-Journal*'s first Derby Day edition in 1875, in which B. G. Bruce had predicted that the Derby would still be a major happening one hundred years later. Nichols commented, "Never in the history of an activity to which predictions are a very part of its existence has any prophecy been so accurate."[55] Another writer previewing the centennial Derby tried to explain why there was such a popular fascination with the Derby's past: "For an instant, for one blessed instant the first Saturday afternoon of each May, the world pauses in its headlong plunge to nowhere. What transpires here? Why this concentration of attention on a contest between animals long outmoded as a means of transportation? Nostalgia has its part in the degree of fascination. Even the youths are transported here to an earlier and perhaps a happier time."[56]

Steve Cady, writing for the *New York Times*, explained the appeal of the Derby in terms of "My Old Kentucky Home":

Played on any other day, it sounds like a minstrel-show anachronism. Played on the first Saturday of May, while America's finest three-year-old thoroughbreds step onto the track at Churchill Downs, the cornball flavor of "My Old Kentucky Home" turns to pure magic. It can transform a cynic into a romanticist, make a poet out of an engineer, bring a horse-lover to the verge of tears. Even touts and pickpockets and ladies of the night have been known to pause long enough to hoist their mint juleps when they hear it. They'll all be there next Saturday in Louisville when racing's most nostalgia-drenched song is played again before the 100th running of the Kentucky Derby. Millions of other Americans, many of whom don't know a fetlock from a furlong, will be watching—and listening—on television.[57]

Sports Illustrated's Frank Deford was similarly moved by the magnitude of the hundredth Derby, writing, "Under the twin spires, in the aura of the bluegrass spring, any good man will cloud up when they play *My Old Kentucky Home* and cry outright when he realizes he is standing in one of those rare places where beauty and history bisect for an instant. He'll order a mint julep or two—not minding that it is corny—and salute a hundred Derbies past and a hundred more ahead."[58]

England's Princess Margaret was one of over 163,000 in attendance that year. The *New York Times* described the enormity of the crowd: "In a swirl of 163,626 spectators that ranged from streakers and flagpole climbers to a princess, the 100th Kentucky Derby was staged today in such a sea of humanity that Custer's last stand might have been held in the infield without special commotion."[59] The record crowd on hand to be a part of centennial Derby history, and the millions watching—and listening—at home saw Cannonade defeat a record field of twenty-three starters for two well-respected horsemen, trainer Woody Stevens and jockey Angel Cordero. In a decade in which Americans were inundated with reports about an unpopular and losing war, presidential scandal, and a floundering economy, the Derby was a part of both the American past and present that Americans could be proud of. The equine heroes celebrated in the 1970s were not capable of singing their own praises, but they were also incapable of lying, cheating, stealing, or negatively affecting domestic or foreign policy.

Part of the celebration of a romantic past at the Derby in the 1960s and 1970s included a "rediscovery" of its connection to memories of the Old South that had been downplayed in the 1940s and 1950s. In 1961, the one hundredth anniversary of the start of the American Civil War, souvenir concessionaires at the Derby did "rapid business" selling replicas of Civil War soldiers' hats. Sales were "about evenly divided between Confederate and Union caps."[60] In 1963 Churchill Downs president Wathen Knebelkamp recalled a strange ticket request that he had received from an Iowa man who told the Churchill executive that although he was from the North, he'd always admired the South. He concluded his letter, "I hate Lincoln, he was a heel," presumably under the assumption that this declaration would increase his chance of acquiring tickets.[61] The United States was a century removed from the Old South, yet the idea that social order and racial harmony had existed in that time and place continued to be attractive, and the Derby continued to be a place where people could celebrate such a memory. In 1965 the *Courier-Journal* described faces of modernity confronting images of the past at a time when the United States was itself approaching a cultural crossroad: "To some—the romantic and the curious—the Kentucky Derby is a pilgrimage, a hopeless hope for an intimate glimpse into history's pages of a bygone era. It's a little jolting, though, to those who have conjured up a soft image of the Old South's gracious living suddenly to be charged $20 to park an automobile on somebody's front lawn. But inside the Old South's heritage and tradition come to life, softly and elegantly."[62] Despite the signs of modernity all around, patrons found the Derby's southern flavor pacifying.

Churchill Downs president Lynn Stone attempted to articulate what the attraction of the Derby was for the thousands who made their way to Louisville each year to witness the event. "It's the South," he explained. "It's the horses, the gambling, the tobacco, the whiskey. It's the river town, the farms, the mint juleps. It creates an antebellum image."[63] This lingering association between the Derby and the Old South, the "antebellum image," might well have contributed to President Richard M. Nixon's decision to attend the Kentucky Derby in 1969, making him the only sitting president to witness the event (although at least seven other former or future presidents have attended the Derby while out of office).

Nixon had attended the previous year's Derby as a guest of Kentucky governor Louie B. Nunn while campaigning for the presidential election to be held in the fall, promising to return the following year if elected, which was quite a promise since no sitting president had attended any horse race since Rutherford B. Hayes. Nunn held Nixon to his promise, glad to have some positive national attention for the Derby after the doping scandal the previous year. The governor boldly claimed that the visit was "the greatest thing that ever happened to Kentucky."[64] The president tried to articulate his own enthusiasm over attending another Derby but missed the mark. "I have been sports-minded all my life. I like the intense competition and skill of the participants, and there is a great thrill in watching great horses run," Nixon told reporters, in what may be the least colorful description of a Derby experience ever offered.[65]

After a brief stint in the governor's box, Nixon became restless. "I can't stay up here . . . where they think all these rich folks are," Nixon complained. "I've got to get down there where the bettors are and where the horse people are."[66] He managed to maneuver through the crowd for a quick tour around the ground level, Secret Service in tow, for a round of handshakes, but the presidential security team balked at Nunn's suggestion that the president join him in the infield after the race for the trophy presentation. To Nixon, ever politically conscious, even a decision to back one horse over another was a risky venture: after the race Nixon turned to reporters and said, "I guess I lost," but some of his aides insisted that the president had in fact been cheering for the winner, post-time favorite Majestic Prince.[67]

Nixon's decision to attend the Derby at all is telling. On the surface, his presence could be viewed simply as a chance to enjoy a day of racing with friends and to relax like the rest of the one hundred thousand spectators at the Downs that day. But "Derby

Dick," as some sportswriters were calling him that weekend, was at the Downs only long enough to be able to claim to have been there. Despite the signs of modernity all around, the Derby's lingering connection to the Old South in the minds of Americans suggests that Nixon's presence at the Derby, like with his decision to attend a college football game in Arkansas later that year, might have had another motivation.

On December 6, 1969, the University of Texas and the University of Arkansas met in Fayetteville, Arkansas, for the Southwest Conference football championship. The two teams were undefeated and ranked one and two in the Associated Press college football poll. Journalists were predicting a showdown for the ages. Adding to the significance of the game was the fact that both teams' players were all white. Prior to kickoff a group of black students threatened to storm the field if the Arkansas band played "Dixie" after a Razorback score as it usually did. The band did not play "Dixie," and the president's visit was capped off by a locker room presentation of a plaque to the victorious Longhorns.[68]

Nixon's appearances at these major sporting events in Arkansas and Kentucky seem to fit into his "southern strategy." In 1967 Kevin P. Phillips was working on a groundbreaking book (that would be published two years later), *The Emerging Republican Majority,* in which he argued in favor of exploiting various prejudices for political gain. Hired to join Nixon's 1968 campaign, Phillips advocated an "outer South strategy," encouraging the Nixon camp to abandon the Deep South strategy that Barry Goldwater had used to carry "George Wallace States" in 1964. He argued that an attempt to appeal to the Deep South would alienate voters in other states. Instead, Phillips suggested that the campaign concentrate on voters in the Appalachians, the Ozarks, and the Piedmont Regions of the (politically safer) South. In time, the outer South strategy worked. After carrying only thirty-two states in his narrow 1968 presidential win, Nixon won landslides throughout the nation in 1972, winning forty-nine states in one of the most lopsided presidential elections in American history.

Even as late as 1969 the Kentucky Derby still qualified as a "southern" event. But Kentucky was not the politically danger-ous Deep South; it fit into what Kevin Phillips would have called the outer South. Even in an attempt to win more southern minds and votes, Nixon could not have risked alienating a silent majori-ty of Americans who still had fresh memories of fire hoses and at-tack dogs in Alabama with a presidential appearance at an event that was off mainstream America's collective radar. The Derby was safe; it was benignly "southern" and still very much "Ameri-can." Derby fans found solace in the sanitized version of Dixie they encountered at the Derby.

Advertisers tying Kentucky and the Derby to the Old South in their marketing campaigns did so in a more subtle fashion in the 1960s and 1970s than they had earlier in the century. Overt references to plantations, white masters, and black servants in whiskey advertisements, which had been popular in the 1930s, had disappeared in the 1940s, yet a perception among Americans that a quiet connection existed between the modern Kentucky Derby and the Old South had remained. Whiskey advertisers had generally been reluctant to market their products as southern in the 1960s. But in the 1970s products were advertised as afford-ing consumers a chance to access a simpler and gentler time— free from "uppity" blacks and "contemptuous" feminists—with an escape to the Old South. Rebel Yell, "the unreconstructed Bourbon," was advertised in local newspapers to Derby-goers throughout the 1970s. "If you're visiting from the North, this could be your only chance to enjoy the South's most luxurious libation," one print ad claimed, "because like this one Saturday and this one race, this one bourbon is available only below the Mason-Dixon line."[69] J&B Scotch, a product not generally as-sociated with the South, tried a similar approach in an ad that depicted a luxurious home situated on a Deep South plantation beneath live oak trees with the caption "For your old Kentucky Home."[70]

No less an authority than Bill Corum, coiner of the phrase "Run for the Roses" and the president of Churchill Downs from 1950 to 1958, acknowledged the major role that the memory of the Old South played in the creation of the identity and experience of the Derby. "To some of us, the echoes of the old starting drums still linger over the ancient Downs," Corum explained. "The rustle of taffeta, the sense of a world apart, the gentle laughter, the rebel scarlet silk of the Lost Cause, and the reverence for the Thoroughbred are there like an unseen mist, an unforgettable aura when you're a part of it for the first time."[71]

This nostalgia for a place that never really existed in a time no one could actually remember pervaded descriptions of the Derby in the 1970s, but not everyone savored the preservation of the memory of the Old South. "While the singing of 'My Old Kentucky Home' at the Kentucky Derby is a cherished tradition and brings tears to the eyes of whites," Clarence L. Matthews wrote in the *Louisville Times,* "the song's lyrics are likely to evoke resentment from blacks. Most black people are equally chagrinned at the sight of other blacks dressed in antebellum costumes and wearing 'Aunt Jemima' like bandanas [while] serving burgoo" at the Kentucky Colonels' reunion barbecue that traditionally concluded Derby Week festivities. "There is no nostalgia in slavery," Matthews concluded.[72]

Journalistic references to the Old South in conjunction with the Derby would again dissipate in the 1980s, but the popularity of the event would not, demonstrating the complex nature of its appeal in that it could accommodate accelerating changes in American society and culture and thrive in the increasingly global environment of Thoroughbred racing and breeding. In the 1960s and 1970s various groups had used the national stage at Louisville at Derby time to challenge the status quo and to influence the nation, and these efforts had further increased the national visibility of the Derby. The success of national equine heroes at the Derby at a time when Americans needed diversion also helped to further entrench Kentucky and its signature event in American culture. This in turn fueled growth in the Kentucky breeding industry, a development that would raise the stature and significance of the Derby to international levels in the coming years.

6

Globalization and
the American Dream

1980–2010

The first half of the 1980s were extraordinary times in Kentucky: the Bluegrass State experienced unprecedented growth in the horse industry, a high-profile couple occupied the governor's mansion, and opulence and excess characterized the state's elite circles. The national profile of the Kentucky Derby continued to rise, the beneficiary of the glamour that was increasingly connected with the state and its horse industry during these boom times in the Bluegrass. By the turn of the century the Derby would be an annual goal for horse owners around the world in an increasingly global Thoroughbred industry. American media focused on tales of redemption and unlikely heroes at the Derby, again proving that the malleable identities of Kentucky and its Derby could adapt to—and affirm—the ever-changing notion of "American values."

For Kentucky the Big '80s began a month early, with the inauguration of Governor John Y. Brown Jr., in December 1979. Brown and his new wife, former Miss America and television personality Phyllis George, immediately raised Kentucky's national profile by virtue of their many prominent social and professional connections. Brown had purchased Kentucky Fried Chicken from Colonel Sanders in 1964 and had been involved in ownership groups of various professional sports franchises, including the Boston Celtics. During Brown's tenure in office, he and George entertained scores of celebrities at the Kentucky Derby and Derby-related functions, adding some additional Hollywood-style panache to the event in an era of excess and materialism. Two of the Browns' most famous guests were Muhammad Ali and Colonel Harland Sanders, two of the most recognized figures on the planet in the early 1980s, and both with strong Kentucky ties.

The Indiana-born Sanders began selling his famous chicken in the 1930s and was soon granted an honorary colonelship by Kentucky governor Ruby Laffoon in acknowledgment of Sanders's culinary contributions to the Commonwealth. In 1952 the first Kentucky Fried Chicken franchise opened in Salt Lake City. Today KFC's corporate offices in Louisville are located in a giant antebellum-style mansion, and Colonel Sanders's visage adorns over eleven thousand Kentucky Fried Chicken stores in more than eighty countries around the globe. When Brown and his partners purchased Kentucky Fried Chicken from Sanders, the colonel was retained as a spokesman for the company and became the face of an international fast-food empire. After Sanders's death at the age of ninety, Brown called the colonel "the best salesman we ever had" at the pre-Derby Kentucky Colonels' Dinner in 1981.[1] Whether Brown's use of the word "we" referred to Kentucky Fried Chicken, the Honorable Order of Kentucky Colonels, or the state of Kentucky, his statement was probably correct.

In 1980 Louisville native Muhammad Ali attended the Derby as the guest of the Browns months before he lost the world heavyweight boxing title for the final time. "I'm bigger than the whole Derby," Ali dryly told reporters.[2] The "Louisville Lip's" connection to Kentucky added to the state's global fame, and his frequent presence at the Derby was a treat for celebrity spotters, adding both levity and gravity to the festival atmosphere. In addition to Ali and Sanders, other guests of the Browns at the Derby included Kenny Rogers, Barbara Walters, Waylon Jennings, and Walter Cronkite. In a culture that celebrated stardom, the Kentucky Derby held its place as an A-list event in the 1980s. Racing had attracted wealthy people and high society for centuries. But in the 1980s most of the celebrities who attended the Derby would not visit another race track all year, unlike in decades past, when racing had a much larger place in American society.

Part of the Derby's appeal for decades had been that it provided the middle classes an opportunity to experience the "good life" while giving high society a chance to get close—but not too close—to the hedonistic behavior of the masses. In decades past, newspapers had published lists of society members who attended the Derby, including information on what fashion the women wore, seat location, and local hosts. But by the 1980s, American popular culture was much more focused upon actors, musicians, and athletes than faceless aristocrats. Society swells still showed up to the Derby, but celebrities from the entertainment industries received much more attention in the newspapers. Some of the celebrities made the trip to Churchill Downs as owners of Derby horses, including filmmaker Steven Spielberg, rapper M. C. Hammer, songwriter Bert Bacharach, Motown Records founder Barry Gordy, and New York Yankees owner George Steinbrenner. These celebrities who were involved in the actual race were doubly effective in bringing attention to Louisville at Derby time.

The Derby had to some degree always been "glamorous," but in the 1980s, *Kentucky* became glamorous in its own right, which only helped to raise the stature of the Derby. In 1985 Lexington, Kentucky, hosted the NCAA Men's Basketball Final Four, an opportunity typically reserved for much larger cities. Weeks later, an editorial in the *Courier-Journal* proclaimed, "It's a giddy F. Scott Fitzgerald time, a flapper week for modern times" above an article about Derby Week festivities in Kentucky.[3] They were certainly high times for the state's horse community. Lavish parties at central Kentucky horse farms rivaled any in the nation. Robin Leach filmed a segment of his *Lifestyles of the Rich and Famous* television program at one of these parties, at which television personality Gary Collins said, "This must be what it was like before the crash in '29. Everybody's happy, there are no problems. It has a very unreal quality that takes you away from all the craziness in our day-to-day events."[4]

This sense of glamour and giddiness in Kentucky equine circles in the early 1980s was fueled by the unprecedented boom in the Thoroughbred bloodstock market that had begun in the 1970s. The beginning of the boom could be partially attributed to a growing international presence at American horse auctions attracted by a weak U.S. dollar, and European interest in the offspring of 1964 Kentucky Derby champion Northern Dancer, whose son Nijinsky captured the English Triple Crown in 1970 and was later named "Horse of the Millennium" in a poll of British racing fans. By the early 1980s the market for top equine racing stock in Kentucky had reached astronomical levels. Fees for top Kentucky stallions' services approached $1 million per "cover." Yearlings were selling in Lexington's Keeneland July sale for eye-popping figures, reaching a peak of $13.1 million for a half brother to Seattle Slew in 1985.

One of the key contributors to this boom market was the ruling family of Dubai, led by Sheikh Mohammed bin Rashid al Maktoum. In 1983 Sheikh Mohammed paid $10.2 million for a horse later named Snaafi Dancer, who never raced and was practically infertile. The following year Mohammed spent more than $41 million on a handful of yearlings. The sheikh's aspiration of establishing the most successful Thoroughbred operation in the world was part of a larger goal of promoting Dubai as a global tourist destination in the face of the fact that the oil reserves that had produced the immense wealth of Dubai and its ruling family were diminishing. Sheikh Mohammed was proud of the

Seattle Dancer brought a world record $13.1 million as a yearling at the 1985 Keeneland July yearling sale. (Photos by Z.)

Sheikh Mohammed bin Rashid al Maktoum. Sheikh Mohammed took the world of horse racing by storm and injected hundreds of millions of dollars into the industry beginning in the 1980s. (Photos by Z.)

Thoroughbred's Arabian roots, and had been a lifelong sportsman and equestrian. Excellence in Thoroughbred racing was one way he sought to raise the international profile of Dubai, located on the Persian Gulf at the crossroads of Europe, Asia, and Africa. He had long-term ambitions of turning Dubai into an Arabian Hong Kong.

In the late 1980s and 1990s, as the sport of Thoroughbred racing became increasingly international, the Maktoums dominated racing in England and won many of the world's most important races, but the Kentucky Derby was a prize that eluded this most decorated family in racing, despite vast expenditures of time, money, and energy in pursuit of the roses. Since its initial foray into the sport, the Maktoum family has spent well over $1 billion on racehorses worldwide. For Mohammed the Derby was a race whose preeminent place both on the American racing calendar and in American culture made it an essential part of his larger goal of bringing international attention and glory to Dubai.

In 1992 Mohammed was part owner of the Derby favorite Arazi. The colt was French trained but had won America's most important race for two-year-olds, the Breeders' Cup Juvenile, the previous fall in spectacular fashion. Racing fans hoped that Arazi might be the next Secretariat. That year members of the international press showed up in record numbers to Churchill Downs: more than one hundred foreign journalists from nine different countries. A German film crew was on hand to shoot a documentary about the Derby, and the race itself would be broadcast that year in countries around the world, including, for the first time, Russia. Aired only months after the collapse of the Soviet Union, the Russian broadcast included advertisements for Kentucky, Louisville, and a cigarette company, and concluded with a Russian-language rendition of "My Old Kentucky Home" performed by the Louisville Chorus.

Arazi finished a disappointing eighth, but his performance did not deter foreign owners. In 1995 a horse with a Japanese owner, trainer, and jockey finished fourteenth in the Derby. "Make no mistake about it," a journalist for the *Courier-Journal* wrote, "the Kentucky Derby no longer is as homemade as a bottle of bourbon. . . . A good interpreter has become as critical as a good set of binoculars" in a milieu where "a Japanese television network questions a Brooklyn horse trainer about the running ability of an English colt while a Canadian sports writer scribbles notes."[5]

The racing world had become more international with the advance in transportation and information technology. But the internationalization of the Derby was more than just a product of these phenomena. A victory in the Kentucky Derby represented the ultimate achievement in American racing, but it also guaranteed a horse and its owner a place in American popular culture and public consciousness (not to mention the possibility of unfathomable riches as the owner of a Derby-winning stud horse in the breeding shed).

In 1999 Sheikh Mohammed returned to the Derby with a colt named Worldly Manner. At a press conference he pledged to win the Derby within four years. "If we fail this time, we'll try again. That's a promise," Mohammed told the *New York Times*.[6] Worldly Manner, for which Mohammed reportedly paid $5 million as a two-year-old, finished seventh. When asked what he and his horse had accomplished in the race the Sheikh responded, "The success is in this [Derby] atmosphere you see. We'll be back, Inshallah. We'll be back."[7]

Mohammed, who raced under the name Godolphin Racing as a tribute to one of the original Arabian ancestors of all Thoroughbred horses, did not just want to win the Derby. He wanted to win it by training and preparing his horses in Dubai, a tactic that flouted conventional wisdom. He was convinced that his training facilities in Dubai were the finest in the world, and there was no better time or place to demonstrate his program's efficacy than at Churchill Downs on the first Saturday in May. Mohammed had not insisted on winning other major American races in this manner. He had dozens of horses in training in the United States at any one time, but the Kentucky Derby was different.

In 2000 Mohammed returned to the Derby with two colts, China Visit and Curule. The horses' trainer, Saeed bin Suroor, reiterated the operation's commitment to achieving success at the Derby: "We win the biggest races in the world. The Kentucky Derby is a target for us. We need to win this. This is very important for us. It's the biggest race in the world—one of the biggest. We need to win it."[8] They did not win, but finished a respectable sixth and seventh. When asked about his training strategy Mohammed asserted, "We can win from Dubai, and we will do it."[9]

That year the Derby roses went to Fusaichi Pegasus, a colt purchased for $4 million at the Keeneland July yearling sale by Fusao Sekiguchi, who told Derby reporters through an interpret-

Fusaichi Pegasus winning the Kentucky Derby in 2000. (Photos by Z.)

er, "When I laid eyes on this colt, I knew he was going to be a Derby winner."[10] Sekiguchi, a Japanese venture capitalist, had raced horses in Japan since the 1970s. He had been interested in American culture since American G.I.s occupied his hometown at the end of World War II. It was through the soldiers that he first became aware of the Kentucky Derby. After realizing success in Japanese racing in the 1990s, he set his sights on American racing and its ultimate prize, the Kentucky Derby. Sekiguchi's entourage that accompanied him to the winner's circle included three geishas carrying roses and paper parasols, symbolically emphasizing a Japanese victory in an American event.

The reaction of one Japanese racing fan in Tokyo underscores the significance of a victory in the Kentucky Derby to a non-American. "Sure I'm happy," Tsuyoshi Yamada told a reporter for the Associated Press outside a Tokyo betting shop after Fusaichi Pegasus's Derby win. "But I'd be a whole lot happier if it had been a horse that had raced and proven itself in Japan."[11] Though "Fu Peg" was Japanese owned, he had been born, raised, sold, and trained in the United States, which in some ways reduced the symbolic significance of a Japanese victory in "America's race." By insisting on winning the Derby with a horse trained in Dubai, Sheikh Mohammed ensured that if he were to win a Kentucky Derby, his victory would be thorough.

Two years after Sekiguchi's triumph at the Derby, Saudi prince Ahmed bin Salman won the race in wire-to-wire fashion with a horse named War Emblem. Prince Ahmed explained, "It's a great achievement. This was important for me and it's an honor to be the first Arab to win the Kentucky Derby."[12] "I love you guys in America," the prince continued, in a line reminiscent of comments from northern American winners in the 1920s who praised the Kentucky "southerners" and the hospitality that they encountered in Louisville.[13] Before the previous year's Derby, in which Ahmed's favored Point Given finished a disappointing fifth, the prince had admitted, "One of the great ambitions of my life is to win the Kentucky Derby. I have dreamed of it since I was a child."[14] Ahmed's trainer Bob Baffert was also aware of his ambition: "The Prince wants to be the first Arab to win the Derby, and so does Sheikh Mo[hammed]. Let's face it, for those guys, bragging rights are what it all comes down to, because they have more money than they'll ever be able to spend. What they really want is the best horse, and that means winning the Derby."[15]

Prince Ahmed had purchased War Emblem for a reported $1 million (a relative bargain in hindsight) only three weeks before the Derby, after the colt's victory in the Illinois Derby. This last-minute acquisition rubbed some horsemen the wrong way. "Never in my life has a horse been given to me, ready-made, just sitting on a win like that," said four-time Derby-winning trainer Wayne Lukas. Two-time Derby-winning trainer Nick Zito suggested that others around the racetrack had similar complaints about Ahmed's trainer: "A lot of guys resent Baffert because he had enough [Derby] horses, then he had to go out and buy one."[16] War Emblem went on to win the Preakness Stakes and had a

Victor Espinoza celebrates as he crosses the wire first in the 2002 Kentucky Derby aboard War Emblem. (Photos by Z.)

Prince Ahmed bin Salman (left) with Bob Baffert, owner and trainer, respectively, of 2002 Kentucky Derby winner War Emblem. (Photos by Z.)

chance to win the Triple Crown in the Belmont Stakes but stumbled at the start and finished a distant fifth.

To American and foreign owners alike, a victory in the Kentucky Derby represented an ultimate achievement in American horse racing. But the Derby took on added significance for foreign owners, who saw the race as part of Americana and took their own national pride to the starting gate and to the winner's circle. English-born Michael Tabor won in 1995 with Thunder Gulch and later said, "I've always loved America, especially the vitality of the country and the people, and to me the [Kentucky] Derby is the greatest race of them all."[17] Tabor was an associate of John Magnier and his Coolmore Stud in County Tipperary, Ireland, the only serious challenger to the Maktoum family in terms of power and influence in Thoroughbred racing and breeding in the 1990s. In the fifteen years after Thunder Gulch's Derby victory, Coolmore and its associates owned over a dozen Derby starters outright or in partnership. Some of Coolmore's Derby horses traveled from Europe for the race, but others prepped in the United States. Still, Sheikh Mohammed was determined to win on his own terms and to win from his homeland. "The more they say that [it is impossible], the more possible Sheikh Mohammed will make it," Godolphin racing manager Simon Crisford declared, leaving no mistake about the sheikh's unwavering ambition.[18] The next chance for the sheikh to prove that a Dubai-based horse could win the Derby came in 2002 when Mohammed entered Essence of Dubai, a $2.3 million yearling purchase and major stakes winner in Dubai; he finished ninth.

In the fall of 2008, Churchill Downs announced the creation of a race called the Kentucky Derby Challenge Stakes, to be contested in England the following March. The winner of the Challenge Stakes would be guaranteed a place in the starting gate at the Kentucky Derby.[19] Churchill Downs president Steve Sexton explained, "The Kentucky Derby is a naturally compelling and exciting event, but the presence of international con-

Jockey Gary Stevens stands in triumph as he crosses the finish line aboard winning horse Thunder Gulch in the 1995 Derby. (Photos by Z.)

tenders always adds to the anticipation and intrigue surrounding America's greatest race. A consistent international presence in the Derby will strengthen worldwide interest in our race and, in the long term, boost demand for the event as we work to expand distribution of wagering opportunities into new international markets."[20] Sheikh Hamdan bin Rashid al Maktoum, Mohammed's brother, won the inaugural running of the Kentucky Derby Challenge Stakes (and that will likely prove to be the only running; Churchill Downs put the event on indefinite hiatus in 2010) with a colt named Mafaaz, but decided not to run in the Derby when the horse finished eighth in Keeneland Race Course's Bluegrass Stakes, a key April Derby prep run in Lexington, seventy miles from Churchill Downs. Mohammed returned to the Kentucky Derby in 2009 with two runners, Regal Ransom and Desert Party. Both had been running well in Dubai in the months prior to being shipped to Louisville, and team Godolphin held higher hopes for its Derby prospects than it had in previous years. The results, however, were no better: Regal Ransom and Desert Party finished eighth and fourteenth, respectively.

The Derby's persistent place of importance in the wider consciousness of the American public led to the recognition of the race by foreign horsemen as emblematic not just of American racing, but also of American society and culture. The foreign recognition of the Derby's significance only added to the race's importance within the American Thoroughbred industry. But whereas journalists gravitated toward foreign owners' quests to win at Churchill Downs, the American public was not always as willing to embrace a foreign owner or horse at the Derby.

Both the Preakness and Belmont drew large crowds in 2002 when Prince Ahmed bin Salman's War Emblem was on the Triple Crown trail, but the national attention that War Emblem received was dwarfed by the fanfare and praise that would be heaped upon Funny Cide and Smarty Jones and their American human connections during their Triple Crown bids the next two years. Perhaps the discrepancy was due to the public disapproval of the manner in which Ahmed had acquired his horse (only weeks before the Derby). Another, more likely, explanation is that Americans were not prepared to fully embrace a Derby-winning Arab owner when the attacks of September 11, 2001, were still fresh in their minds and the possibility of American military action in the Middle East loomed.

Funny Cide, winner of the 2003 Derby, was a relatively inexpensive New York–bred gelding (once purchased for $22,000 from Fasig-Tipton's New York–bred sale) who was owned in partnership by a group that included six high school buddies from upstate New York. The group raced under the name Sackatoga Stables—derived from a combination of the name of their hometown and their favorite race meet—and the owners followed their gelding on the Triple Crown trail in a rented school bus. In winning the Derby, Funny Cide defeated the regally bred post-time favorite, Empire Maker, owned by a Saudi prince named Khalid

Jack Knowlton of Sackatoga Stables holds the 2003 Kentucky Derby trophy with trainer Barclay Tagg (left) and jockey Jose Santos (right) following Funny Cide's victory. (Photos by Z.)

Abdullah, becoming the first gelding since Clyde Van Dusen in 1929 to win the race, and the first New York–bred horse ever to wear the Derby roses.

The victory of these American "regular guys" over Saudi royalty resonated with an American public that had made hits of jingoistic saber-rattling songs like country music star Toby Keith's "Courtesy of the Red, White and Blue (The Angry American)."[21] The lyrics are a vague threat and shake-of-the-fist imprecisely directed toward the Middle East in general (or anywhere any Muslims might be found). They struck a chord with Americans in the aftermath of the attacks of September 11, 2001. That same sentiment helped to create a following for Funny Cide, many of whose fans embraced him as an equine American who did his own part to strike a blow against a wealthy and influential Arab.

The American public's propensity to embrace Funny Cide's story was also increased by the immense popularity of Laura Hil-

Funny Cide wins the 2003 Kentucky Derby. (Photos by Z.)

lenbrand's *Seabiscuit,* published in 2001, about a hard-luck horse who captures the hearts of Depression-era Americans and wins a climactic match race against a regally bred colt owned by American racing royalty.[22] *Seabiscuit* enjoyed a long run atop national best-seller lists and was still very popular during Funny Cide's improbable bid for the Triple Crown. A major motion picture based upon the book was released later that summer, garnering box-office success, critical acclaim, and seven Academy Award nominations.

Funny Cide's success in the late spring of 2003 spawned the production of countless pieces of Funny Cide–related memorabilia, including—among other trinkets, gadgets, and knickknacks—a Funny Cide beer. The beer was produced in a Saratoga, New York, brewery not far from a Funny Cide retail store. A Web site devoted to the gelding is still up and running; here fans can sign up for the Funny Cide fan club and purchase assorted products bearing the horse's name or likeness, including hats, T-shirts, poker chips, wine corks, snow globes, mugs, mouse pads, key

Smarty Jones and jockey Stewart Elliott win the 2004 Derby on a sloppy Churchill Downs track. (Photos by Z.)

chains, and dozens of other items. Though Funny Cide failed to capture the Triple Crown, NBC's telecast of Funny Cide's attempt in the Belmont Stakes was the highest-rated program in America that week. Americans rallied that year behind "America's horse," winner of America's race, at a time when patriotism was at a fever pitch. Today Funny Cide resides at the Kentucky Horse Park's Hall of Champions near Lexington and is visited by thousands of fans every year.

Though no Web site celebrates Ahmed bin Salman's War Emblem, there is one devoted to 2004 Kentucky Derby winner Smarty Jones, who attracted even more attention and fanfare than Funny Cide had the previous year. After his Derby victory, Smarty appeared on the cover of *Sports Illustrated* beneath the headline "Why Everybody Loves Smarty Jones." The article explained the recipe for the colt's popularity: "He has a breathtaking story—aging, kindhearted owners; a trainer and a jockey from a small-time track testing their chops against the best, and a timeline sprinkled with tragedy, nearly including his own demise. But he also has the goods."[23]

In June 2004 more than 120,000 fans showed up for the 2004 Belmont Stakes hoping to witness Smarty Jones capture the Triple Crown, shattering attendance and betting records at the New York racetrack. It was the largest crowd ever to witness a sporting event in New York. Fans not at the racetrack were also paying attention as Smarty Jones's Belmont had the highest-rated television audience for the race since 1977 when Seattle Slew won the Triple Crown. Bucking a twenty-year trend of dwindling American viewership of horse racing, NBC's Belmont broadcast drew a higher rating than that year's NCAA Men's Basketball Championship game and the final round of the Masters golf tournament. An estimated 8,500 people came to Philadelphia Park to watch a Smarty Jones workout prior to the Belmont, and the colt received a police escort, followed by news helicopters, to Belmont Park for the big race.

Smarty's fans were disappointed, as the colt chased a fast early pace, tired, and finished second. Some expressed their displeasure vocally as the spoiler named Birdstone and his connections (including owner Marylou Whitney, the fourth wife of Cornelius Vanderbilt Whitney, whose father, H. P. Whitney, had owned 1915 Derby-winning filly Regret) made their way to the winner's circle. Despite his loss in the Belmont, the only loss of his career in what would be his final race, Smarty had made a mark on American culture. He was named one of *Time* magazine's "People Who Mattered [in] 2004" along with the likes of Democratic presidential nominee John Kerry, Apple, Inc., cofounder Steve Jobs, and Israeli prime minister Ariel Sharon. Fans spent hundreds of thousands of dollars on Smarty merchandise, and reporters from across the globe flocked to cover the horse and speak with Smarty's human connections. Such unprecedented attention for a horse in a sport whose heyday had passed decades before begged the question "Why?" Why that horse? Why that year? Before Smarty Jones, six of the previous seven horses to win the Kentucky Derby had gone on to win the Preakness. Each came to Belmont Park with a chance to win the Triple Crown. But none of those horses received the attention and fanfare that Smarty did.

Unlike the others, Smarty entered the Belmont undefeated. Smarty was trying to become the first undefeated Triple Crown winner since Seattle Slew in 1977. This circumstance must have added something to Smarty's appeal, but it was by no means the only reason for the horse's popularity. His owners were an elderly husband-and-wife team, Roy and Patricia Chapman. Roy "Chappie" Chapman was suffering from emphysema. The horse's jockey had overcome problems with alcohol. The trainer was enjoying his time in the spotlight after years of hard work and relative anonymity. The horse had overcome a near-fatal injury as a youngster. Any of these stories would have been compelling by themselves. Taken together, at a time when American headlines were dominated by stories of war and a contentious presidential election, these stories made Smarty Jones a symbol of what was "right" with America when so many things seemed to be wrong. But the sine qua non of Smarty's popularity was his victory in the Kentucky Derby. Like Funny Cide the year before, he was an "all-American" champion of America's horse race. Since Derby-winning horses could not tell their own stories, journalists and fans were left to sculpt an identity for them. In the cases of Smarty Jones and Funny Cide, the American public embraced them and their human connections as examples of Americans who overcame obstacles to achieve greatness in affirmation of the "American Dream."[24]

The Derby could provide a story line that could fit almost any national mood or set of tastes, and the malleable identity of Kentucky mixed well with the malleable identity of a horse. Journalists covering the Derby had the option to ascribe an almost limitless assortment of "personality" traits to the Derby horses they covered, depending on the pervading cultural climate. Throughout the twentieth century journalists who covered the event tended to gravitate to stories that reflected and reaffirmed the dominant social and cultural values of their era. Beginning in the 1980s the stories that emerged from the Kentucky Derby tended to be those of redemption, the triumph of the underdog, and the reward of patience and perseverance. These themes reflected the hope and assumption that opportunity existed in the United States for anyone to succeed, regardless of age, gender, or background. Of the countless "human interest" stories available to journalists at the Derby, in the 1980s and 1990s journalists were inclined to focus on those that spoke to the belief that the American Dream was alive and well at the Kentucky Derby.

For the first hundred years, newspaper reports about Derby-winning horses tended to fall into the category of "superhorse" or "dark horse," but later journalists found many other ways to "spin" their stories. Each racehorse had people who had cared for it as a foal. Some were sold at auction. Each was taught to carry a rider. Each was introduced to the racetrack and starting gate by some human. Each horse had an owner, a trainer, a jockey, an exercise rider, a groom, a breeder, a veterinarian, a blacksmith, and countless other people who had helped the horse along the way to the Derby. In every Derby-winning team there was someone who was an example of outstanding achievement, or someone who had overcome substantial obstacles to reach the pinnacle of his or her career. Sometimes it was the horse itself who had overcome obstacles or was an example of excellence. The stories that journalists discovered, reported, and promoted at Churchill Downs each May became the Derby experience for millions of Americans. In a sport with so many human-interest stories from which to choose, each Derby was almost guaranteed to have a memorable image or an attractive storyline attached to it for posterity.

Beginning in the 1980s, stories of individuals overcoming adversity and embodying an American spirit largely replaced

Genuine Risk became the second filly to win the Derby in 1980. She is pictured with her first foal. (Photos by Z.)

connections to the Old South (with the obvious exceptions of "My Old Kentucky Home" and mint juleps) as the imagery most readily associated with the Derby. Photographs and descriptions of beautiful women were still a part of the journalistic coverage of the Derby, but stories of female success on the racetrack were increasingly part of that coverage as well. In order to retain its status as a part of Americana, the Derby needed to reflect some of the values of an ever-changing American culture and society or risk becoming an irrelevant anachronism. In an era when Americans placed a high value on the notion that their society was one in which anyone could succeed with enough desire, effort, and perseverance, stories of unlikely victors helped to affirm this belief.

In 1980 Genuine Risk became the first filly to run in the Kentucky Derby since 1959, and the first to win the race since Regret in 1915. After the race Dick Young of the *New York Daily News* commented, "Let's admit it, fellows. It's a different world. Equal pay for equal work. Women at the head of large corporations. And now this, the ultimate step in the sexual revolution—a filly beating the colts in the Kentucky Derby."[25] In reality, women did not actually receive equal pay for equal work and that year the Republican Party would remove support for the Equal Rights Amendment from their party platform; however, Genuine Risk's gender was the major focus of journalists' reports from the Derby in 1980.

In 1984 females were again in the Derby spotlight, and the race was referred to as the "female Derby" by local media. The betting favorites that year were a coupled entry of two fillies, Althea and Life's Magic. That year Patty Cooksey became the second female jockey to start in the race, and Dianne Carpenter the fourth woman to train a Derby starter. Governor Martha Layne Collins, a former Derby Festival Queen, brought as guests to the Derby vice presidential nominee Geraldine Ferraro and astronaut Sally Ride. Collins presented the trophy to the winning owners from Claiborne Farm, after Seattle Slew's son Swale stomped a full field of twenty under jockey Laffit Pincay Jr.

In 1988 Winning Colors became the second filly to win the Derby in less than a decade, a much shorter gap than the sixty-five years between Regret and Genuine Risk. Dave Anderson attempted to put the feat in perspective for his *New York Times* readers. "It's as if Martina Navratilova won the Wimbledon men's singles. As if Nancy Lopez won the Masters. As if Jackie Joyner-Kersee won the men's Olympic decathlon." After the trophy presentation the winning owner, former San Diego Chargers owner Eugene Klein, exclaimed, "I'd like to salute all the women of America. This one's for you gals."[26] D. Wayne Lukas, the filly's trainer, found the win somewhat bittersweet as it brought back memories of the death of a favorite filly, Landaluce, who had died suddenly five months before the 1983 Derby. "She had a head like a princess, a butt like a washerwoman, and a walk like a hooker," the trainer recalled.[27] Lukas's description served as a

(*Above*) Winning Colors, winning the 1988 Kentucky Derby with jockey Gary Stevens. (Photos by Z.)

(*Right*) D. Wayne Lukas, winner of four Kentucky Derbies. (Photos by Z.)

reminder that if Winning Colors's victory represented some kind of a triumph for womankind, it was a superficial one.

Journalistic portrayals of the Derby reflected what Americans wanted to see in their culture and society. Americans valued the notion that their nation was one in which women were treated as the equals of men. When females competed in the Derby as owners, trainers, and jockeys in the latter part of the twentieth century, they garnered plenty of attention from the media, which also gravitated to stories about people who played by the rules and waited patiently for the fruits of their labor.

In 1986 seventy-three-year-old Charlie Whittingham was one of the most successful and well-respected trainers in racing history, but a horse of his had never won the Kentucky Derby. Fifty-four-year-old jockey Bill Shoemaker had ridden more winners than any rider in history, but hadn't won a Derby in twenty years; and it had been more than thirty years since he had won his first. Both men had long since been inducted into American racing's Hall of Fame. After sitting off of a fast early pace aboard Ferdinand (a son of the top international stallion Nijinsky), Shoemaker weaved through the pack of tiring frontrunners in the homestretch, guiding the chestnut colt to Derby victory. With their triumph, Whittingham and Shoemaker became the oldest trainer and jockey of a Derby winner, and were greeted with great fanfare in the winner's circle and lauded the next day in the newspapers.

After the race Whittingham explained what a Derby victory meant to him. "You tell people what business you've been in since 1934 and the first thing they ask you is, 'Did you ever win the Kentucky Derby?' When you tell them no, they walk away. Now, I guess they won't."[28] Shoemaker had been confident all week, telling anyone who would listen that forty-six-year-old Jack Nicklaus's win in the Masters golf tournament earlier that spring was an omen and that he and Ferdinand would win on Saturday. Though the horse was a 17-1 long shot, the producer of

Jockey Bill Shoemaker after winning the 1986 Derby
with Ferdinand. (Photos by Z.)

ABC's Derby telecast chose to focus a camera on Ferdinand during the race because of a "gut feeling and sentiment."[29] The decision paid off and viewers were treated to a replay of one of the
more memorable rides in Derby history.

A similar choice in camera positioning allowed ABC to capture another of the Derby's most memorable moments in 1990,
and another example of a popular and emotionally evocative
Derby victory for an elderly person, this time a nonagenarian
owner. None of the millions who watched the 1990 Derby tele-

Charlie Whittingham, the oldest trainer to win a Kentucky Derby, won two: Ferdinand (1986) and Sunday Silence (1989). (Photos by Z.)

cast would soon forget the image of trainer Carl Nafzger describing to nearly blind ninety-two-year-old owner Frances Genter (whose late first husband was involved in the development of the pop-up toaster) the progress of her colt Unbridled as jockey Craig Perret urged him toward the front in the race's final turn, took the lead in the stretch, and extended it as the finish line approached. "He's gonna win," Nafzger shouted as the colt approached the wire. "He's a winner, Mrs. Genter. We won it! You won the Kentucky Derby! Oh, Mrs. Genter, I love you!"[30] Mrs. Genter, who had been involved in racing for fifty years, was finally rewarded by what racing fans and journalists often call the "Derby gods," deities who preside over the Derby from on high, dispensing racing luck with particular regard to the elderly, those who have overcome adversity, and those who have "paid their dues."

This praise for Derby-winning horsemen and horsewomen

Jockey Craig Perret celebrates as he wins the 1990 Derby on Unbridled. (Photos by Z.)

who had paid their dues and waited their turn soon reappeared. In 1993 Sea Hero won the Derby for eighty-five-year-old owner Paul Mellon, son of billionaire financier and former secretary of the treasury Andrew Mellon, and seventy-one-year-old trainer Mackenzie "Mack" Miller. Hall of Fame jockey Jerry Bailey, who rode Sea Hero to Derby victory, described the significance of the race in his autobiography. "[The Kentucky Derby] epitomizes the American Dream," Bailey explained, "offering hope that enough sweat can allow anyone to smell the roses. With the joyful mayhem it compresses into two minutes and change, the Derby affirms life itself."[31] Thomas Meeker, president of Churchill Downs, praised the winning connections in the winner's circle. "The Kentucky Derby is a collage. Sometimes the new people win it, and sometimes the old people win it. There is something for everybody."[32] Though perhaps not overly profound in his observations, Meeker was right. The winners of the Derby were sometimes new and sometimes old. In either case, journalists were ready to frame the event in a favorable light, one that appealed to popular American sensibilities at the time.

In 1996 the storyline was repeated for seventy-eight-year-old William T. Young when his colt Grindstone (a son of Mrs. Genter's Unbridled) just caught Cavonnier at the wire in the closest finish in the Derby in almost forty years. While the press praised Young and trainer D. Wayne Lukas (Grindstone's victory was the trainer's record sixth-straight win in Triple Crown events), many felt sorry for Cavonnier's trainer—the excitable and affable Bob Baffert. Baffert, a prematurely white-haired character from Southern California, was then relatively unknown, but he would soon become a media darling. Baffert later recalled in his autobiography, "As much as I hated to lose and hated to get beat by D. Wayne Lukas, at least here was a good man [Young] who had won. He was just the chosen one this year."[33] Baffert graciously congratulated Young, but later admitted that the loss was devastating. His disappointment with Cavonnier and his grace in defeat would serve as preludes to the realization of another prevalent theme in the coverage of modern Derbies—that of redemption—the following year.

In the last quarter century turf writers have often referenced the "Derby gods," and it was to these Baffert was referring when he called Young the "chosen one." These references, typically made in hindsight, are efforts to explain the significance of a Derby result and to justify how it was the right and fair result. When Silver Charm survived a photo finish to win the 1997 Derby for Baffert the year after he had narrowly missed with Cavonnier, the Derby gods were smiling upon Baffert, who in this victory was, according to journalists, granted his just reward for his perseverance. A headline in the *New York Times* read, "Baffert Makes Good on a Second Chance."[34] Adding a bit of spice to Baffert's tale of redemption was the fact that the trainer won the 1997 Derby for owners Bob and Beverly Lewis. The Lewises were also clients of Wayne Lukas, who often received the own-

Bob Baffert, three-time Derby-winning trainer. (Photos by Z.)

ers' more expensive yearlings, leaving Baffert with what he called "ham sandwiches."[35]

At the trophy presentation, Baffert thanked his friend Mike Pegram for helping him get his start in Thoroughbred training. The following May, Baffert again won the Derby, this time with Real Quiet, a skinny $17,000 yearling purchase owned by none other than Mike Pegram. "The Gods smiled on me today," Pegram said after Real Quiet's Derby win.[36] The Derby gods seemed to share a sense of justice with the nondenominational American God evoked by presidents in speeches ending with the line "May

Silver Charm on his way to the winner's circle after the 1997 Derby. (Photos by Z.)

God bless America." Americans like to think that the American God rewards those who play by the rules, work hard, and wait their turn for their just desserts. Journalists and fans assumed that, as an important American cultural tradition, the Derby and its gods adhered to a compatible set of ethics.

The following year the resonant story to emerge from the Derby was again a tale of redemption, this time for a jockey: Chris Antley returned from drug and weight problems to win aboard Charismatic, a 31-1 long shot. "A forgotten horse, a trainer who had been upstaged, and a jockey trying to find his way back to the top combined for one of the biggest payoffs in Kentucky Derby history," Maryjean Wall summarized in the *Lexington Herald-Leader.*[37] Antley had experienced a meteoric rise to the top of American racing, culminating in his 1991 Derby victory aboard Strike the Gold, but had found himself out of racing only sixth months before his improbable 1999 Derby score. With Charismatic's victory in the 1999 Derby, trainer Wayne Lukas

Charismatic (right) narrowly defeats Menifee in the 1999 Derby. (Photos by Z.)

ended Bob Baffert's streak of consecutive Derby wins at two. Baffert's first Derby win in 1997 had itself deprived Lukas of a third consecutive victory, making the 1999 Derby a tiebreaker of sorts between the two. Both had achieved great success and national prominence from well-documented roots as outsiders to the world of Thoroughbreds. Both were former Quarter Horse trainers. Lukas was a former high school basketball coach from Wisconsin, and Baffert was an irreverently playful character from rural Arizona (his autobiography, published that year, was titled *Dirt Road to the Derby*). The rivalry between two of the most visible characters in the sport of horse racing was covered by the Derby press corps, but it was overshadowed by the story of Antley's redemption that year.

In fact, this tale of Antley's return from drug problems to win America's greatest race had already been told—in 1991, on the heels of his earlier well-publicized drug problems. Antley's success in overcoming a cocaine addiction had been part of the *New York Times*'s coverage of the 1991 Derby, in which George

Vecsey credited the jockey for testing clean since the previous March. The story could have had a much different emphasis—an irresponsible former drug abuser had managed to hold it together just long enough to win the Kentucky Derby—but the race had achieved such a place in American culture and society that such a story would be unacceptable. The Derby represented a nation and a culture, and the stories that emerged through Derby journalists tended to reflect the ideals and values of that nation and culture.

Antley and Charismatic would go on to capture the Preakness Stakes two weeks after the 1999 Derby, setting up a chance for the Triple Crown with a win in the Belmont Stakes. Alas, Charismatic fractured his leg sixty yards from the finish line and finished third. Antley again made headlines for the great care he took in holding the horse's leg until vets arrived on the scene. Charismatic would make a full recovery, but Antley died the next year from a drug overdose. His passing would have received little or no attention had he not been twice celebrated by the media as a redeemed champion of the Kentucky Derby. Since Antley was a two-time Derby champion, his death was widely reported in news outlets across the country. Redemption at the Derby made a good story, but so did the fall from grace of a Derby winner.

Perhaps the greatest story of redemption in recent Derby lore was that of Arthur B. Hancock III. Americans first became aware of the central Kentucky horseman's story in 1982, when his colt Gato del Sol won the Derby. Hancock, a fourth-generation horseman, was the oldest son of Arthur "Bull" Hancock II, whose father had founded world-renowned Claiborne Farm in Paris, Kentucky. Arthur III had been a black sheep in the family, a self-described "freewheeling, hard-drinking, guitar-picking, bar-brawling, skirt-chasing fool."[38]

According to racing journalist William Nack, "Hancock bridled at authority and this compromised his chances for ever wielding it at Claiborne."[39] When his father died in 1972, the trustees of his estate recommended that Arthur's younger broth-

Arthur Boyd Hancock III. (Photos by Z.)

er Seth be put in charge of the farm. Arthur left Claiborne and established a breeding operation at Stone Farm just down the road. In the 1989 Derby, Sunday Silence, a colt owned in partnership by Hancock, defeated two-year-old champion and odds-on favorite Easy Goer, who was owned by one of the trustees of Bull Hancock's estate and had been born and raised at Claiborne Farm. The fact that Charlie Whittingham was a co-owner and trainer of the colt only added to the storyline. Sports journalists and racing enthusiasts fully embraced the story, which seemed tailor-made for a Hollywood drama as it played out on the bright stage of the Kentucky Derby and became another important entry into the race's anthology of lore. Sunday Silence and Easy Goer would meet three more times that year, in the Preakness, Belmont, and Breeders' Cup Classic. Of the four meetings, Easy Goer managed only one win, but it cost Sunday Silence a Triple Crown in the Belmont Stakes. Their rivalry, though brief, was horse racing's most compelling since Affirmed-Alydar, and it began at the Kentucky Derby.

In the absence of a tale of redemption in the Derby, journalists covering the race in recent years have often relied on the "unlikely victor" or "underdog" angle. There can only be one betting favorite in any race, and in a race that often consists of twenty starters there are many horses who can qualify as surprise winners. A horse can qualify on the merits of an unusual place of origin or breeding, a small price tag at auction, or long odds as determined by Derby bettors. More often than not, a Derby winner can meet at least one of these criteria. In a sport that is thought to be dominated by extremely wealthy men, the underdog Derby winner can be attractive to followers of America's race as proof that there is room for "the little guy" on such a bright and significant stage.

In 2007 jockey Calvin Borel became the latest unlikely victor to be celebrated at the Derby after his come-from-behind victory aboard Street Sense. Borel left school in the eighth grade to ride the minor Louisiana bush track circuit. Journalists lauded him as a hard-working, polite, unassuming man, and he quickly became the favorite story of that year's Derby. When asked how it felt to perform in front of "the queen," Borel was confused until told by his fiancé that Queen Elizabeth of England had made a much-publicized visit to the Derby that year.[40] The following night Borel joined the queen at a state dinner at the White House, where he sat next to "a football player, I forget his name."[41] The football player was reigning Super Bowl MVP Peyton Manning.

Borel's story seemed to be taken straight from the pages of a Horatio Alger novel. In reality Borel's life had already included

(*Left*) Charlie Whittingham and Sunday Silence. (Photos by Z.)

(*Below*) Sunday Silence (saddle cloth #8) and Easy Goer, one of the great rivalries in Thoroughbred racing history. (Photos by Z.)

Jockey Calvin Borel, the only rider to win three Kentucky Derbies in four years, celebrating his first Derby triumph aboard Street Sense in 2007. (Photos by Z.)

many rags-to-riches elements before his Kentucky Derby victory. But his victory at Churchill Downs on the first Saturday in May made Borel's name familiar to millions of people, and the Kentucky Derby was again shown to be a place where American dreams can come true. "Riding in the Derby is a dream every jock has, much less winning it," Borel explained after the race.

Calvin Borel, hoisting the 2009 Derby trophy, with connections of surprise winner Mine That Bird. (Photos by Z.)

"It's the greatest moment of your life, to win the Kentucky Derby."[42] Borel's performance on one of American sport's grandest stages was an affirmation of what Americans like to believe is possible for good people and hard workers in the United States.

Two years later Borel again found his name in the headlines when he won his second Derby, this time aboard 50-1 long shot Mine That Bird.[43] No horse had won with higher odds since Donerail in 1913, and no horse had won by a greater margin since Assault's eight-length victory in 1946. Purchased as a yearling for $9,500, the horse had been driven from New Mexico to Louisville by his trainer, Bennie L. "Chip" Woolley Jr., the week before the race. The trainer, a former bareback rodeo rider, was forced to drive the fifteen hundred miles with his left foot because of a broken leg sustained in a motorcycle accident. On the way to the Derby he stopped at Lone Star Park outside of Dallas so that his horse could exercise. Borel and his mount were featured on the cover of *Sports Illustrated* the following week, and

213

the Cajun jockey brought lumps to the throats of millions of television viewers as he lamented that his deceased parents could not witness his victory. "This just shows what can be done with two buddies who have fun together who like to go to the races and dream a little bit," explained Mine That Bird's co-owner Leonard Blach.[44]

News media and the American public had gravitated to stories about the realization of the dream of Derby success for decades. Whatever the mood of the nation, the Derby could provide a storyline that would affirm the collective values and ideals of the American people. In the case of Mine That Bird, journalists focused on the fact that the horse had been sold as a yearling for a relatively modest purchase price, or on the romantic cross-country journey of horse and trainer to reach the Derby. Buried beneath the headlines and deep within stories that celebrated the unlikely success of an underdog horse was the fact that Mine That Bird had been a champion two-year-old in Canada. He had been purchased by his owners for $400,000—a far less modest sum than his cost as a yearling—after he won four races in a row as a two-year-old.[45] Mark Allen, one of the horse's two co-owners, had been granted immunity from prosecution in exchange for his father's guilty plea in an Alaska bribery and corruption scandal involving the state legislature and former U.S. senator Ted Stevens.[46] Allen first became friends with the trainer Woolley when the latter assisted the former in a fight he had gotten himself into at a New Mexico bar called Annie Get Your Guns. But these less romantic elements of the Mine That Bird story were not widely reported by journalists.

Because the Derby is such an important piece of American culture, people want their Derby champions to "deserve" the title and to reflect the salient "American values" of their time. These values are not static; they evolve, disappear, and resurface at the whim of the pervading cultural, political, and social climate. However, one of the most enduring elements of American national identity has been the idea that America is a place in which people can make whatever they want of themselves if they work hard and play by the rules—a theme that has been reflected in journalistic coverage of America's most famous horse race over the past thirty years.

The morning after their Derby win with Mine That Bird, trainer Chip Woolley and owners Mark Allen and Leonard Blach returned to Churchill Downs and held court in front of a newly unveiled statue honoring widely beloved 2006 Derby champion Barbaro, whose untimely death, caused by complications resulting from a racetrack injury, captured the hearts of people around the world.[47] The trio distributed roses from the blanket worn by Mine That Bird in the winner's circle to fans visiting the statue in the shadows of the Kentucky Derby Museum. Woolley, Allen, and Blach had become part of Derby lore with Mine That Bird's victory the day before, but their decision to ceremonially share a symbol of their Derby experience at that memorial site revealed an understanding of the centrality of history to the identity, meaning, and significance of the Kentucky Derby.

Technically speaking, the race that Mine That Bird won was no longer called simply "the Kentucky Derby." Three years earlier Churchill Downs, Inc., had made international headlines when it announced a five-year sponsorship agreement with Yum! Brands, the parent company of Kentucky Fried Chicken, that included a provision to change the name of the most famous horse race in America to "The Kentucky Derby, presented by Yum! Brands." The agreement marked the first time in the event's long history that the race would be called something other than simply the Kentucky Derby. A *Chicago Sun-Times* columnist opined that the agreement "may well be the most repellent sponsorship deal . . . in marketing history."[48] Traditionalists and purists concerned that the sponsorship would detract from the race echoed this opinion. Downs officials did not share those concerns; they rang the opening bell of the NASDAQ stock market live from the

The ill-fated Barbaro, winning the 2006 Derby by six and a half lengths. (Photos by Z.)

racetrack during Derby Week, underscoring the corporate nature of their operation.

Two months after the Derby's name change was made public, Woodford Reserve Distillery announced that it would be selling fifty premium mint juleps for $1,000 each at the 2006 Derby, with the proceeds to benefit charity. Latter-day colonels of conspicuous consumption who shelled out such big money were presented with hand-prepared concoctions consisting of ice from the Arctic Circle, mint from Morocco, sugar from the South Pacific, and bourbon from Kentucky, served in a gold-plated cup. In addition to the fifty "Ultimate Mint Juleps," well over one hundred thousand more modestly priced mint juleps would be sold at the track during Derby weekend that year, suggesting that many at the Derby were disobeying "polite" society's rules for moderation in ways that called to mind the old tales of reckless and lawless Kentucky in bygone days. These symbols of decadence and exuberance were part of the Derby culture that had drawn Christian evangelical protesters to the sidewalks surrounding Churchill Downs in droves each Derby Day for decades.

Their presence demonstrated that the Derby was still an important cultural battleground in the twenty-first century. But the 157,536 fans who witnessed Barbaro's dominant six-and-a-half-length win that day were not thinking about colonels or hillbillies, sin or salvation. They were too busy marveling at the magnificence of the winning horse, whose margin of victory was the largest in sixty years and whose final quarter mile was the fastest since the great Secretariat. They were taking in all the sights, sounds, and smells of Derby Day at Churchill Downs beneath the twin spires on a warm spring afternoon in Kentucky. They were experiencing one of the great sporting environments in the entire world.

Today overt references to the Old South around Churchill Downs and the Kentucky Derby are few. However, the "sense of a world apart" is still perceptible to anyone who visits the Downs on Derby Day: the gleaming white façade of the clubhouse, the roses, the mint juleps, fashionable ladies in hats, and "My Old Kentucky Home" are each in their own way a small nod both to Derbies of yesteryear and, less directly, to nostalgic memories of

Old Kentucky. The myths and stereotypes associated with Kentucky and Kentuckians that helped to make the Derby an attractive destination in the first part of the twentieth century are no longer as prominent in American culture as they once were. But they persevere: Elements of the old mythology and identity of the state now live on in the identity and experience of the Kentucky Derby. The rich and famous in the clubhouse, luxury boxes, and dining rooms perform their best impersonations of colonels and belles. Meanwhile, in the infield, the rowdy hedonists flout societal rules by drinking, smoking, gambling, and shedding clothes, helping to preserve the contradictory dualistic elements of Kentucky's identity that trace back to the first published reports of Daniel Boone.

According to the master newscaster Walter Cronkite, the cultural cachet of Kentucky remained a part of the attraction of the event at the end of the twentieth century. In the introduction to a coffee-table book about the Derby, Cronkite asked, "What is it about the 'Run for the Roses' that so captures our imagination?" He answered his own question, explaining, "Those viewing the Derby on television somehow feel—if only for a moment—a part of the nostalgia of Old Kentucky. And those who attend the event in person sense they are witnessing history."[49]

Each person experiences the Derby in a different way. But the history, mythology, and imagery that have become associated with Kentucky over the course of more than two centuries still comprise an important part of what makes the Derby unique and attractive as a spectacle and as an event. It is Old Kentucky for which Derby fans feel an affinity. But what that is and what it means have varied drastically over the years. That evolutionary process is bound to continue as the meaning of Kentucky and the Derby continues to be reinvented by Derby fans and the journalists who cover the race. Despite an uncertain future for the sport of horse racing, Kentucky remains the capital of the American Thoroughbred industry, and its Derby is unquestionably America's greatest horse race. The bold predictions of the Derby's potential for longevity made in 1875 proved to be remarkably prescient. Today, Derby fans have every reason to be just as optimistic about its prospects in the twenty-first century.

Acknowledgments

Any acknowledgment of the many people who helped make this book possible must begin with Joanne Pope Melish, who inspired and encouraged me to pursue the study of history and has served as an advisor, mentor, sounding board, and editor. Without her support and belief in my capabilities as a writer and a scholar, this book would never have been attempted, let alone completed. Tracy Campbell read multiple early drafts of this book that were quite rough and gave constructive criticism that allowed me to learn from mistakes without losing focus or confidence. Meetings in his office were always a source of laughter, a valuable commodity in the occasionally-too-serious world of history. Ron Eller, Ellen Furlough, and Ron Formisano read early drafts and encouraged me to go further. Dennis Domer, Rhoda-Gale Pollack, Karl Raitz, and Maryjean Wall read later drafts and provided helpful feedback.

In the course of this long process, I have received cheerful assistance from a number of libraries and archives. The staff at the reference desk of the William T. Young Library at the University of Kentucky in Lexington indulged me and what must have seemed like a limitless appetite for all periodicals published in the month of May in the last 135 years. The staff and volunteers at the University of Kentucky Archives, the Louie B. Nunn Center for Oral History at the University of Kentucky, Ekstrom Library at the University of Louisville, the Kentucky Historical Society in Frankfort, and the Curt Teich Postcard Archives in the Lake County, Illinois, Discovery Museum were all very courteous, diligent, knowledgeable, and cooperative. Phyllis Rogers and Cathy Schenck at the Keeneland Library in Lexington, Kentucky, were especially obliging. Laura Sutton, Larry Malley, and Robbie Hare answered many questions and pointed me in the right direction in my initial exploration of the world of publishing. Tina Hagee, Carol O'Reilly, and their various assistants at the UK history department always had answers to my myriad questions.

Everyone at the University Press of Kentucky has been extremely friendly and accommodating. They have made this first book experience a pleasure. Anne Dean Watkins has been my guide as I have blindly made my way through the publishing forest for the first time. Along the way I have met (some in person, others via e-mail) some very helpful people at the University Press of Kentucky, including David Cobb, Pat Gonzales, Bailey Johnson, Cameron Ludwick, Ann Malcolm, Allison Webster, and Steve Wrinn. Robin DuBlanc asked pertinent questions in her capacity as editor and helped to disguise many of my limitations of grammar and diction.

I have been fortunate to be surrounded by an outstanding group of friends that has often had more confidence in my ability to see this project to fruition than I have. I am especially grateful to those, including Hanzly Albina, Zack Bray, Eric Buckley, Alex Bushel, Will Coffman, and Walt Robertson, who have indulged my periodic desire for long-winded conversations about horse racing's fascinating past and uncertain future. I would also like to give a corny but sincere nod to the hundreds of journalists who have covered the Derby over the years. While I could list my favorites, I learned as much from the bad ones as the good. The words of all the men and women who covered the Derby have provided me a window into the American past and have helped me to better appreciate the timeless nature of racetrack culture.

Throughout this process my entire family, especially my parents and my sister Kelsey, have been extraordinarily supportive even when they didn't necessarily understand what the hell I was doing. My gratitude for their encouragement cannot be measured. Finally, my wife, Maegan, has always been patient and understanding with the serious time commitment that this project has often required. There is no one with whom I would rather spend a Derby Day.

For each person who has the chance to witness a Kentucky Derby, the experience is both unique and shared. Similarly, the process of writing a book is both maddeningly isolating and inescapably collaborative. I am grateful to all who have facilitated this project—those who have been mentioned above and those who remain nameless. This rewarding experience would not have been possible without their contributions great and small, but all of this book's shortcomings are entirely my own.

Notes

Introduction

1. Legend has it that he won a coin flip with Sir Charles Bunbury to decide whose name the race would carry. The Derby Stakes is run at Epsom Downs over one and a half miles and is now internationally known as the Epsom (or English) Derby.

2. John Filson, *The Discovery, Settlement, and Present State of Kentucke* (New York: Corinth Books, 1962), originally published in 1784 in Wilmington, Delaware.

3. See Maryjean Wall, *How Kentucky Became Southern: A Tale of Outlaws, Horse Thieves, Gamblers and Breeders* (Lexington: University Press of Kentucky, 2010) for an explanation of why Kentucky became a national Thoroughbred center. The term *place* carries much more meaning than simply geographical location. The identity of a place (a city, state, region, nation, monument, or other site) is shaped both by its own physical characteristics, history, and so on, and the perspectives, values, and expectations of the person visiting, imagining, or referencing that site.

4. Boone was the subject of numerous biographical works in the nineteenth century, becoming one of the first pop culture heroes in the United States, and the archetypical frontiersman. He was lauded by Lord Byron in his epic poem *Don Juan,* and served as a model for James Fenimore Cooper's hero Natty Bumppo (Hawkeye) in the *Leatherstocking Tales.*

5. Given Boone's significant association with the history and iconography of Kentucky, it is ironic that he was buried in the state capital of Frankfort against his will. Boone had left specific instructions stating he did not wish to be buried in Kentucky because of continued disagreements with the state government. He had not set foot in Kentucky since 1799. He spent the final two decades of his life in Missouri, where he died and was originally buried in 1820. He was reinterred in the Bluegrass State in 1845 after the Kentucky state legislature appropriated funds at the request of a Frankfort cemetery to relocate Boone, with the permission of Boone's descendants. See John Mack Faragher, *The Life and Legend of an American Pioneer* (New York: Henry Holt, 1992), 356.

6. The fact that slaves in Kentucky were geographically closer to freedom in the North than slaves in the Lower South, and that Kentucky was home to two vocal abolitionists, Cassius M. Clay and John Fee, may also have contributed to this perception.

7. Harriet Beecher Stowe, *Uncle Tom's Cabin* (New York: Penguin Books, 1966), 21. The book was first published serially in 1851.

8. Vickie Mitchell, "Derby Anthem's Dark Roots," *Kentucky Derby Souvenir Magazine,* May 3, 2003, 66–68.

9. I use the term *myth* here and throughout this book not to signify untruth, but to refer to the kinds of legends and stories that become part of a cultural fabric without regard to whether they actually occurred.

1. Early Struggles and Foundations for Success

1. B. G. Bruce, "Derby Day," *Louisville Courier-Journal,* May 17, 1875.

2. "A Voice from Kentucky," *New York Times,* August 12, 1874, 4.

3. The racetrack was called Churchill Downs as early as 1883, and the name entered common parlance a few years later. Over the years the business entity that began as the Louisville Jockey Club and Driving Park Association would have numerous names under numerous ownership umbrellas, including the New Louisville Jockey Club, the Kentucky Jockey Club, and the American Turf Association. It would not officially be called Churchill Downs, Inc. (its current moniker) until well into the twentieth century. For simplicity's sake I use the name

Churchill Downs to describe both the racetrack and the various business entities that conducted race meets at the facility.

4. "Louisville Jockey Club Opens Meeting," *New York Times,* May 18, 1875, 5.

5. Nelson Dunstan, "Reflections," *Daily Racing Form,* May 3, 1952, 64.

6. "The Kentucky Derby," *New York Times,* May 9, 1886, 2.

7. *Louisville Courier-Journal,* May 14, 1886, in William S. Butt, ed., *They're Off: A Century of Kentucky Derby Coverage by the* Courier- Journal *and the* Louisville Times (Louisville: Courier-Journal and Louisville Times, 1975).

8. This was not the only time that Haggin threatened to take his horses and go home if he did not have his way. According to a July 17, 1890, *New York Times* article, Haggin pulled a similar stunt after a St. Louis racetrack official banned Haggin's jockey for impudence. Haggin threatened to remove his horses from the track immediately if he were not reinstated, and the track relented.

9. "A Cake Walk," *Louisville Commercial,* May 16, 1894.

10. "Brooklyn Handicap Horses," *New York Times,* February 24, 1894, 11.

11. See Wall, *How Kentucky Became Southern,* 180.

12. "A Very Poor Derby," *Kentucky Leader,* May 13, 1891; *New York Times,* May 14, 1891, 2.

13. "No More American Derby," *New York Times,* October 15, 1894, 1.

14. T. J. Jackson Lears, *Something for Nothing: Luck in America* (New York: Viking, 2003), 152–53.

15. *Louisville Courier-Journal,* September 2, 1894.

16. *Louisville Courier-Journal,* September 30, 1879.

17. *Louisville Courier-Journal,* April 23, 1899.

18. *Louisville Courier-Journal,* May 6, 1896.

19. *Louisville Courier-Journal,* February 4, 1895. The twin spires were designed by twenty-four-year-old draftsman Joseph Dominic Baldez, who was working for the Louisville firm D.X. Murphy & Brother. The new grandstand even had "toilet rooms."

20. "Colonel M. Lewis Clark a Suicide," *New York Times,* April 23, 1899, 13.

21. *Louisville Courier-Journal,* April 23, 1899.

22. Jim Bolus, *Kentucky Derby Stories* (Gretna, LA: Pelican, 1993), 68.

23. Recipients of the title have included Jimmy Buffet, Ronald Reagan, Hunter S. Thompson, Walt Disney, and "Colonel" Harland Sanders, the founder of Kentucky Fried Chicken. In the 1940s Indiana governor Ralph Gates was granted a colonelship in the days leading up to that year's Derby and decided to create "Sagamore of the Wabash" as an honorary title in his state, but somehow it lacked the majesty of Kentucky's version.

24. See "Old Kentucky's Last Stand," *New York Times*, May 14, 1927, 18; "Party Lines Waver in Kentucky Campaign," *New York Times*, November 6, 1927, N1.

25. In a statement to the *Louisville Courier-Journal*, leaders of the New Louisville Jockey Club claimed that the track never lost money. Winn stated that he and his partners saved the club from certain financial ruin. The answer lies somewhere in between. But given Winn's penchant for self-aggrandizing embellishment, it is likely that the situation was not nearly as dire as he would recall four decades later.

26. Matt J. Winn and Frank G. Menke, *Down the Stretch: The Story of Colonel Matt J. Winn, as Told to Frank G. Menke* (New York: Smith and Durrell, 1944), 1–2.

27. Samuel W. Thomas, *Churchill Downs: A Documentary History of America's Most Legendary Race Track* (Louisville: Kentucky Derby Museum, 1995), 110.

28. Joe H. Palmer, *This Was Racing* (Lexington, KY: Henry Clay, 1973), 75.

29. *Louisville Courier-Journal*, March 26, 1908; Winn and Menke, *Down the Stretch,* 72–73. There is some disagreement among racing historians and journalists over the number of machines that were in place for the 1908 race. Winn claims there were six in his autobiography. Other historians, including William H. P. Robertson (*The History of Thoroughbred Racing in America* [Englewood Cliffs, NJ: Prentice-Hall, 1964]), have the number at eleven. The precise number is not as significant as is the fact that the machines helped to save the Derby and racing in Louisville in general.

30. "Stone Street Wins Derby: Parimutuel Betting Machines Reinstated Satisfactorily at Louisville," *New York Times*, May 6, 1908, 8.

31. Lears, *Something for Nothing,* 195.

32. Robertson, *History of Thoroughbred Racing in America*, 214.

33. Bolus, *Kentucky Derby Stories*, 192.

34. Edward Hotaling, *The Great Black Jockeys: The Lives and Times of the Men Who Dominated America's First National Sport* (Rocklin, CA: Prima, 1999), 236.

35. *Louisville Courier-Journal*, May 17, 1884.

36. "The Colored Archer," *Louisville Courier-Journal*, May 15, 1890.

37. *Louisville Courier-Journal*, May 5, 1898.

38. *Louisville Courier-Journal*, April 30, 1901.

39. *Louisville Courier-Journal*, May 4, 1902.

40. *Louisville Courier-Journal*, May 3, 1903.

41. See Joe Drape, *Black Maestro: The Epic Life of an American Legend* (New York: HarperCollins, 2006); Edward Hotaling, *Wink: The Incredible Life and Epic Journey of Jimmy Winkfield* (Camden, ME: McGraw-Hill, 2004).

42. Hotaling, *The Great Black Jockeys*, 192.

43. *Baltimore Afro-American*, May 24, 1930.

44. Ibid.

45. "A Kentucky Pastoral," *New York Times*, December 7, 1878, 4.

46. Much of the violence in the region at that time can be attributed to the interaction between forces of modernization, including the invasion of northeastern industrialists, and traditional mountain society. At the heart of many of the mountain feuds was a competition for access to resources in the competitive commercial environment. See Ronald D. Eller, *Miners, Millhands, and Mountaineers: Industrialization of the Appalachian South, 1880–1930* (Knoxville: University of Tennessee Press, 1982). See also Altina Waller, *Feud: Hatfields, McCoys, and Social Change in Appalachia, 1860–1900* (Chapel Hill: University of North Carolina Press, 1988); John Ed Pearce, *Days of Darkness: The Feuds of Eastern Kentucky* (Lexington: University Press of Kentucky, 1994).

47. "A Tale of Savage Personal Warfare Unparalleled in the History of Civilized Communities," *New York Times*, July 3, 1904, 9–10.

48. "Breathitt County Again a Battlefield," *New York Times*, November 7, 1909, SM9.

49. "Breathitt County to Go," *New York Times*, June 18, 1909, 6.

50. See Tracy A. Campbell, *The Politics of Despair: Power and*

Resistance in the Tobacco Wars (Lexington: University Press of Kentucky, 1993).

51. James C. Klotter, *Kentucky: Portrait in Paradox, 1900–1950* (Frankfort: Kentucky Historical Society, 1996), 50.

2. The "Southern" Path to National Prominence

1. *Louisville Courier-Journal,* May 24, 1883. Since blacks were not allowed in the grandstand after the 1890s (until Churchill Downs integrated its facilities in the early 1960s), the variety of people in the free infield helped to create an environment of dangerous excitement at the Derby that contributed to the appeal of the event. *Louisville Commercial,* May 11, 1893, reported that the infield crowd included "all colors and nationalities."

2. "Condensed History of the Running of the Kentucky Derby," *Daily Racing Form,* April 2, 1912, 1.

3. "Bad Weather for Derby," *Kentucky New Era,* May 14, 1912, 1.

4. See Derek Birley, *Playing the Game: Sport and British Society, 1910–1945* (Manchester: Manchester University Press, 1995), 17.

5. "Old Rosebud Wins Kentucky Derby," *New York Times,* May 10, 1914, S2.

6. "Slow Track for Derby," *Daily Racing Form,* May 9, 1914, 1.

7. "Regret from End to End," *Daily Racing Form,* May 9, 1915, 1.

8. *Thoroughbred Record,* May 16, 1915.

9. *Thoroughbred Record,* May 4, 1918.

10. Many records indicate that Exterminator ran exactly one hundred times, but according to the *Binghampton Press,* September 26, 1945, one of those "races" was an uncontested exhibition that did not add to his win total and should not be counted as an actual start.

11. "Geldings to Be Barred," *Daily Racing Form,* August 7, 1918, 1.

12. Rothstein was also the inspiration for the character of Meyer Wolfsheim in F. Scott Fitzgerald's *The Great Gatsby.*

13. Percy Hammond, "Derby a Sacred Ceremonial for Kentucky Folks," *Chicago Tribune,* May 11, 1919. Henry Watterson was the editor of the *Louisville Courier-Journal* from 1868 to 1919. He was a former Confederate soldier and a leading advocate of a "New South" that would integrate itself into the national industrial economy.

14. *Thoroughbred Record,* May 17, 1919.

15. "Ral Parr's Paul Jones Leads Field of Seventeen Fleet Racers," *New York Times,* May 9, 1920, S1.

16. *Thoroughbred Record,* May 16, 1920.

17. "Cox Again Attacks Curris Publication," *New York Times,* October 29, 1920, 15.

18. *Thoroughbred Record,* May 10, 1919.

19. Henry L. Farrew, "Upset Bradley's Dope," *St. Petersburg Evening Independent,* May 18, 1928, 15.

20. *Time,* May 7, 1934.

21. "All on Bradley Farm Are Richer for Derby Victory," *New York Times,* May 11, 1921, 24.

22. *Louisville Courier-Journal,* May 8, 1921.

23. Henry McLemore, "Roman Soldier and Whiskolo Follow In," *Milwaukee Journal,* May 5, 1935, 13.

24. See Mitchell, "Derby Anthem's Dark Roots," 66–68.

25. In 1986, Carl Hines, the only black member of Kentucky's House of Representatives, presented a bill to change the lyrics from "'tis summer, the darkies are gay" to "'tis summer, the people are gay." The resolution passed, and today the modified lyrics are sung at the Derby.

26. *Time* reported on May 16, 1932, that a band had played Stephen Foster's "Suwannee River (Old Folks at Home)" during that year's Derby post parade. It seems most likely that the writer was confused because no other report of that occurrence has been found. In either case—a factual report or simple confusion—it demonstrates that much of the significance of "My Old Kentucky Home" lay in its connection to—and evocation of—the Old South.

27. *Thoroughbred Record,* May 20, 1922.

28. Ibid.

29. "Morvich Wins Kentucky Derby by Two Lengths," *New York Times,* May 14, 1922, 1.

30. Ibid.

31. Winn and Menke, *Down the Stretch,* 135.

32. Ibid., 178.

33. Louisville parks were segregated beginning in the 1920s, much later than in some southern cities.

34. George C. Wright, *Life behind a Veil: Blacks in Louisville, Kentucky, 1895–1930* (Baton Rouge: Louisiana State University Press, 1985), 76.

35. J. Winston Coleman Jr., *Lexington during the Civil War* (Lexington, KY: Henry Clay, 1968), 52.

36. See "A Dream Realized," *Louisville Courier-Journal*, August 2, 1883.

37. See Joseph F. Wall, *Henry Watterson, Reconstructed Rebel* (New York: Oxford University Press, 1956); C. Vann Woodward, *Origins of the New South, 1877–1913* (Baton Rouge: Louisiana State University Press, 1951); Henry Watterson, *Marse Henry: An Autobiography* (New York: George H. Doran, 1919).

38. "Going Down to Dixie Land," *New York Times*, September 13, 1894, 1.

39. Michael Veach, "Grand Army of the Republic at the Filson," *Filson News Magazine* 2, no. 3 (2002).

40. "Ready for the Grand Army Men," *New York Times*, September 9, 1895, 8.

41. "The G.A.R. Encampment," *New York Times*, June 21, 1882, 5.

42. See David Blight, *Race and Reunion: The Civil War in American Memory* (Cambridge, MA: Belknap Press of Harvard University Press, 2001).

43. "Amusements," *Nebraska State Journal*, December 20, 1894, 3.

44. Silas Bent, "My Old Kentucky Home: In June All the Exiles Are Invited to Return and Taste True Hospitality," *New York Times*, April 6, 1924.

45. Genevieve Forbes, "Crowd Goes Mad as Slim Black Beauty Races In," *Chicago Tribune*, May 18, 1924.

46. *Black Gold*, dir. Phil Karlson (Allied Artists Pictures, 1947).

47. J. E. Crown, *New Orleans States*, February 25, 1923, in Jim Bolus, *Derby Magic* (Gretna, LA: Pelican, 1997), 205.

48. Bolus, *Derby Magic*, 205.

49. Jim Bolus, *Run for the Roses: 100 Years at the Kentucky Derby* (New York: Hawthorne Books, 1974), 42. A WGN broadcast of the 1927 Derby included a "special program to lend atmosphere to the race" ("Devise New System of Broadcasting," *New York Times*, May 14, 1927, 24).

50. "Air Description of Race Given," *Louisville Courier-Journal*, May 20, 1928.

51. "WHAS Gives Race Details from Downs," *Louisville Courier-Journal*, May 17, 1925. By the late 1920s Derby results were published

in newspapers as far away as Austrailia: *Melbourne Argus,* May 16, 1927; *Sydney Mail,* June 6, 1928.

52. "Kentucky Derby Booked for WGN," *New York Times,* May 8, 1927.

53. *Thoroughbred Record,* May 20, 1925.

54. Gerold Griffin, "Negroes Offer Prayer for Rain," *Louisville Courier-Journal,* May 18, 1929.

3. Conflict at the Derby in the Great Depression

1. Harvey Woodruff, "Turf Classic Only a Gallop for Favorite," *Chicago Tribune,* May 13, 1922; Hugh Fullerton, "Greatest of Crowds Jams Churchill Downs for Derby," *Chicago Tribune,* May 20, 1923.

2. Henry R. Ilsley, "Bubbling Over Wins the Kentucky Derby by a 5-Length Margin," *New York Times,* May 16, 1926, S1.

3. Bryan Field, "Gallant Fox Takes Derby as Lord Derby and 60,000 Look On," *New York Times,* May 30, 1930, 1.

4. "Great Asset," *Blood-Horse,* May 23, 1931, 803.

5. *Louisville Courier-Journal,* May 17, 1931. Interestingly, within the article that fell beneath the headline "Throng at Race Is Orderly One: Police Fail to Receive Complaint for First Time in Forty-three Years" came the admission that three men, who were "known pickpocket men," were arrested that day. All were from out of town, and one was a "Negro." Thirty-three detectives had been placed in the clubhouse, around the betting sheds, and in the crowd.

6. *Louisville Courier-Journal,* May 17, 1931.

7. "Exams and the Derby," *Blood-Horse,* March 12, 1932, 433.

8. The winning colt was named after Jim Mooney, a Lexington grocer whose burgoo had achieved some substantial recognition.

9. Bryan Field, "50,000 to See Race at Churchill Downs," *New York Times,* May 7, 1932, 19.

10. Bryan Field, "Burgoo King Wins Kentucky Derby as 50,000 Look On," *New York Times,* May 8, 1932, S1.

11. *Louisville Courier-Journal,* May 6, 1934.

12. *Time,* May 14, 1934.

13. Dave Brown, "Human Tide Is Thrill at Derby Scene," *Louisville Courier-Journal,* May 6, 1934.

14. *Los Angeles Times,* May 5, 1935.

15. "Rain Spoils Parade of Finery at Derby," *Milwaukee Journal,* May 5, 1935.

16. *Pittsburgh Post-Gazette,* May 1, 1936.

17. "Derby Notes," *Blood-Horse,* May 11, 1935, 612.

18. *Louisville Courier-Journal,* May 4, 1932.

19. *Blood-Horse,* May 23, 1936.

20. Marion Porter, "Hotel Expands Facilities for Derby," *Louisville Courier-Journal,* May 6, 1937; Judy Marchman and Tom Hall, *Kentucky Derby Glasses Price Guide: A Comprehensive Guide to Collecting Kentucky Derby Mint Julep Glasses and Shot Glasses* (Lexington, KY: Eclipse, 1999).

21. Bryan Field, "Can't Wait Is Third," *New York Times,* May 8, 1938, 75.

22. "Louisville Flood Toll 90," *New York Times,* February 28, 1937, 26; "Louisville Flood Loss $52,575,741," *New York Times,* March 27, 1937, 30. See also Rick Bell, *The Great Flood of 1937: Rising Water, Soaring Spirits* (Louisville: Butler Books, 2007).

23. Bryan Field, "Gallant Fox Beats Whichone 4 Lengths in $81,340 Belmont," *New York Times,* June 8, 1930, 147.

24. The three tracks had recently been moved under a single ownership and management umbrella called the Kentucky Jockey Club. The group was headed by James Graham Brown, founder of Louisville's Brown Hotel, among his many other business interests. In 1925 Latonia Racecourse offered a $5,000 bonus to the winner of the Kentucky Derby if he could also win the Latonia Derby.

25. *St. Petersburg Times,* April 27, 1935.

26. Gerald Carson, *The Social History of Bourbon: An Unhurried Account of Our Star-Spangled American Drink* (Lexington: University Press of Kentucky, 1963), 60.

27. Joe Nickell, *The Kentucky Mint Julep* (Lexington: University Press of Kentucky, 2003), 67.

28. The Preakness and Belmont Stakes have their own traditional drinks, the "black-eyed Susan" and the "Belmont breeze," respectively, though neither begins to approach the sales figures of the mint julep at Churchill Downs on Derby weekend.

29. J. Soule Smith, *The Mint Julep: The Very Dream of Drinks from the Old Receipt of Soule Smith down in Lexington, Ky.* (Lexington, KY: Gravesend, 1949).

30. *Thoroughbred Record,* May 17, 1919.

31. *Milwaukee Journal,* May 9, 1920.

32. *Louisville Times,* May 12, 1923, quoted in Butt, *They're Off.*

33. *Chicago Tribune,* May 2, 1935. The ad also ran in other papers, including the *Louisville Courier-Journal* and the *Washington Post,* during the week leading up to the Derby.

34. *Time,* May 14, 1934.

35. R. L. Duffus, "Kentucky Pays a Debt to Daniel Boone," *New York Times,* September 2, 1934, SM7.

36. J. W. Williamson, *Hillbillyland: What the Movies Did to the Mountains and What the Mountains Did to the Movies* (Chapel Hill: University of North Carolina Press, 1995); Anthony Harkins, *Hillbilly: A Cultural History of an American Icon* (New York: Oxford University Press, 2004), 75–78.

37. See Harkins, *Hillbilly,* 103–40.

38. Webb's *Mountain Boys* drawings often appeared next to essays by Kentucky author Jesse Stuart in *Esquire* magazine. Stuart described mountaineers in his native state as living in harmony with nature, lacking in formal education, possessing a propensity for violence, and existing in isolation from modern civilization. The subjects of Stuart's essays and Webb's cartoons were capable of weathering any storm and could be seen as models for Americans trying to endure economic and social upheaval.

39. Contradictory identities and stereotypes need these dualistic sets of imagery to survive. If only one set were available, it would be too easy to disprove popular perceptions about people or places. Also, changing needs and wants of societies often render one set of stereotypical assumptions unattractive. The longevity of Kentucky's special place within American culture can be attributed to the fact that, regardless of whether the colonel or the hillbilly image is dominant during a given era, the "recessive" flip side is always present, ready to meet the ever-changing tastes and needs of Americans and Derby fans.

40. James Gosle, "Paddock Show Before Race Offers a Behind-Scenes Thrill," *Louisville Courier-Journal,* May 7, 1939.

4. An American Institution

1. "Owner Overjoyed by Derby Triumph," *New York Times,* May 5, 1940, 94.

2. Milky Way Stables was by no means a small racing operation.

In fact, it was one of the largest and most successful in America at the time. But in the spring of 1940, Milky Way had been unable to achieve any measure of success at the Derby, Gallahadion had an unspectacular race record, and Bimelech was a potential superhorse. These elements combined to allow Milky Way and Gallahadion to qualify as underdogs on that day.

3. *Louisville Courier-Journal,* May 3, 1941.

4. *Louisville Courier-Journal,* April 30, 1941.

5. Winn and Menke, *Down the Stretch,* 279.

6. "The Kentucky Derby Runs," *Blood-Horse,* February 20, 1943, 278.

7. Winn and Menke, *Down the Stretch,* 279.

8. In 1951 Count Fleet's son Count Turf would become the first third-generation Derby winner, joining his sire Count Fleet and grand-sire Reigh Count on the Derby champions list.

9. "Count Fleet 1-2 Favorite among Twelve Entries in 'Street Car' Derby," *New York Times,* May 1, 1943, 19; Matt Winn's memoirs place the attendance at around sixty-five thousand (Winn and Menke, *Down the Stretch,* 280).

10. "War Derby," *Blood-Horse,* May 8, 1943, 610.

11. Winn and Menke, *Down the Stretch,* 278.

12. "Stir Up Still Rated as 'the Horse to Beat' in Kentucky Derby," *New York Times,* May 5, 1944, 23.

13. "Derby Fans Arrive at 4 A.M.," *New York Times,* May 7, 1944, 54; "GI Joes in Naples Wager on the Derby," *New York Times,* May 7, 1944, S1.

14. *Louisville Courier-Journal,* May 7, 1944.

15. This was a process that worked to the advantage of major league baseball as well. After the attack on Pearl Harbor, President Franklin Roosevelt issued a "green light" for baseball to continue during the war at the request of major league team owners, under the theory that it was in the nation's best interest. Wartime teams were made up of those not fit for military service, including the old, young, and crippled. Despite the reduced quality of play on the field, wartime baseball provided fans a sense of continuity in a world that had dramatically changed. Games took on a patriotic feel as the "Star-Spangled Banner" was played before every game, ticket prices were reduced, servicemen were often let in ballparks for free, and teams regularly conducted

drives to sell war bonds as well as to collect blood, rubber, paper, aluminum, and other materials needed for the war effort. Baseball's survival during World War II demonstrated that it was an important part of American culture before the war. Its survival also helped to reinforce that status. See William Marshall, *Baseball's Pivotal Era, 1945–1951* (Lexington: University Press of Kentucky, 1999), 6–7.

16. Robertson, *History of Thoroughbred Racing in America*, 364. The ban was lifted on V-E Day, May 8, 1945, and racing resumed three days later.

17. Ibid., 365. "Handle" refers to the gross money wagered at a racetrack.

18. "65,000 Jam Downs," *New York Times,* June 10, 1945, S1.

19. Lizabeth Cohen, *A Consumers' Republic: The Politics of Mass Consumption in Postwar America* (New York: Vintage Books, 2003).

20. *Louisville Courier-Journal,* May 4, 1902.

21. *Time,* January 22, 1945.

22. *Blood-Horse,* May 4, 1946.

23. *Louisville Courier-Journal,* May 7, 1950; "Derby Fans Hear 4 Bands," *Chicago Tribune,* May 4, 1952.

24. *Southern Fried Rabbit* (Warner Bros., 1953).

25. "Derby Festival Parade," *Louisville Courier-Journal,* May 6, 1962.

26. *Louisville Times,* May 1, 1959.

27. Don Freeman, "Holiday Spirit Prevails," *Louisville Courier-Journal,* May 3, 1957.

28. The official Web site of the Kentucky Derby Festival, http://www.kdf.org., March 1, 2009. In 1957 festival organizers also added the "They're off Luncheon" to the festivities. By the late 1960s, organizers regularly invited black entertainers and athletes to host the event, including actor James Earl Jones, baseball legend Hank Aaron, and basketball star Magic Johnson. As a result, the connection between the Derby and the South now includes an element of black triumph instead of (or in addition to) black subservience.

29. Hank Messick, "Tradition as Thick as the Steaks as Colonels Hold Their 24th Dinner: Singing Waiters Bring in Juleps," *Louisville Courier-Journal,* May 4, 1957.

30. John Eisenberg, *Native Dancer: The Grey Ghost, Hero of a Golden Age* (New York: Warner Books, 2003), 93.

31. Ann Hagedorn Aurbach, *Wild Ride: The Rise and Tragic Fall of Calumet Farm, Inc., America's Premier Racing Dynasty* (New York: Henry Holt, 1994), 57.

32. Ibid., 10; generally speaking, the "breeder" of a horse is the person or persons who owned its mother at the time the horse was born.

33. Citation's jockey, Eddie Arcaro, was the subject of a cover story in *Time* magazine the week after his Derby victory.

34. The Standardbred is a breed of horse developed in North America that is capable of trotting and "pacing" at high speeds while in harness. The name refers to the original requirement that a horse be able to meet the "standard" time of two and a half minutes for a mile in a trot. In Standardbred races the horses pull a "driver" in a sulky rather than being ridden by a jockey as in Thoroughbred races.

35. Aurbach, *Wild Ride,* 36.

36. "Devil Red and Plain Ben," *Time,* May 30, 1949; Margaret Glass, *The Calumet Story* (Lexington, KY: Calumet Farm, 1979), 18.

37. Alex Bower, "The 78th Kentucky Derby," *Blood-Horse,* May 10, 1952, 880.

38. James Roach, "8-1 Shot Triumphs," *New York Times,* May 5, 1957, 217.

39. *Time,* May 27, 1957.

40. Roach, "8-1 Shot Triumphs," 217. Bold Ruler would have a greater influence on the Derby as a stallion. The family trees of Triple Crown champions Secretariat and Seattle Slew both include Bold Ruler.

41. The Hall of Fame horses were Gallant Man, Round Table, and Bold Ruler.

42. James Roach, "Hampden Is Third," *New York Times,* May 5, 1946, S1; Eva Jolene Boyd, *Assault: Thoroughbred Legends* (Lexington, KY: Eclipse, 2004), 70, 72.

43. Boyd, *Assault,* 84.

44. "Two-Race $195,520 Caps Assault Rush," *New York Times,* May 13, 1946, 38.

45. See Cohen, *A Consumers' Republic,* 6–15.

46. This was the second third-generation winner of the Derby, the first trio being Reigh Count (1928), Count Fleet (1943), and Count Turf (1951).

47. John Steinbeck, *Louisville Courier-Journal,* May 5, 1956.

48. William Faulkner, "Kentucky: May: Saturday," *Sports Illustrated,* May 16, 1955, 22.

49. Ibid.

50. "Air Description of Race Given," *Louisville Courier-Journal,* May 20, 1928.

51. Arthur Daley, "The Passing of a Legend," *New York Times,* October 19, 1949, 42.

52. Winn and Menke, *Down the Stretch,* 104, 249–56. Winn also spent significant time at Chicago's Drake Hotel.

53. Arthur Daley, "Disclosing a Secret," *New York Times,* June 10, 1948, 35.

54. *Time,* May 10, 1937.

55. "Derby on Live TV for the First Time," *New York Times,* May 4, 1952, S4. There had been limited national television coverage on a delayed basis the two previous years. This was the first live national broadcast.

56. The figure grew to 30 million by 1955, according to *Louisville Times,* May 7, 1955.

57. Eisenberg, *Native Dancer,* 149. This is an impressive percentage despite the fact that there were significantly fewer options for television viewers, and fewer televisions, in the 1950s than today.

58. Ibid., x.

59. Ibid.

60. *Time,* May 31, 1954. Native Dancer appeared on the cover of this issue.

61. Arthur Daley, "A Shattered Romance," *New York Times,* May 4, 1953.

62. *Time,* March 17, 1958.

63. Whitney Tower, "The Hobo and the Gent," *Sports Illustrated,* April 28, 1958, 8.

64. "The Fizzle of a Legend," *Time,* May 12, 1958.

65. Frank Deford, "The Sun Shines Bright," *Sports Illustrated,* April 29, 1974, 86.

66. In some cases, Derby winners are internationally recognized. According to the manufacturer's Web site, Tim Tam, "Australia's favourite chocolate biscuit," is named after Calumet's Derby-winning colt.

5. A Stage for Social Protest and a Site of National Healing

1. James S. Tunnell, "Madras Coasts Home in the Infield Derby," *Louisville Courier-Journal*, May 2, 1965.

2. David Gordon, "Shades of Huck Finn!" *Chicago Tribune*, May 1, 1963.

3. Eisenberg, *Native Dancer*, 132. He is in good company. Broadcasting legend Mel Allen once made the same mistake on the air.

4. *Louisville Times*, May 7, 1966.

5. Arthur Daley, "A Taste of Mint Julep in Kentucky," *New York Times*, May 4, 1966, 56.

6. David Alexander, "The Post Parade," *Thoroughbred Record*, May 14, 1966, 1254.

7. "A Tough Act to Follow," *Thoroughbred Record*, May 11, 1974, 1202. The anonymous commentator's choice of language was a reference to John Olin, that year's Derby-winning owner, who declared after the race, "There were just too damned many [horses]."

8. Deford, "The Sun Shines Bright."

9. Steve Cady, "Derby Week: When the South Rises," *New York Times*, April 25, 1976, 163.

10. Sir Peter Teazle, "Sour Juleps," *Thoroughbred Record*, May 16, 1979. Sir Peter Teazle was the name of the horse who in 1787 won the English Derby in his first start for his owner, the twelfth Earl of Derby.

11. W. B. Park, "When the Sun Shines Bright," *Sports Illustrated*, May 1, 1972, 37.

12. Ibid., 37–38.

13. Kent Hollingsworth, "What's Going on Here," *Blood-Horse*, May 12, 1975, 1837.

14. *Louisville Courier-Journal*, May 14, 1911.

15. Hunter S. Thompson, "The Kentucky Derby Is Decadent and Depraved," in *The Great Shark Hunt: Strange Tales from a Strange Time (Gonzo Papers, vol. 1)* (New York: Simon and Schuster, 2003).

16. Ibid.

17. Howard Fineman and Jim Adams, "Beer-Drinking, Socializing Are Favored Sports," *Louisville Courier-Journal*, May 8, 1977, 11.

18. "Only One Horse Could Wear the Roses, but the Derby's Real

Winners Were 130,564 People," *Louisville Courier-Journal*, May 7, 1972, B1.

19. "Jockeys Won't Swerve to Miss Demonstrators," *Louisville Times*, May 3, 1967.

20. "Five Youths Dash in Front of Horses during Race," *Louisville Courier-Journal*, May 3, 1967, B1.

21. "Remains of Isaac Murphy Are Placed in New Grave," *Daily Racing Form*, May 5, 1967, 3.

22. David Alexander, "Delayed Honors," *Thoroughbred Record*, May 6, 1967, 1176.

23. "Traditional Security Planned for Derby Day," *Louisville Courier-Journal*, May 3, 1967, A1.

24. *Louisville Times*, May 2, 1967.

25. Douglas Robinson, "Louisville Is Shocked at the Canceling of Parade," *New York Times*, May 3, 1967, 32.

26. "Louisville Mayor Requests Nat. Guard, State Police," *Daily Racing Form*, May 3, 1967, 7.

27. Douglas Robinson, "Protest at Derby Is Reported Off," *New York Times*, May 6, 1967, 19.

28. James E. Bassett III and Bill Mooney, *Keeneland's "Ted" Bassett: My Life* (Lexington: University Press of Kentucky, 2009), 118.

29. "Jockeys Won't Swerve to Miss Demonstrators."

30. Douglas Robinson, "Dr. King Presses Louisville Fight," *New York Times*, May 4, 1967, 30.

31. Bassett and Mooney, *Keeneland's "Ted" Bassett*, 118.

32. Gerald Henry, "Crowd Has Good Time Despite Drizzle," *Louisville Courier-Journal*, May 7, 1967, A4.

33. Ibid.

34. *Louisville Times*, May 6, 1967.

35. It was the second Derby victory for Darby Dan Farm, which was owned by John W. Galbraith, who was born in Derby, Ohio, and won three World Series as the owner of the Pittsburgh Pirates.

36. Jobie Arnold, "Notes from among the Roses," *Thoroughbred Record*, May 11, 1968, 1233.

37. *Thoroughbred Record*, May 4, 1968.

38. Bob Hohler, "Thorns and Roses," *Boston Globe*, May 2, 2008.

39. *Thoroughbred Record*, May 18, 1968. See also Louie B. Nunn Interview, May 14, 1998, 48, Louie B. Nunn Oral History Project,

980H42 LBN 10, Louie B. Nunn Center for Oral History, University of Kentucky Special Collections, Collections and Digital Programs, Lexington. Nunn recalls telling Kentucky Racing Commission chairman George Eggers, "Call a press conference as fast as you can, tell everything that you know about it, implicate everybody and everybody that's involved that you are aware of, and call for a complete and thorough investigation of everything." Concerned about possible political repercussions over the scandal, Nunn told his children, who had correctly predicted the order of finish at the Derby, "Don't be bragging about having the winners at the Derby. They were drugged. Somebody may think [chuckle] your father knew about it" (49).

40. William Robertson, "Pick Up the Pieces, and Hold Up Your Head," *Thoroughbred Record,* May 18, 1968, 1296.

41. Ibid.

42. Hohler, "Thorns and Roses."

43. See Curt Sampson, *The Lost Masters: Grace and Disgrace in '68* (New York: Atria Books, 2005).

44. Whitney Tower, "It Was a Bitter Pill," *Sports Illustrated,* May 20, 1968.

45. Robertson, "Pick Up the Pieces."

46. "Rehearsal for Busing," *Time,* September 8, 1975; "Busing and Strikes," *Time,* September 15, 1975.

47. *Chicago Tribune,* May 2, 1976.

48. Whitney Tower, "Missing Data Not Available," *Sports Illustrated,* May 10, 1971, 20–21.

49. Whitney Tower, "History in the Making," *Sports Illustrated,* June 18, 1973, 16.

50. Frank Deford, "Adieu, Adieu, Kind Friends," *Sports Illustrated,* November 5, 1973, 28.

51. Arnold Kirkpatrick, "Secretariat," *Thoroughbred Record,* June 16, 1973, 1439.

52. M. A. Simmons, "A Tradition Enters Its Second Century," *Louisville Times,* May 2, 1975.

53. Kent Hollingsworth, "What's Going On Here," *Blood-Horse,* May 14, 1973, 1659.

54. Deford, "The Sun Shines Bright," 80.

55. Joe Nichols, "Kentucky Derby: A Rousing Event!" *New York*

Times, May 5, 1974, S2. While longevity can be an indication of a sporting event's success, popularity, and cultural relevance, the longevity of few events is publicized like that of the Derby. For example, even diehard baseball fans would have a difficult time guessing how many World Series have been played. The Super Bowl is a notable exception, though the roman numerals that purport to distinguish each subsequent edition of the game became difficult to decipher for non-"Romaphiles" after the third Super Bowl.

56. Haden Kirkpatrick, "A Significance Far More Important than the Mere Venerability," *Thoroughbred Record*, April 27, 1974, 1068.

57. Steve Cady, "All Eyes Turn to Kentucky on Saturday," *New York Times*, April 28, 1974, 241.

58. Deford, "The Sun Shines Bright," 82.

59. Joseph Durso, "Princess Margaret Adds Royal Flair to Kentucky Derby Centennial Party," *New York Times*, May 5, 1974, 53.

60. "Flock Battles the Elements," *Louisville Courier-Journal*, May 7, 1961, 9.

61. Whitney Tower, "Two Take Dead Aim at Candy," *Sports Illustrated*, May 6, 1963, 21.

62. Robert G. Trautman, "Color—It Abounds at the Downs," *Louisville Courier-Journal*, May 2, 1965, 36.

63. Cady, "Derby Week: When the South Rises," 163.

64. Bill Peterson, "People Watching 2nd Only to Sport of Kings at Derby," *Louisville Courier-Journal*, May 4, 1969, A2.

65. *Blood-Horse*, May 10, 1969.

66. Louie B. Nunn Interview, May 14, 1998, 78.

67. James S. Tunnel, "Nixon Mixes Politics with a Visit to Derby," *Louisville Courier-Journal*, May 4, 1969.

68. Terry Frei, *Horns, Hogs, and Nixon Coming: Texas vs. Arkansas in Dixie's Last Stand* (New York: Simon and Schuster, 2002).

69. *Louisville Courier-Journal*, May 4, 1978.

70. *Louisville Times*, May 3, 1974.

71. Bill Doolittle, *The Kentucky Derby: The Run for the Roses* (Del Mar, CA: Tehabi Books, 1998), 53.

72. Clarence L. Matthews, "Few Blacks Join in Derby Festivities," *Louisville Times*, May 3, 1971.

6. Globalization and the American Dream

1. John C. Long, "Governor Salutes Harland Sanders at Colonels' Fete," *Louisville Courier-Journal,* May 2, 1981, B4.

2. Eve Hutcherson and Milton C. Toby, "Derby Notes," *Blood-Horse,* May 10, 1980, 2532.

3. David Fleischaker, "Derbying," *Louisville Courier-Journal,* May 2, 1985, A11.

4. Kevin Nance, "Whitney Scene 'Fabulous,' Leach Pronounces," *Lexington Herald-Leader,* May 5, 1990, C1.

5. Rick Bozich, "Foreign Intrigue Comes to Churchill," *Louisville Courier-Journal,* May 5, 1995.

6. William Orme Jr., "Far From Bluegrass, Dubai Runs Stealthily for the Roses," *New York Times,* April 19, 1999, A1.

7. Jason Levin, *From the Desert to the Derby: The Ruling Family of Dubai's Billion-Dollar Quest to Win America's Greatest Horse Race* (New York: Daily Racing Form Press, 2002), 18.

8. Dave Koerner, "Radical Sheikh: Godolphin Follows Own Path," *Louisville Courier-Journal,* May 5, 2000, F11.

9. Joseph Durso, "In a Crowed Field, Fusaichi Pegasus Stands Out," *New York Times,* May 6, 2000, D2.

10. Joseph Durso, "Fusaichi Pegasus Ends Favorites' Drought," *New York Times,* May 7, 2000, SP1.

11. Eric Prideaux, "Japan Welcomes First-Time Derby Win by Japanese-Owned Horse," *London Independent,* May 8, 2000.

12. William C. Rhoden, "Winning Formula? This Year It Was Money," *New York Times,* May 5, 2002, G7.

13. "Baffert's a Genius, Says War Emblem's Owner," *Waikato (New Zealand) Times,* May 6, 2002, 16.

14. Steve Haskin, *Horse Racing's Holy Grail: The Epic Quest for the Kentucky Derby* (Lexington, KY: Eclipse, 2002), 40.

15. Levin, *From the Desert to the Derby,* 91.

16. Tim Layden, "Triple Threat," *Sports Illustrated,* May 27, 2002.

17. Levin, *From the Desert to the Derby,* 136.

18. Daniel Roth, "The Sheikh Who Would Be King of Horse Racing," *Conde Nast Portfolio,* April 16, 2007.

19. The Derby field is limited to twenty starters, with preference given to the horses with the highest amount of graded stakes earnings

in their careers. This puts European horses at a disadvantage because their racing season starts later than in the United States.

20. Janet Patton, "Derby Adding Foreign Flavor," *Lexington Herald-Leader,* September 18, 2008, B1.

21. Toby Keith, "Courtesy of the Red, White, and Blue (The Angry American)," *Unleashed* (DreamWorks Nashville, 2002).

22. Laura Hillenbrand, *Seabiscuit: An American Legend* (New York: Random House, 2001).

23. Tim Layden, "Smart Money," *Sports Illustrated,* May 10, 2004.

24. See Steven A. Reiss, "Sport and the American Dream," *Journal of Social History* 14, no. 2 (1980): 298, in which he describes the connection between the idea of social mobility in American society and American athletics. For a historical overview of the idea of the "American Dream," see Jim Cullen, *The American Dream: A Short History of an Idea That Shaped a Nation* (New York: Oxford University Press, 2003).

25. Dick Young, quoted in "The Press," *Louisville Courier-Journal,* May 4, 1980, 7.

26. Dave Anderson, "Four Men on a Filly at the Kentucky Derby," *New York Times,* May 8, 1988, S6.

27. Ibid. In 2008 the on-track death of the filly Eight Belles immediately after she finished second to Big Brown was widely covered by national media. Some looking for an explanation for her death felt that the filly should not have been competing against males.

28. Jay Hovdey, *Whittingham: The Story of a Thoroughbred Racing Legend* (Lexington, KY: Blood-Horse, 1993), 164.

29. Michael Goodwin, "TV Sports: On Target with Ferdinand," *New York Times,* May 5, 1986, C7.

30. See William Nack, "Bound for Glory," *Sports Illustrated,* May 14, 1990, 20–27.

31. Jerry Bailey and Tom Pedulla, *Against the Odds: Riding for My Life* (New York: G. P. Putnam's Sons, 2005), 132.

32. George Vecsey, "A Popular Victory by Old Guard," *New York Times,* May 2, 1993.

33. Bob Baffert and Steve Haskin, *Baffert: Dirt Road to the Derby* (Lexington, KY: Blood-Horse, 1999), 18–19.

34. Jay Privman, "Baffert Makes Good on Second Chance," *New York Times,* May 4, 1997, S4.

35. Ibid. Baffert, Lukas, and Nick Zito constituted a training triumvirate in the 1990s. One or another won seven of the ten Derbies run in that decade.

36. Maryjean Wall, "Quiet but Quick," *Lexington Herald-Leader,* May 3, 1998; William Nack, "Coming up Roses: Jockey Kent Desormeaux Capped a Comeback, and Long Shot Real Quiet Made a Lot of Noise with a Victory in the Kentucky Derby," *Sports Illustrated,* May 11, 1998.

37. Maryjean Wall, "Charismagic: 30-1 Shot Gives Trainer Lukas His Fourth Derby Victory," *Lexington Herald-Leader,* May 2, 1999, AA1.

38. Joe Drape, *The Race for the Triple Crown: Horses, High Stakes, and Eternal Hope* (New York: Grove, 2001), 84.

39. William Nack, "A Sunday Stroll," *Sports Illustrated,* May 15, 1989, 23–24.

40. A longtime horse owner and racing enthusiast, the queen had often visited Kentucky horse farms in the past but had never been to Kentucky's signature event.

41. Rick Maese, "Borel a Face for Horse Racing," *South Florida Sun Sentinel,* May 17, 2007, 1C.

42. Malcolm C. Knox, "Borel Inducted into Shrine," *Kentucky Post,* May 24, 2007, C8; Jennie Rees, "Street Sense Beats Long-Term Trends," *Seattle Times,* May 6, 2007, C1.

43. In 2010 Borel would add an unprecedented third win in four years to his impressive Derby résumé aboard WinStar Farm's Supersaver. The win also marked the first Derby score for trainer Todd Pletcher, one of the world's top trainers, who for years suffered a well-documented losing streak at the Derby. The following year top jockey John Velasquez won the Derby for the first time. He had endured a stretch of three straight years in which his Derby horses (each a legitimate contender) were scratched days before the race due to injury or illness. Fans and journalists alike were drawn to this latest version of "redemption" at the Derby.

44. Alicia Wincze, "Rail Bird," *Lexington Herald Leader,* May 3, 2009, AA1.

45. Ed Gray, "135th Kentucky Derby Racing Beat," *Boston Herald,* May 3, 2009, 619.

46. Paul Shockley, "Ex–Grand Junction Resident Eyes Preakness

Win on Heels of Kentucky Derby," *Grand Junction (CO) Daily Sentinel,* May 14, 2009, A1.

47. Barbaro's ashes are buried beneath the statue.

48. Lewis Lazare, "Finger-lickin' Deal for Yum!" *Chicago Sun-Times,* February 6, 2006, 61.

49. Walter Cronkite, introduction to Doolittle, *The Kentucky Derby,* 19–20.

Selected Bibliography

Anderson, James C. *Historic Photos of Louisville*. Nashville: Turner, 2006.

Arcaro, Eddie, and Jack O'Hara. *I Ride to Win*. New York: Greenburg, 1951.

Aron, Stephen. *How the West Was Lost: The Transformation of Kentucky from Daniel Boone to Henry Clay*. Baltimore: Johns Hopkins University Press, 1996.

Ashworth, G. J., and J. E. Tunbridge. *The Tourist-Historic City*. London: Belhaven, 1990.

Aurbach, Ann Hagedorn. *Wild Ride: The Rise and Tragic Fall of Calumet Farm, Inc., America's Premiere Racing Dynasty*. New York: Henry Holt, 1994.

Austin, William W. *"Susanna," "Jeanie," and "The Old Folks at Home": The Songs of Stephen C. Foster from His Time to Ours*. New York: Macmillan, 1975.

Baffert, Bob, and Steve Haskin. *Baffert: Dirt Road to the Derby*. Lexington, KY: Blood-Horse, 1999.

Bailey, Jerry, and Tom Pedulla. *Against the Odds: Riding for My Life*. New York: G. P. Putnam's Sons, 2005.

Bakeless, John. *Daniel Boone*. Harrisburg, PA: Stackpole, 1965.

Bassett, James E., III, and Bill Mooney. *Keeneland's "Ted" Bassett: My Life*. Lexington: University Press of Kentucky, 2009.

Bell, Rick. *The Great Flood of 1937: Rising Water, Soaring Spirits*. Louisville: Butler Books, 2007.

Blight, David. *Race and Reunion: The Civil War in American Memory.* Cambridge, MA: Belknap Press of Harvard University Press, 2001.

Blood-Horse Publications. *Racing's Top 100 Moments.* Lexington, KY: Blood-Horse, 2006.

Bolus, Jim. *Derby Dreams.* Gretna, LA: Pelican, 1996.

———. *Derby Fever.* Gretna, LA: Pelican, 1995.

———. *Derby Magic.* Gretna, LA: Pelican, 1997.

———. *Kentucky Derby Stories.* Gretna, LA: Pelican, 1993.

———. *Remembering the Derby.* Gretna, LA: Pelican, 1994.

———. *Run for the Roses: 100 Years at the Kentucky Derby.* New York: Hawthorne Books, 1974.

Bottorff, William. *James Lane Allen.* New York: Twayne, 1964.

Bowen, Edward L. *At the Wire: Horse Racing's Greatest Moments.* Lexington, KY: Eclipse, 2001.

———. *Bold Ruler.* Lexington, KY: Eclipse, 2005.

———. *The Jockey Club's Illustrated History of Thoroughbred Racing in America.* Boston: Bullfinch, 1994.

———. *Man o' War.* Lexington, KY: Eclipse, 2000.

———. *Nashua.* Lexington, KY: Eclipse, 2003.

———. *War Admiral.* Lexington, KY: Eclipse, 2002.

Bowen, Edward L., et al. *10 Best Kentucky Derbies.* Lexington, KY: Eclipse, 2005.

Boyd, Eva Jolene. *Assault: Thoroughbred Legends.* Lexington, KY: Eclipse, 2004.

———. *Exterminator: Horse Racing's Beloved "Old Bones."* Lexington, KY: Eclipse, 2002.

Broadhead, Fred C. *Here Comes Whirlaway!* Manhattan, KS: Sunflower University Press, 1995.

Brodowsky, Pamela K., and Tom Philbin. *Two Minutes to Glory: The Official History of the Kentucky Derby, in Cooperation with Churchill Downs.* New York: Collins, 2007.

Buchanan, Lamont. *The Kentucky Derby Story.* New York: E. P. Dutton, 1953.

Butler, Carol, and Bill Butler, eds. *Kentucky Derby Festival: Fifty Years of Fun.* Louisville: Butler Books, 2004.

Butt, William S., ed. *They're Off: A Century of Kentucky Derby Coverage by the* Courier-Journal *and the* Louisville Times. Louisville: Courier Journal and Louisville Times, 1975.

Cain, Glenye. *The Home Run Horse: Inside America's Billion-Dollar Racehorse Industry and the High-Stakes Dreams That Fuel It.* New York: Daily Racing Form, 2004.

Campbell, Edward D. C. *The Celluloid South: Hollywood and the Southern Myth.* Knoxville: University of Tennessee Press, 1981.

Campbell, John C. *The Southern Highlander and His Homeland.* New York: Russell Sage Foundation, 1921.

Campbell, Tracy A. *Politics of Despair: Power and Resistance in the Tobacco Wars.* Lexington: University Press of Kentucky, 1993.

Capps, Timothy T. *Affirmed and Alydar.* Lexington, KY: Eclipse, 2002.

———. *Secretariat.* Lexington, KY: Eclipse, 2007.

———. *Spectacular Bid.* Lexington, KY: Eclipse, 2001.

Carson, Gerald. *The Social History of Bourbon: An Unhurried Account of Our Star-Spangled American Drink.* Lexington: University Press of Kentucky, 1963.

Case, Carole. *The Right Blood: America's Aristocrats in Thoroughbred Racing.* New Brunswick, NJ: Rutgers University Press, 2001.

Cherrington, Ernest Hurst. *History of the Anti-saloon League.* Waterville, OH: American Issue, 1913.

Chew, Peter. *The Kentucky Derby: The First 100 Years.* Boston: Houghton Mifflin, 1974.

Clancy, Sean. *Barbaro: The Horse Who Captured America's Heart.* Lexington, KY: Eclipse, 2007.

Clark, Thomas D. *Kentucky: Land of Contrast.* New York: Harper and Row, 1968.

Cohen, Lizabeth. *A Consumers' Republic: The Politics of Mass Consumption in Postwar America.* New York: Vintage Books, 2003.

Coleman, J. Winston, Jr. *Famous Kentucky Duels: The Story of the Code of Honor in the Bluegrass State.* Frankfort, KY: Roberts, 1953.

———. *Historic Kentucky.* Lexington, KY: Henry Clay, 1967.

———. *Lexington during the Civil War.* Lexington, KY: Henry Clay, 1968.

Connelly, Emma M. *The Story of Kentucky.* Boston: D. Lothrop, 1890.

Cooper, Page, and Roger L. Treat. *Man o' War.* Yardley, PA: Westholme, 2004.

Coulter, E. Merton. *The Civil War and Readjustment in Kentucky.* Chapel Hill: University of North Carolina Press, 1926.

Crowgey, Henry G. *Kentucky Bourbon: The Early Years of Whiskey Making.* Lexington: University Press of Kentucky, 1971.

Cullen, Jim. *The American Dream: A Short History of an Idea That Shaped a Nation.* New York: Oxford University Press, 2003.

Dean, John Wesley. *Warren G. Harding.* New York: Macmillan, 2004.

DeBord, Guy. *Society of Spectacle.* New York: Zone Books, 1994.

Degler, Carl. *Place over Time: The Continuity of Southern Distinctiveness.* Baton Rouge: Louisiana State University Press, 1977.

Devito, Carlo. *D. Wayne: The High-Rolling and Fast Times of America's Premiere Horse Trainer.* Chicago: Contemporary Books, 2002.

Doolittle, Bill. *The Kentucky Derby: The Run for the Roses.* Del Mar, CA: Tehabi Books, 1998.

Drager, Marvin. *The Most Glorious Crown.* New York: Winchester, 1975.

Drape, Joe. *Black Maestro: The Epic Life of an American Legend.* New York: HarperCollins, 2006.

———. *The Race for the Triple Crown: Horses, High Stakes, and Eternal Hope.* New York: Grove, 2001.

———, ed. *To the Swift: Classic Triple Crown Horses and Their Race for Glory.* New York: St. Martin's, 2008.

Eisenberg, John. *The Great Match Race: When North Met South in America's First Sports Spectacle.* Boston: Houghton Mifflin, 2006.

———. *The Longest Shot: Lil E. Tee and the Kentucky Derby.* Lexington: University Press of Kentucky, 1996.

———. *Native Dancer: The Grey Ghost, Hero of a Golden Age.* New York: Warner Books, 2003.

Eller, Ronald D. *Miners, Millhands, and Mountaineers: Industrialization of the Appalachian South, 1880–1930.* Knoxville: University of Tennessee Press, 1982.

———. *Uneven Ground: Appalachia since 1945.* Lexington: University Press of Kentucky, 2008.

Emerson, Ken. *Doo-dah! Stephen Foster and the Rise of American Popular Culture.* New York: Simon and Schuster, 1997.

Fabian, Ann. *Card Sharps, Dream Books, and Bucket Shops: Gambling in Nineteenth-Century America.* Ithaca, NY: Cornell University Press, 1990.

Falvey, William D., and Aaron Chase. *The Official Collector's Guide to Kentucky Derby Mint Julep Glasses*. Louisville: Louisville Manufacturing, 1991.

Faragher, John Mack. *Daniel Boone: The Life and Legend of an American Pioneer*. New York: Henry Holt, 1992.

Farr, Finis. *Black Champion: The Life and Times of Jack Johnson*. New York: Scribner's, 1964.

Filson, John. *The Discovery, Settlement and Present State of Kentucke*. 1784. Reprint, New York, Corinth Books, 1962.

Finney, Humphrey S. *Fair Exchange: Recollections of a Life with Horses*. New York: Scribner's, 1974.

Flake, Carol. *Tarnished Crown: The Quest for a Racetrack Champion*. New York: Doubleday, 1987.

Foster, Gaines. *Ghosts of the Confederacy: Defeat, the Lost Cause, and the Emergence of the New South, 1865–1913*. New York: Oxford University Press, 1987.

Frei, Terry. *Horns, Hogs, and Nixon Coming: Texas vs. Arkansas in Dixie's Last Stand*. New York: Simon and Schuster, 2002.

Gatto, Kimberly. *Churchill Downs: America's Most Legendary Racetrack*. Charleston: History Press, 2010.

Georgeff, Phil. *Citation: In a Class by Himself*. Lanham, MD: Taylor, 2003.

Glass, Margaret. *The Calumet Story*. Lexington, KY: Calumet Farm, 1979.

Goad, Jim. *The Redneck Manifesto: How Hillbillies, Hicks and White Trash Became America's Scapegoats*. New York: Simon and Schuster, 1998.

Goldberg, David J. *Discontented America: The United States in the 1920s*. Baltimore: Johns Hopkins University Press, 1999.

Gorman, Bob. *Churchill Downs 100th Kentucky Derby: Compiled under the Auspices of Churchill Downs, 1875–1974*. Louisville: Churchill Downs, 1973.

Greenberg, David. *Nixon's Shadow: The History of an Image*. New York: Norton, 2003.

Greenburg, Kenneth S. *Honor and Slavery*. Princeton, NJ: Princeton University Press, 1996.

Gulliver, Lucille. *Daniel Boone*. New York: Macmillan, 1925.

Hall, Colin Michael. *Hallmark Tourist Events: Impacts, Management and Planning*. London: Belhaven, 1992.

Halliwell, Martin. *American Culture in the 1950s*. Edinburgh: Edinburgh University Press, 2007.

Harkins, Anthony. *Hillbilly: A Cultural History of an American Icon*. New York: Oxford University Press, 2004.

Harrison, Lowell, and James Klotter. *A New History of Kentucky*. Lexington: University Press of Kentucky, 1997.

Harwell, Richard Barksdale. *The Mint Julep*. Charlottesville: University of Virginia Press, 1975.

Haskin, Steve. *Horse Racing's Holy Grail: The Epic Quest for the Kentucky Derby*. Lexington, KY: Eclipse, 2002.

———. *Tales from the Triple Crown*. Lexington, KY: Eclipse, 2008.

Heckman, Lucy. *Damascus*. Lexington, KY: Eclipse, 2004.

Henry, Jim. *Galloping Ghosts: The Story of the Kentucky Derby, 1875–1933*. Louisville: Herald Post, 1934.

Hirsch, Joe. *The Grand Senor: The Fabulous Life of Horatio Lugo*. Lexington, KY: Blood-Horse, 1987.

Hirsch, Joe, and Jim Bolus. *Kentucky Derby: The Chance of a Lifetime*. New York: McGraw-Hill, 1988.

Hogan, Lawrence D. *Shades of Glory: The Negro Leagues and the Story of African-American Baseball*. Washington, DC: National Geographic, 2006.

Hollingsworth, Kent. *The Kentucky Thoroughbred*. Lexington, KY: University Press of Kentucky, 1976.

———. *Madden: The Wizard of the Turf: John E. Madden of Hamburg Place*. Lexington, KY: Blood-Horse, 1965.

Hood, Fred J., ed. *Kentucky: Its History and Heritage*. St. Louis: Forum, 1978.

Hotaling, Edward. *The Great Black Jockeys: The Lives and Times of the Men Who Dominated America's First National Sport*. Rocklin, CA: Prima, 1999.

———. *Wink: The Incredible Life and Epic Journey of Jimmy Winkfield*. Camden, ME: McGraw-Hill, 2004.

Hovdey, Jay. *Whittingham: The Story of a Thoroughbred Racing Legend*. Lexington, KY: Blood-Horse, 1993.

Howard, John Tasker. *Stephen Foster, American Troubadour*. New York: Thomas Y. Crowell, 1953.

Hunter, Avalyn. *American Classic Pedigrees, 1914–2002*. Lexington, KY: Eclipse, 2003.

Jenkins, Sally. *Funny Cide*. New York: G. Putnam's Sons, 2004.

Jillson, Wilard Rouse. *The Boone Narrative*. Louisville: Standard, 1932.

Keppler, Dean. *Betting the Kentucky Derby: How to Wager on and Win America's Biggest Race*. New York: Daily Racing Form, 2008.

Kirby, Jack Temple. *Media-Made Dixie: The South in the American Imagination*. Baton Rouge: Louisiana State University Press, 1978.

Klotter, James C. *Kentucky: Portrait in Paradox, 1900–1950*. Frankfort: Kentucky Historical Society, 1996.

———. *William Goebel: The Politics of Wrath*. Lexington: University Press of Kentucky, 1977.

Klotter, James C., and Hambleton Tapp. *Kentucky: Decades of Discord, 1865–1900*. Frankfort: Kentucky Historical Society, 1977.

Knight, Grant C. *James Lane Allen and the Genteel Tradition*. Chapel Hill: University of North Carolina Press, 1935.

Leach, Brownie. *The Kentucky Derby Diamond Jubilee, 1875–1949*. New York: Dial, 1949.

Lears, T. J. Jackson. *Fables of Abundance: A Cultural History of Advertising in America*. New York: Basic Books, 1994.

———. *Rebirth of a Nation: The Making of Modern America, 1877–1920*. New York: Harper-Collins, 2009.

———. *Something for Nothing: Luck in America*. New York: Viking, 2003.

Levin, Jason. *From the Desert to the Derby: The Ruling Family of Dubai's Billion-Dollar Quest to Win America's Greatest Horse Race*. New York: Daily Racing Form, 2002.

Levy, Bill. *The Derby: A Lively and Entertaining Look at the Greatest Horse Race in America—The Kentucky Derby*. Cleveland: World Publishing, 1967.

Lofaro, Michael A., and Joe Cummings, eds. *Daniel Boone: An American Life*. Lexington: University Press of Kentucky, 2003.

———. *The Life and Adventures of Daniel Boone*. Lexington: University Press of Kentucky, 1978.

Magnum, William Preston, II. *A Kingdom for the Horse: A Classic Epic of the Brightest Star in American Race Horse Breeding History*. Louisville: Harmony House, 1999.

Marchman, Judy, and Tom Hall. *The Calumet Collection: The History of the Calumet Trophies*. Lexington, KY: Eclipse, 2002.

————. *Kentucky Derby Glasses Price Guide: A Comprehensive Guide to Collecting Kentucky Derby Mint Julep Glasses and Shot Glasses*. Lexington, KY: Eclipse, 1999.

Margolies, Jacob. *The Negro Leagues: The Story of Black Baseball*. New York: Franklin Watts, 1994.

Marshall, William. *Baseball's Pivotal Era, 1945–1951*. Lexington: University Press of Kentucky, 1999.

McDowell, Robert Emmett. *City of Conflict: Louisville in the Civil War, 1861–1865*. Louisville: Louisville Civil War Round Table, 1962.

McEvoy, Hallie. *Genuine Risk*. Lexington, KY: Eclipse, 2003.

McEvoy, John. *Round Table*. Lexington, KY: Eclipse, 2002.

McGuinniss, Joe. *The Big Horse*. New York: Simon and Schuster, 2004.

Mearns, Dan. *Seattle Slew*. Lexington, KY: Eclipse, 2000.

Mellon, Paul. *Reflections in a Silver Spoon*. New York: William Morrow, 1992.

Mickle, Shelley Fraser. *Barbaro: America's Horse*. New York: Aladdin, 2007.

Morgan, Robert. *Boone: A Biography*. Chapel Hill, NC: Algonquin Books, 2007.

Nack, William. *Secretariat: The Making of a Champion*. New York: Da Capo, 1975.

Nickell, Joe. *The Kentucky Mint Julep*. Lexington: University Press of Kentucky, 2003.

O'Connor, John. *History of the Kentucky Derby, 1875–1921*. New York: Rider, 1921.

Olson, Keith W. *Watergate: The Presidential Scandal That Shook America*. Lawrence: University Press of Kansas, 2003.

Ours, Dorothy. *Man o' War: A Legend Like Lightning*. New York: St. Martin's, 2006.

Owen, David. *The Making of the Masters: Clifford Roberts, Augusta National, and Golf's Most Prestigious Tournament*. New York: Simon and Schuster, 1999.

Pace, Mildred Mastin. *Kentucky Derby Champion*. Ashland, KY: Jesse Stuart Foundation, 1993.

Palmer, Joe H. *This Was Racing*. Lexington, KY: Henry Clay, 1973.

Parmer, Charles B. *For Gold and Glory: The Story of Thoroughbred Racing in America.* New York: Carrick and Evans, 1939.

Paulick, Ray. *Sunday Silence.* Lexington, KY: Eclipse, 2009.

Pearce, John Ed. *Days of Darkness: The Feuds of Eastern Kentucky.* Lexington: University Press of Kentucky, 1994.

Peterson, Robert. *Only the Ball Was White: A History of Legendary Black Players and All-Black Professional Teams.* New York: Oxford University Press, 1970.

Philbin, Tom. *Barbaro: A Nation's Love Story.* New York: Collins, 2007.

Phillips, Kevin P. *The Emerging Republican Majority.* New Rochelle, NY: Arlington House, 1969.

Pudup, Mary Beth, Dwight Billings, and Altina Waller, eds. *Appalachia in the Making: The Mountain South in the Nineteenth Century.* Chapel Hill: University of North Carolina Press, 1995.

Rader, Benjamin. *American Sports: From the Age of Folk Games to the Age of Televised Sports.* Englewood Cliffs, NJ: Prentice-Hall, 1990.

Renau, Lynn. *Jockeys, Belles and Bluegrass Kings: An Official Guide to Kentucky Racing.* Louisville: Herr House, 1995.

Richey, Ish. *Kentucky Literature, 1784–1963.* Tompkinsville, KY: Monroe County, 1963.

Roberts, Randy. *Papa Jack: Jack Johnson and the Era of White Hopes.* New York: Free Press, 1983.

Robertson, James Oliver. *American Myth, American Reality.* New York: Hill and Wang, 1980.

Robertson, William H. P. *The History of Thoroughbred Racing in America.* Englewood Cliffs, NJ: Prentice-Hall, 1964.

Robinson, Patrick, and Nick Robinson. *Horse Trader: Robert Sangster and the Rise and Fall of the Sport of Kings.* London: Harper Collins, 1993.

Rutherford, Susan B. *The Derby Dixienary.* Lawrenceburg, KY: Susan B Rutherford, 1941.

Sampson, Curt. *The Lost Masters: Grace and Disgrace in '68.* New York: Atria Books, 2005.

Saunders, James Robert, and Monica Renae Saunders. *Black Winning Jockeys in the Kentucky Derby.* Jefferson, NC: McFarland, 2003.

Saunders, Steven, and Deane L. Root. *The Music of Stephen C. Foster*. Vol. 1, *1844–1855*. Washington, DC: Smithsonian Institution Press, 1990.

Scanlan, Lawrence. *The Horse God Built: The Untold Story of Secretariat, the World's Greatest Race Horse*. New York: St. Martin's, 2007.

Shapiro, Henry. *Appalachia on Our Minds: The Southern Mountaineers in American Consciousness, 1870–1920*. Chapel Hill: University of North Carolina Press, 1978.

Silber, Nina. *The Romance of Reunion: Northerners and the South, 1865–1900*. Chapel Hill: University of North Carolina Press, 1993.

Smith, J. Soule. *The Mint Julep: The Very Dream of Drinks from the Old Receipt of Soule Smith down in Lexington, Ky*. Lexington, KY: Gravesend, 1949.

Smith, Pohla. *Citation*. Lexington, KY: Eclipse, 2003.

Steadman, Ralph. *The Joke's Over: Bruised Memories, Gonzo, Hunter S. Thompson, and Me*. Orlando, FL: Houghton Mifflin Harcourt, 2006.

Tallant, Harold D. *Evil Necessity: Slavery and Political Culture in Antebellum Kentucky*. Lexington: University Press of Kentucky, 2003.

Taylor, William R. *Cavalier and Yankee: The Old South and American National Character*. New York: Harper and Row, 1961.

Thayer, Bert Clark. *Whirlaway: The Life and Times of a Great Racer*. New York: Abercrombie and Fitch, 1966.

Thomas, Samuel W. *Churchill Downs: A Documentary History of America's Most Legendary Race Track*. Louisville: Kentucky Derby Museum, 1995.

Thompson, Hunter S. *The Great Shark Hunt, Gonzo Papers*. Vol. 1, *Strange Tales from a Strange Time*. New York: Simon and Schuster, 2003.

Thoroughbred Champions: Top 100 Racehorses of the 20th Century. Lexington, KY: Blood-Horse, 1999.

Titus, W. I. *John Fox, Jr*. New York: Twayne, 1971.

Townsend, John Wilson. *Kentucky in American Letters, 1784–1912*. Cedar Rapids, IA: Torch, 1913.

Tyler, Bruce M. *African-American Life in Louisville*. Charleston: Arcadia, 1998.

Wall, Joseph F. *Henry Watterson, Reconstructed Rebel*. New York: Oxford University Press, 1956.

Wall, Maryjean. *How Kentucky Became Southern: A Tale of Outlaws, Horse Thieves, Gamblers and Breeders*. Lexington: University Press of Kentucky, 2010.

Waller, Altina. *Feud: Hatfields, McCoy's, and Social Change in Appalachia, 1860–1900*. Chapel Hill: University of North Carolina Press, 1988.

Waller, Gregory A. *Main Street Amusements: Movies and Commercial Entertainment in a Southern City, 1896–1930*. Washington, DC: Smithsonian Institution Press, 1995.

Watterson, Henry. *Marse Henry: An Autobiography*. New York: George H. Doran, 1919.

Wenner, Jann S., and Corey Seymour. *Gonzo: The Life of Hunter S. Thompson*. New York: Little, Brown, 2007.

White, Dan. *Kentucky Bred: A Celebration of Thoroughbred Breeding*. Dallas: Taylor, 1986.

Williamson, J. W. *Hillbillyland: What the Movies Did to the Mountains and What the Mountains Did to the Movies*. Chapel Hill: University of North Carolina Press, 1995.

Wilson, Charles R. *Baptized in Blood: The Religion of the Lost Cause, 1865–1920*. Athens: University of Georgia Press, 1980.

Wilson, James Boone. *The Spirit of Old Kentucky*. Louisville: Glenmore Distilleries, 1945.

Winn, Matt J., and Frank G. Menke. *Down the Stretch: The Story of Colonel Matt J. Winn, as Told to Frank G. Menke*. New York: Smith and Durrell, 1944.

Woodward, C. Vann. *The Burden of Southern History*. Baton Rouge: Louisiana State University Press, 1960.

———. *Origins of the New South, 1877–1913*. Baton Rouge: Louisiana State University Press, 1951.

Wright, George C. *A History of Blacks in Kentucky*. Vol. 2, *In Pursuit of Equality, 1890–1980*. Frankfort: Kentucky Historical Society, 1992.

———. *Life behind a Veil: Blacks in Louisville, Kentucky, 1895–1930*. Baton Rouge: Louisiana State University Press, 1985.

———. *Racial Violence in Kentucky, 1865–1940: Lynchings, Mob Rule, and "Legal Lynchings."* Baton Rouge: Louisiana State University Press, 1990.

Yater, George H. *Two Hundred Years at the Falls of the Ohio*. Louisville: Filson Club, 1987.

Zeitz, Joshua. *Flapper: A Madcap Story of Sex, Style, Celebrity and the Women Who Made America Modern*. New York: Random House, 2007.

Index

Index